W9-AXU-190

BIBLE ALMANAC

Anna Trimiew

Consultant:
Gary Burge, Ph.D.

Publications International, Ltd.

Louis Weber, C.E.O.
Publications International, Ltd.
7373 North Cicero Avenue
Lincolnwood, Illinois 60646

Manufactured in U.S.A.

8 7 6 5 4 3 2 1

ISBN: 0-7853-2496-8

Library of Congress Catalog Card Number: 97-66700

Anna Trimiew is a freelance writer and a former school teacher who holds a master's degree from Gordon-Conwell Theological Seminary. Her previously published work includes *Who's Who in the Bible, Images of Heaven, The Wisdom of Jesus,* and other religious literature, including Christian educational materials.

Gary Burge is a professor in the department of Biblical, Theological, Archaeological & Religious Studies at Wheaton College. He holds a Ph.D in New Testament from King's College, The University of Aberdeen in Aberdeen, Scotland and a Master of Divinity degree from Fuller Theological Seminary. He is a member of the Biblical Archaeological Society.

Picture credits:
Front cover: **Biblical Archaeology Society:** Courtesy of Israel Antiquities Authority (bottom right); Zev Radovan: (top right); **The Crosiers:** (top right center); **Erich Lessing/Art Resource:** (top left center); **Richard T. Nowitz:** (bottom right center); **Zev Radovan:** (top left, bottom left, bottom left center & bottom center); **SuperStock:** (background); Sistine Chapel: (center).
Back cover: **Zev Radovan.**
Archive Photos: 83, 88; **Art Resource:** 250, 270, 299; Cameraphoto: 290–291, 308; Giraudon: 192, 217; Jewish Museum: 236, 248; Erich Lessing: 7, 20, 42, 73, 105, 120–121, 133, 134, 145, 151, 153 (bottom), 178 (top), 211, 228, 260, 304 (right), 310; Pierpont Morgan Library: 107; Scala: 30, 41, 148, 190, 205, 218–219, 241, 249, 259, 261, 267, 285, 296, 313; **Biblical Archaeology Society:** Werner Braun: 271; Sonia Halliday: 150; Gard Nalbandian: 143; Hershel Shanks: 239; P. Wernerbraun: 238 (left); **Bettmann Archive:** 114; **Bridgeman Art Library:** 234–235; **The Crosiers:** 29, 33, 52, 57, 61, 62, 64, 65, 67, 69, 71, 98, 104, 198, 222 (left), 226, 283, 292, 294, 300, 302, 303, 304 (left), 305, 312, 314; **FPG International:** 193; David Bartruff: 206; Josef Beck: 85 (bottom); **International Stock:** Roberto Arakaki: 130; Bob Firth: 131 (bottom); Miwako Ikeda: 265; Hal Kern: 131(top); **Richard T. Nowitz:** table of contents: (bottom left), 12 (top), 78, 84 (top), 86 (top), 122 (bottom), 124, 129, 140, 142, 158, 165, 169, 222 (right), 227, 230; Black Star: 154 (bottom); **Zev Radovan:** table of contents (top right, left center & bottom right), 14, 79, 81, 82, 84 (bottom), 86 (bottom), 119, 125, 126, 132 (bottom), 136, 149, 152, 154 (top), 155, 160, 161, 162, 163, 166, 170, 172, 175, 178 (bottom), 182, 184, 185, 186, 194, 197, 201, 207, 214, 215 (top), 221, 223, 224, 229, 231, 233, 238 (right), 288; BLMJ Borowski Collection: 85 (top), 204; **Noah Satat/Animals Animals:** 132 (top); **SuperStock:** table of contents (top left & right center), 10–11, 12 (bottom), 19, 27, 32, 36, 37, 38, 43, 45, 53, 56, 58, 63, 66, 100, 113, 118, 139, 180, 202, 210, 212, 245, 251, 254, 258, 264, 273, 276, 278, 307, 315; A.K.G., Berlin: 96; Accademia Pattavina, Paudua/M. Magliani: 275; American Bible Society, New York City: 17, 24, 25; Archbishopric, Udine,Venetia, Italy/M. Magliani: 31; Art Museum, Basel/A.K.G., Berlin: 18; Baptistery of the Cathedral, Padua: 49; Birmingham City Gallery & Museum, England: 50–51; Leonid Bogdanov: 244; British Museum/ET Archive, London: 13; Christie's Images: 55, 89, 101, 188–189; Church of San Luigi de Francesi, Rome/Canali Photobank, Milan: 92; Church of San Vitale, Ravenna, Italy/Canali Photobank, Milan: 116; Civic Museum, Padua, Italy: 287; Correr Civic Museum, Venice/ET Archive, London: 74, 255; Detroit Institute of Arts, Michigan/Bridgeman Art Library, London: 171; By permission of the Trustees of the Dulwich Picture Gallery, London: 268–269; Explorer, Paris: 87; Galleria Degli Uffizi, Florence, Italy/Bridgman Art Library, London: 216; Guildhall Art Gallery, Corporation of London/Bridgeman Art Library: 146–147; Hermitage Museum, St. Petersburg, Russia: 109; The Huntington Library, Art Collections, and Botanical Gardens, San Marino, California: 110; The International Fine Art Auctioneers, Phillips/Bridgeman Art Library, London: 47; Jewish Museum, New York City: 102, 253, 256, 257; Kunsthalle, Mannheim, Germany: 95; Metropolitan Museum of Art, New York City/J. Barnell: 112; Musee du Louvre, Paris: 297; Musee du Louvre, Paris/ET Archive, London: 106; Musee du Louvre, Paris/Giraudon, Paris: 97, 208; Musee Granet, Aix-en-Provence, France/Bridgeman Art Library, London: 215 (center); Museo del Prado, Madrid, Spain: 243; Museo del Prado, Madrid, Spain/Bridgeman Art Library, London: 247; Museo di San Marco, Florence, Italy: 279; Museo di San Marco dell'Angelico, Florence/Bridgeman Art Library, London: 277; Museum of Fine Arts, Rouen, France/ET Archive, London: 70; National Gallery of Scotland, Edinburgh/Bridgeman Art Library, London: 60; Pinacoteca Di Brera, Milan, Italy/Canali Photobank, Milan: 225; Pinacoteca Di Brera, Milan, Italy includes The Jesi Collection/M. Magliani: 159; Prenestino Museum, Rome, Italy/ET Archive, London: 266; Rijksmuseum Vincent Van Gogh, Amsterdam, Netherlands A.K.G., Berlin: 91; Russian State Museum, St. Petersburg, Russia/Lonid Bogdanov: 153 (top); Saint Anne's Museum, Lubeck, Germany: 309; Society S Giorgio Degli Sciavone, Venice/ET Archive, London: 76–77; Toledo Cathedral, Castile/Bridgeman Art Library, London: 93; Vatican Museums & Galleries, Rome: 293; Vatican Museums & Galleries, Rome/A.K.G., Berlin: 242; Courtesy of the Board of Trustees of the Victoria & Albert Museum, London/Bridgeman Art Library, London: 174.

Diagrams and map illustrations: Myron Netterlund.
Map colorization: Brian Warling.

Contents

UNDERSTANDING THE WORLD OF THE BIBLE

THE BIBLE has been described as the world's greatest book. It is filled with drama, action, emotion, and inspiration. Readers everywhere are guided, encouraged, and fascinated by its message and by the sheer variety of information within its pages. In its hundreds of translations, the Bible is the world's all-time best-seller. Three major religions—Christianity, Judaism, and Islam—claim the Bible, or portions of it, as a sacred book. Christianity acknowledges the Bible as its only holy writings, believing the Bible to be God's word to ancient and modern readers alike.

Although people are attracted to its timeless stories and truths, the Bible is still, in many ways, an unfamiliar book. Its setting is nothing like our own ordinary neighborhoods. Its clothes, customs, and family patterns are different from ours. The ancient world of buying and selling, with its system of bartering and weights and measures, is very unlike today's convenient shopping, handy malls, and easy access to banks and teller machines. Even the biblical world of worship seems unfamiliar. Many of the sacred rituals of ancient times seem to have little in common with contemporary styles of worship.

It is also important to remember that the Bible was not originally written in our language. The Old Testament was written mostly in Hebrew, and the New Testament in Greek. As we read through the Scriptures today, we are looking at the ancient writings through the wisdom and eyes of translators. In addition, we discover that the Bible is not one book, but a collection of 66 books (plus the Deuterocanonical writings) written by several different authors—kings, priests, and fishermen among them—spanning nearly 2,000 years of history.

All these things make the Bible difficult to understand, and even though we love to turn its pages, questions invariably arise. Why was the Bible written? Who were the writers? How do we know that the Bible is true? Who were the people we are reading about? What did they do? Where did they live? When did these events take place?

This book was written to answer questions like these, and to reveal other mysteries, wonders, and curiosities of the Bible, its people, and cultures. *Bible Almanac* is designed to bring the biblical world to life in a readable, accurate, and up-to-date way. And each chapter provides a unique look at an important and specific subject, starting with how the Bible came to be in the first place.

THE STORY OF THE BIBLE

During the 19th century, Bible scholars made several important discoveries about the Bible, its message, and the way it was handed down to us. First, they came to see that the Bible was a set of writings from different places and times—a magnificent collection of Hebrew and Greek literature that probably took more than 1,000 years to reach the form from which the English Bible was eventually translated. Also, many well-preserved manuscripts of the Scriptures were found that helped scholars determine the accuracy of the Bible. Then, in the

"Christ and the Samaritan woman at the well," by Paolo Veronese

20th century, the discovery of the Dead Sea Scrolls revealed that hundreds of years of copying and recopying had barely altered the original text.

As the story of the Bible unfolds in Chapter One, it becomes clear that all the books of the Bible and the writers belong together in a remarkable way, from Genesis to Revelation, from the works attributed to Moses to the writings of the apostle John.

Events in the Bible

From the story of creation to the final ministry of the apostles and Paul's activities in Rome, the glorious events of the Bible are traced in Chapter Two. The history of the Bible can be divided into the Old Testament and the New Testament periods, with a stretch of 400 years between the Testaments.

Old Testament history paints a colorful, unfolding picture of God's dealings with humanity. The New Testament provides the final brushwork in revealing God's plan of redemption; it introduces the Messiah, Jesus Christ, his life and ministry, and the beginning of Christianity.

The Language and Literature of the Bible

The term "Bible" comes from the Greek word for a book, "Biblos." This amazing work includes laws, poetry, sermons, prophecies, and much more. This chapter emphasizes important language and writing discoveries. It also takes a look at important Bible themes, and common literary threads interwoven throughout Scripture. We are all familiar with the Ten Commandments, the Beatitudes, and the Lord's Prayer. However, the Bible also includes many other wonderful prayers, songs, and wise sayings. Greetings, farewells, and blessings also form an integral part of biblical literature. And we discover that some common phrases of ours actually come from the Bible.

The Land of the Bible

The people of the Old Testament lived in a very small section of the world, not much bigger than the state of Oregon. The area is made up of mountains and desert, with a narrow band of lush land along the river valleys known as the Fertile Crescent. This strip begins at the river Nile in Egypt, extends along the Mediterranean coast, through the land of Canaan (modern Israel, Lebanon, and part of Syria), and then curves down the Tigris and Euphrates rivers and on to the Persian Gulf.

The fourth chapter of *Bible Almanac* explores the environment of the Bible—its land and water, climate, vegetation, animals, and plants. The geography of this small area at the end of the Mediterranean Sea is all-important to understanding the story of the Bible.

THE EVERYDAY WORLD OF THE BIBLE

What was ordinary, daily living like back during biblical times? It is hard enough to imagine life when our grandparents were children. Imagine how much more difficult it is to get an accurate picture of home and family life in Bible times. The fast-paced life of our 20th century would seem strange to anyone living in biblical times.

Chapter Five takes a look at life within the average Bible family—how they lived, worked, and worshiped. Besides family life and special occasions, this chapter covers a variety of other aspects of everyday life, including food and health issues, money, war and weaponry, the world of work, and what people did just for fun back then.

RELIGION AND WORSHIP IN THE BIBLE

In every age, the spiritual dimension of life has always been extremely important, and for the Israelites and their neighbors of ancient times, this was certainly true. The Ten Commandments, the ark of the covenant, the tabernacle, false gods, and the temple in Jerusalem are all elements of religion and worship presented in the Bible. Israel's religion began when God spoke to Abraham, telling him to journey to a new place to live. He made a covenant with Abraham, promising to make him the founder of a great and "holy" nation. In the New Testament, the coming of Jesus—the promised Messiah—is seen as the fulfillment of God's covenant with his people.

Chapter Six introduces us to the development of religion under Moses the lawgiver, and the worship practices among the Israelites while they struggled to obey God in the wilderness. This chapter explores the work of priests and prophets, as well as the importance of animal sacrifices, religious festivals, feasts, fasts, music and other significant elements. It also looks at the teachings of Jesus, the birth of Christianity, and the explosive growth of the early church.

TRADE AND INDUSTRY IN THE BIBLE

In ancient times, the Israelites were primarily shepherds wandering around with their flocks. A self-supporting group, pottery, spinning, weaving, and some metal work were likely their main crafts. After they settled in towns and cities, however, new trades and small industries developed including masonry, sculpture, engraving, architecture, and jewelry making. In some cities, entire streets were occupied by one particular trade.

Chapter Seven explores trade development among the Israelites, including trade routes, camel caravans, the risky business of buying and selling, and the great trading nations. We learn about the ancient practice of bartering, the principal goods in the world of trade, and the growth of industry in the Bible.

PEOPLE OF THE BIBLE

Chapter Eight explores the fascinating world of Bible personalities. Besides heroes of the faith, outstanding military geniuses, great kings and queens, and other marvelous mentors, the Bible also takes note of thieves, murderers, and prostitutes—some of whom redeemed themselves to become exemplary characters. Although by no means a complete list, this section covers a wide variety of notable people.

This chapter also provides a valuable look at God, Jesus, and the Holy Spirit as presented in the Scriptures. There is even a biblical character sketch of the personality and work of Satan. We've also included several other nations and people, including the industrious and ambitious Egyptians, the literary Canaanites, the conquering Assyrians, and the Babylonians—with their great structures and works of art.

IDEAS AND BELIEFS OF THE BIBLE

The Bible is much more than an ancient history of people, places, and events. It is the handbook of faith to followers of two of the world's religions, Judaism and Christianity. Old Testament teachings—especially the law of Moses and the traditions of the elders—form the foundation for the ideas and beliefs in Judaism. Christians accept the Old and New Testament Scriptures as the entire counsel of God, and his written instruction to all believers everywhere.

Chapter Nine presents key ideas and beliefs of the Bible, explaining some of the Bible's important teachings. Besides dealing with sin, forgiveness, and salvation—staples of Christian theology—this section also highlights the nature of miracles and wonders, a description of what heaven is like, and ways to worship God.

BIBLE QUESTIONS AND ANSWERS

What makes the Bible important? What were the first human beings like? Who were the Nephilim? Where was the garden of Eden? These and other fascinating questions are posed and answered in the final chapter. The Bible is filled with riveting history, interesting characters, and valuable wisdom for everyday living. However, many people are puzzled by Scripture passages that are hard to understand, numbers that seemingly do not add up, curious names and terms, and unlikely events. Included in this section are questions that deal with common, puzzling Bible issues, such as the authenticity of the Bible and the story of Creation.

Turning to the New Testament, questions include the date of Christ's birth, the star of Bethlehem, and the identity of the wise men who visited Jesus. Several New Testament names and terms are explained, along with curious Bible trivia.

Bible Almanac is your "guided tour" through the pages of the Scriptures. It aims to provide a clearer view of the Bible, the God of the Scriptures, and life in the ancient world. We are introduced to each Bible book, to historical events, and to the language. The people, customs, religion, beliefs, and ideas are all drawn into focus. As the story of the Bible is brought to life, the people of this ancient world become familiar, rooted in real places with their lives spread plainly before us. We discover that these biblical characters loved and hated, succeeded and failed, cried and celebrated—just like people everywhere. In a refreshing way, the kings, queens, priests, farmers, and carpenters of the Bible become part of our own world.

Within these pages, you'll find a wealth of information, with answers to many of your questions about the Bible. Discover some fascinating—and sometimes humorous—scriptural facts. Deepen your knowledge and understanding of the world's best-selling book, and enjoy its richness.

THE STORY OF THE BIBLE

MANY OF US are familiar with the sight of a big, black Bible on a bookshelf. When we take it down and open its pages, we discover that the Bible is, in fact, not just one book. It is made up of an entire collection of books containing many different writings: law, history, poetry, prophecy—even sermons, hymns, and personal letters. A deeper look reveals that the Bible is composed of two main sections: the Old Testament and the New Testament (and some Bibles include a third section—the Apocrypha). But how did the books of the Bible come to be written? How and why were they divided into these sections? Who were the writers? When did they write these books? This chapter will help provide some insight on the history behind this body of work.

With painstaking accuracy, a Yemenite scribe corrects a Torah scroll. Among several important functions performed in biblical times, scribes devoted themselves to preserving and transcribing the Old Testament text, and teaching the law to Jewish believers.

THE OLD TESTAMENT

The first 39 books of the Bible are known as the Old Testament. They were first written down in Hebrew and Aramaic, the ancient languages of the Jews. We do not have any of the original manuscripts (known as *autographs*) today. When the Old Testament authors finished their scrolls, they did not have modern copy machines or mechanical presses to duplicate their writings. The work of copying belonged to Jewish scribes, who would laboriously make handwritten copies of the original writings. When the documents became worn out, the scribes made new copies from the old copies. Unfortunately, many of these scrolls have not survived over time. They deteriorated in the climate of the Bible lands. As a result, today there are few surviving original copies of these early holy books, first written down about 1400 B.C.

Before 1947, the oldest known manuscripts of the Hebrew Old Testament dated from the ninth and tenth centuries A.D. These were copies of the Pentateuch—the first five books of the Bible. In 1947, however, there was an amazing discovery. Bedouin shepherds found a priceless treasure in the caves near the Dead Sea. They discovered the Dead Sea Scrolls. These second-century B.C. copies of all the books of the Old Testament (except Esther) were from the library of a Jewish religious group (called the Essenes) at Qumran who lived about the time of Jesus. This remarkable find revealed that the Old Testament text had changed very little over a thousand years. In fact, the Qumran manuscripts were so similar to the ninth-century documents, it showed that the scribes had done an outstanding job of accurately passing on the sacred writings. By this we know that the Old Testament

An important discovery, these portions of ancient Old Testament texts written on papyrus and leather parchment are from the group of manuscripts known as the Dead Sea Scrolls, found hidden in caves near the Dead Sea in 1947.

as we now have it is probably very similar to the way it was originally written.

How the Old Testament Was Put Together

Jewish tradition holds that the scribe Ezra (whose story is told in the Book of Ezra) compiled the books of the Old Testament. Lacking evidence, however, we do not know for certain how the books actually came together in the collection we now have. We do know that by the time of Jesus, the Hebrew sacred writings usually comprised the 39 books we accept as the Old Testament. And Jesus himself makes it clear which books he and his apostles accepted as their "Bible."

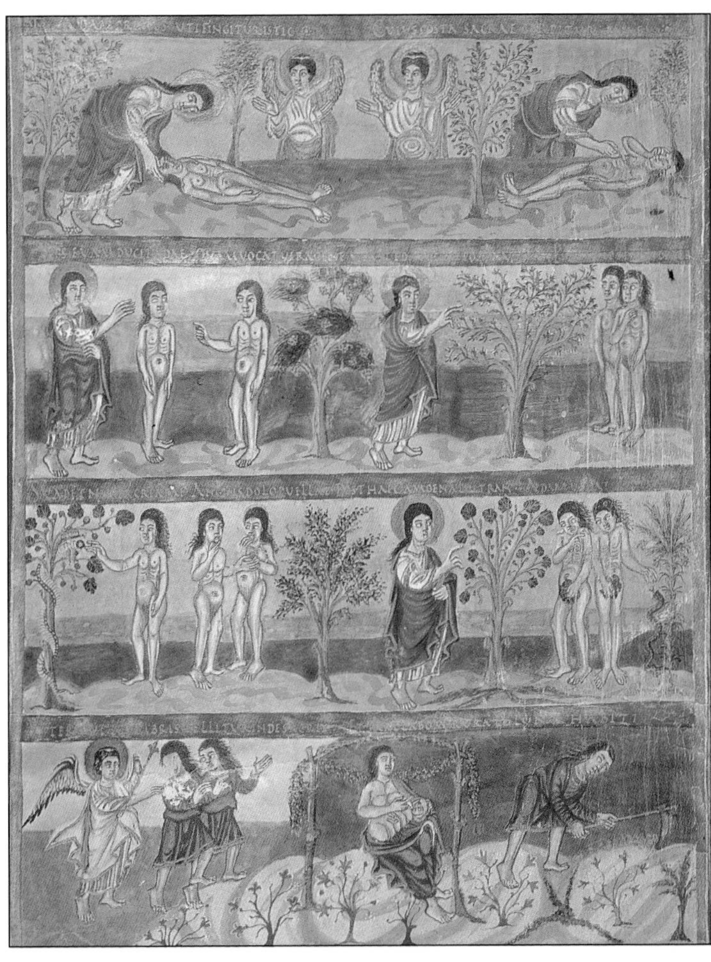

God made the first man and woman and placed them in the Garden of Eden. There they ate the forbidden fruit of the tree of knowledge of good and evil, and were subsequently banished from the garden for their transgression. These scenes from the Moutier Granval Bible Manuscripts, British Museum, London, depict these early stories from the Book of Genesis.

The Jews arranged their sacred books into three major divisions: the Law, the Prophets, and the Writings. When Jesus spoke to his disciples about the Old Testament, he referred to these same groupings. Besides, most of the books of our Old Testament are quoted somewhere in the New Testament. It seems, then, that Jesus and his followers were familiar with the same Old Testament we have today.

Besides the 39 Old Testament books, the Jews had other holy texts. These books and chapters are known as the *Apocrypha* or *Deuterocanonical writings,* and may be found in some Bibles. In the Greek version, these writings were given the same respect as other Old Testament books. However, in the Hebrew Bible, they were not considered to have the same authority as the other books of the Bible.

Other Ancient Versions of the Old Testament

One of the most important translations of the Old Testament is the Greek version known as the *Septuagint*. Jews who spoke Greek and many Christians of the first centuries A.D.

used the Septuagint. It has been suggested that this text was put together at the request of Pharaoh Ptolemy Philadelphus, who reigned from 285–246 B.C. The Pharaoh wished to have a translation for his library at Alexandria. As Christianity spread to people of other cultures and languages, the Old Testament was translated into Latin, Syriac, and Egyptian—and eventually other languages.

These pages from an old Bible belong to Exodus, the second book of the Old Testament. This second of the five books of Moses tells of Israel's departure from Egypt, march to Mount Sinai, the giving of the Law, and the description of the tabernacle of worship, where Israelites met to worship God.

THE NEW TESTAMENT

The writers of the New Testament finished their work in the first century A.D. Today we have many fragments of the New Testament text from as early as the second century A.D. Originally written down in Greek, there are perhaps 15,000 complete manuscripts and fragments available today to help scholars put together the final 27 books of the Bible. In addition, scholars have available several early translations of the New Testament. There are also New Testament quotations in the writings of the early church fathers. With all this information, scholars have had to be cautious in selecting and preserving the most accurate texts of the original writings.

By the fifth century A.D., the text of the New Testament was standardized from a common text found in many Greek manuscripts.The first printed edition of the standard Greek text came in 1516, prepared and published by the Dutch scholar Erasmus. Up to this point, there had been no thought to examine the accuracy of this text. During the next two centuries, however, some Bibles noted certain alterations from the standardized version, including the text of Stephanus used in translating the King James Version in England (1611), and the edition of Elzevir (1633), which became the model for New Testament translations in Europe. They had discovered older texts that were quite different from the fifth-century standard text.

As scholars continued their work of translation, they became more involved in the history and accuracy of texts. It became clear that certain texts were more reliable than others. Manuscripts were then grouped together according to their similarities. We now know that certain families of older texts (such as the Alexandrian and the Western texts) are closer to the original writings than the standard fifth-century text.

HOW THE NEW TESTAMENT BOOKS WERE COLLECTED

When the first Christians met together to worship, they probably read from the Old Testament, following the Jewish synagogue tradition. Since the focus of their worship was Jesus Christ, they likely added to their meetings an account of some part of his life and ministry. At first, the reports might have been first-hand accounts from people who knew Jesus. But as the church grew in numbers (and eye-witnesses began to die), it became important to write these stories down. This was how Matthew, Mark, Luke, and John came into being. These four Gospels became an important part in the worship and life of the early church.

As the Christian movement expanded, the apostles wrote letters to the young churches and various key individuals,giving guidance on Christian beliefs. These letters were useful to the church as a whole, and so they were preserved. This also occurred with the Book of Acts, which was accepted because it continued Luke's Gospel account and provided the only full record of the beginnings of Christianity.

MANUSCRIPT MAKING

In ancient days, the art of making books was very different from printing and publishing as we know it. Back then, scribes used a quill pen and ink to write on parchment or vellum scrolls (made from animal skins) to make individual copies of the Bible. In Egypt, a writing surface was made from papyrus reeds. Scrolls were usually attached to two wooden handles and could be as long as 40 feet! When scrolls became tattered or old, copies were made and the old ones were buried in special ceremonies.

Although we do not have original scrolls of any Bible book today, we believe that we have reliable copies of the earliest texts. Scribes took painstaking care to copy out the sacred writings by hand generation after generation. Copyists usually worked together, writing at the dictation of the chief scribe. Seldom did they make mistakes, and when errors were found, the copy was corrected. These expensive handwritten manuscripts were generally owned and used by churches or groups. Few individuals could afford to purchase such costly writings. The well-known Masoretes (a group of European Jewish scribes), working from the sixth century and into the tenth century A.D., produced several Old Testament manuscripts that still exist. The Masoretic texts are highly regarded and still widely used today.

At first, the New Testament books were written in the traditional manner—on papyrus or parchment scrolls. However, by the late first century A.D. a new way of making copies of the Scriptures developed. Sheets of papyrus or vellum were folded and sewn together at the spine to make a book, known as a *codex*. This book form was a great improvement over the long, awkward scroll, and copyists could write on both sides of each page.

Many important papyrus manuscripts of the New Testament exist today. In fact, the Revised Version of the Bible was based on Codex Sinaiticus and Codex Vaticanus, produced during the fourth century by professional scribes at Alexandria. Over the past 250 years, scholars have worked hard to ensure that our New Testament today is as close as possible to the original words of the authors.

TEN QUICK BIBLE FACTS

- The first Bible books were written nearly 3,500 years ago.
- Approximately 40 different people wrote the books of the Bible.
- Some Bible authors dictated their words to a scribe or secretary who wrote them down.
- The first five books of the Bible were written about 1400 B.C., and the last books (Revelation, 3 John, and John) were written about 96–100 A.D.
- The grouping of books in the Hebrew Bible is different from the ordering of the books in the Christian Bible.
- The Hebrews hid or buried old copies of their Bible.
- Scribes were so careful in copying that they counted all the words and letters in the original and in the copy to check for errors.
- The Dead Sea Scrolls were found in old jars in caves by the Dead Sea.
- The New Testament was written within the span of 50 years.
- The New Testament books came together because of the needs of the church.

By 200 A.D., the church was officially using the four Gospels as their authority for the life and teaching of Jesus. By this time also, Paul's letters were accepted as equally important. Then, during the third and fourth centuries, the remaining books of the New Testament were generally approved by the church.

This process was formally established when church leaders compiled a list of books similar to our New Testament at the Council of Laodicea (363 A.D.) and the Council of Carthage (397 A.D.).

Now we have the entire Bible in our hands, Old and New Testaments, all 66 books. Many scholars and critics believe that the world's best-seller (often referred to as the "Holy Writ" or the "Word of God") is an accurate record of the authors' words, handed down without significant loss from generation to generation throughout the centuries.

TRANSLATING THE SCRIPTURES

Before printing began, all copies of the Bible had to be written by hand—first by scribes, then later by monks. After the New Testament was written and Christianity began spreading, the work of translation started. The Bible appeared in Latin, Armenian, Gothic, Coptic, and other languages. People wanted to read the Bible in their own tongue. These translations were not produced on scrolls but in codex form. This was a step forward in Bible making and the growing work of translation. Today, the Bible has been translated in more than 1,700 languages. The history of this work is both fascinating and far-reaching.

ANCIENT VERSIONS OF THE BIBLE

Common Version: Jerome is the first Bible translator known to us. His Latin translation, the Vulgate (or Common Version) was the standard Bible of the Roman Catholic Church for centuries. A respected scholar, Jerome wrote his famous translation around 400 A.D.

These New Testament pages from an old Arabic Bible show an illustration of Jesus and his disciples at the last supper. The first Bible translations in Arabic likely appeared in the eighth century.

Syriac Bible: Although Syriac, a dialect of Aramaic (the language of Jesus), is no longer spoken, this fourth-century translation (known as the Peshitta) is still used in Syria, Iran, India, and elsewhere.

Coptic Bible: A Coptic version was needed as Christianity spread south to Egypt and beyond. Translation began in the third century, and the Coptic Bible is still used today.

Gothic Version: When Christianity swept through the Roman Empire after Emperor Constantine's conversion (312 A.D.), new Bible translations were needed. The Germanic Goths received almost the whole Bible in their language, Gothic, from the missionary translator, Ulfilas.

Armenian Bible: Translated by St. Mesrop in the fifth century, this Bible is still the standard version used today in the ancient Armenian Church scattered throughout the world.

The Ge'ez and Georgian Bibles: Still used in Ethiopia and Russia, these Bibles were probably also from the fifth century.

Old Slavonic Bible: St. Cyril invented the Cyrillic alphabet, and before long the entire Bible was translated in Old Slavonic. This version is the official Bible of the Russian Orthodox Church.

MIDDLE AGES—ENGLISH TRANSLATIONS

When the Roman Empire broke up, Christianity spread to northern and eastern Europe, and the need for new Bible translations increased. Early English translations were made from the Latin Bible, which was first read and taught in England by monks. It is believed that the first English translation was done by a seventh-century monk named Caedmon. Another English churchman, named Bede, is said to have translated the Gospels into English. He died in 735 A.D while working on his translation. King Alfred the Great (who reigned 871–899 A.D.), another translator, gave his people parts of Exodus, Psalms, and Acts in their own language. He even included parts of the Ten Commandments in the laws of the land! In the 1300s William of Shoreham and Richard Rolle translated the Psalms into English. Both of these popular translations were metrical, and therefore called *Psalters*.

BEFORE THE REFORMATION

John Wycliffe: This Oxford theologian (c. 1329–1384) was the first to translate the entire Bible from Latin into English. He believed that the Bible should be in the hands of every reader, not the exclusive property of churches and church leaders. Wycliffe and his team of translators followed the Latin text closely—even in its awkward order of words! By 1395 John Purvey revised Wycliffe's work in better and clearer English.

Some copies of the Bible had notes that expressed the controversial theological views of Wycliffe and his followers. The pope reproved Wycliffe, and banned his English versions from the popular market. But the appeal of the English Bible continued. Hundreds of copies continued to circulate even up to the time of printing—more than 100 years later.

Jan Hus: Influenced by Wycliffe's teaching, Jan Hus (rector of the University of Prague) was burnt at the stake in 1415. However, his followers began the work of Bible translation. As a result, the Czech New Testament was printed in 1475.

Erasmus of Rotterdam, a well-known Dutch scholar, writer, and humanist was the first editor of the New Testament in Greek. Here, the lover of literature and scholarship is portrayed by the great German Renaissance portraitist, Hans Holbein the Younger (1497–1543).

PRINTING, GUTENBERG, AND THE REFORMATION

At Mainz in Germany, Johann Gutenberg pioneered the process of printing from movable type. The Bible, printed in Latin in 1456, was the first major work to emerge from his press. Ten years later, it was printed in German at Strasbourg. Following this, an Italian Bible and a French New Testament rolled off the press. Next, the first Dutch Scriptures appeared in 1477. Then in 1478, the entire Bible was produced in Catalan for Spain. All these printed versions were based on existing manuscripts and translated from the Latin.

Erasmus: In 1516, the renowned Dutch scholar Erasmus was the first to publish the Greek New Testament. Erasmus himself was not a translator.

Martin Luther: While the young monk Martin Luther was studying his Latin Bible in Germany, he was struck by Paul's teaching in the Book of Romans. Luther's life was transformed by his new understanding of God and salvation, and he became a Bible scholar in earnest. He decided to translate the Bible into plain, everyday German. Luther was determined that everyone should be able to read the Bible. The translation was completed in 1532, and has remained the most famous German Bible since then.

William Tyndale: A Cambridge scholar and follower of Erasmus, Tyndale went to Germany to complete his work of translating the New Testament into English. His first printed version appeared at Worms, Germany, in 1526. Copies soon arrived in England, and were eagerly studied. However, the Bishop of London rejected this work and had the translation burnt in large quantities. Undaunted, Tyndale went on to produce a better version, and by 1566, his second revision had been printed 40 times! He continued to translate other Bible books, but his greatest legacy is his English New Testament.

The founder of the Protestant reformation, Martin Luther. His German translation of the Bible, completed in 1532, is the best-known German Bible today. This portrait by the German artist Lucas Cranach the Elder (1472–1553), is one of many painted throughout the great reformer's life.

Myles Coverdale: In 1535, Coverdale published the entire Bible in English. It was printed overseas but quickly found its way into England. At the request of the clergy, the Coverdale Bible (with a dedication to King Henry VIII included in its pages) was authorized by the king for circulation among the people. Coverdale's work was based on the scholarship of Tyndale, Luther, and the Latin versions of the Bible. His translation of the Psalms is still printed in The Book of Common Prayer. Coverdale is known for including chapter summaries (similar to the Authorized or King James Version), and for separating the Apocrypha from the Old Testament books in his version.

The Great Bible: This translation appeared in 1539 and contained a preface by the Archbishop of Canterbury, Thomas Cranmer, encouraging everyone to read the Bible. The Great Bible was intended for use by churches, and all controversial notes were dropped from its pages.

Before King Henry VIII's death in 1547, large numbers of Tyndale's and Coverdale's translations were destroyed, but the Great Bible remained in the churches (even though services were once more conducted in Latin).

The Geneva Bible: In 1560, English scholars working in Geneva, Switzerland, came out with a Bible revision dedicated to Queen Elizabeth I. The Geneva Bible, as it was called, tried to remain faithful to the style and phrasing of the Hebrew language. It included the Apocrypha, with a note about the importance of these books. The Geneva Bible became popular both in Britain and Switzerland, and was printed 70 times during Elizabeth's reign! It also became the official Bible of the churches in Scotland. It has sometimes been called the Breeches Bible, because in its translation of Genesis 3:7, it notes that Adam and Eve made "breeches" (rather than "loincloths") for themselves.

The Bishops' Bible: The Great Bible, revised by Bishop Parker and others in 1568, became known as the Bishops' Bible. The aim was to improve the text, remove offensive language, and avoid controversial notes and interpretations. In the end, the Great Bible was less popular than the Geneva Bible—and not as good. (However, it was still used in many churches.)

A portrait of James I of England. When James became king in 1603, he became actively involved in a new revision of the Bible, organizing the work and giving his name to the most famous of all English translations—the King James Version, published in London in 1611.

The King James or Authorized Version of 1611: When James I became king of England in 1603, he agreed to a new Bible revision. He helped organize the work, which was then handed to six groups of scholars. The revision was based on the Bishops' Bible, but the original Bible languages were used. Margin notes explained Hebrew and Greek words, linked parallel passages, and new chapter summaries were included.

When it was published, there was a dedication to King James and a long preface explaining how the work of revision and translation was done. This popular version (which, in the beginning, included the Apocrypha) enjoyed great status and authority for 350 years. People enjoyed the flow and dignity of its language. Since the early edition of the King James Version, the spelling has been updated, margin references expanded, and chapter summaries shortened.

The Douai Bible: A year before the King James Version, the first Roman Catholic Bible—the Douai version—was published in France. Gregory Martin and others who worked on this project tried to translate the Vulgate word for word. They ended up with a version that was difficult to understand. Bishop Challoner, unhappy with their results, called for two revisions of the Old Testament—and five of the New Testament! The last revision replaced the original Douai as the official Roman Catholic version.

Dutch, French, and other European Languages: Besides English and German, the Reformation gave rise to Bible translations in many other languages. The first complete Dutch Bible was produced in 1525. During the following century, other versions were published, including the standard Protestant Bible—the States-General version of 1637. This is still used today along with other modern versions.

The French have produced many Bibles, the most popular among Protestants being The Segond Version of 1880 and the Synodale of 1910. *Le Nouveau Testament en Francais Courant,* a modern version in everyday language, is well-liked, especially in French-speaking Africa.

The story of Bible translation in other western Europe countries is similar. However, in eastern Europe old versions were used for centuries. In Russia, the entire Bible was not translated into Russian until 1876. Today there is much Bible translation being done throughout Europe.

MAJOR MODERN ENGLISH VERSIONS

In the centuries following the first publication of the Authorized Version, there were several revisions and new translations. Some of them were based on better manuscripts than the "Received Text" from which the Authorized Version was originally made.

English Revised Version: In 1870, the Church of England decided to make a revision of the King James Version. Talented teams of scholars were appointed and told to make as few changes in the text as possible. When the Revised Version New Testament emerged in 1881, it aroused great interest and speculation in England and America. In the revision,

FOUR VERSIONS COMPARED

	King James Version (1611)	New English Bible (1970)	New International Version (1973 and 1978)	New Revised Standard Version (1989)
Psalm 46:1	God is our refuge and strength, a very present help in trouble.	God is our shelter and our refuge, a timely help in trouble;	God is our refuge and strength, an ever-present help in trouble.	God is our refuge and strength, a very present help in trouble.
John 8:12	Then spake Jesus again unto them, saying, I am the light of the world: he that followeth me shall not walk in darkness, but shall have the light of life.	Once again Jesus addressed the people: 'I am the light of the world. No follower of mine shall wander in the dark; he shall have the light of life.'	When Jesus spoke again to the people, he said, "I am the light of the world. Whoever follows me will never walk in darkness, but will have the light of life."	Again Jesus spoke to them, saying, "I am the light of the world. Whoever follows me will never walk in darkness but will have the light of life."

TRANSLATION, VERSION, REVISION—WHAT'S THE DIFFERENCE?

What type of Bible do you read? Is it a recent translation? An updated version? Perhaps it's a revision of an older version? If this all seems a bit confusing, perhaps some definitions of these terms will help:

Translation: There are two different types of translations. In one instance, the translator tries to render the exact words of the original language into the receptor language—for example, English. Using another approach, the translator takes the words or terms of the original language and tries to find the closest natural meaning in the receptor language. In this second method, the translation should have the same impact on the modern reader as the original had upon its audience.

Version: A translation from the original texts that is prepared by a committee of scholars.

Revision: A revised edition of an existing translation.

many well-known words and verses had been left out because they were lacking any real manuscript authority. The entire Bible was issued in 1885, but because it was oriented toward British spelling and figures of speech, it lost support in the United States.

Revised Standard Version: A special agency of the World Council of Churches began working on a revision of the American Standard Version in 1929. Based on the latest scholarly Greek texts, the New Testament section of the RSV was published in 1946, and the Old Testament came out in 1952. It was considered a more reliable and readable translation than most others up to this point, but it was criticized because of the new wording of some key passages.

New English Bible: Dr. C. H. Dodd was the director of a new translation, suggested by the Church of Scotland in 1946. The New Testament was first published in 1961; the Old Testament appeared in 1970. This official interchurch translation in Britain was the first major version to move away from the Tyndale and Authorized Version tradition.

All the latest biblical research was considered in putting together the New English Bible. The Dead Sea Scrolls gave light to Old Testament texts, and newly discovered manuscripts revealed the meanings of some difficult words. This version, although updated, has not quite captured the idiom of everyday speech.

Good News Bible: This version was produced by the American Bible Society between 1966 and 1976. Its aim was to have a reliable and accurate translation using the language of everyday speech. Based on a careful study of linguistics, it has provided a pattern for translations in many languages all over the world.

Jerusalem Bible: In 1966, the Jerusalem Bible was published by Roman Catholic translators. Based on the original languages, this modern, lively version is widely used by both Catholics and Protestants. The Jerusalem Bible (first translated into French) includes the introduction and notes from

SOME OF TODAY'S ENGLISH VERSIONS

Date	Title	Translator
1901	*The Holy Bible: American Standard Version*	Thomas Nelson and Sons
1903	*The New Testament in Modern Speech*	Richard Weymouth
1913	*The New Testament*	James Moffatt
1917	*The Holy Scriptures According to the Masoretic Text*	The Jewish Publication Society of America
1923	*The New Testament: An American Translation*	Edgar J. Goodspeed
1924	*The Old Testament*	James Moffatt
1944	*The New Testament*	Ronald Knox
1947	*Letters to the Young Churches: Epistles of the New Testament*	J. B. Phillips
1949	*The Old Testament*	Ronald A. Knox
1950	*The New Testament of Our Messiah and Saviour Yahshua*	A. B. Traina
	New World Translation: New Testament	Watchtower Bible and Tract Society, Inc.
1952	*The Holy Bible: Revised Standard Version*	Thomas Nelson and Sons
1958	*The New Testament in Modern English*	J. B. Phillips
1959	*The Holy Bible: The Berkeley Version in Modern English*	Zondervan Publishing Co.
1960	*The Holy Bible (New American Standard)*	Thomas Nelson and Sons
	The New World Translation: Old Testament	Watchtower Bible and Tract Society, Inc.
1966	*The Jerusalem Bible*	Darton, Longman & Todd, Ltd.
1970	*New English Bible*	Oxford/Cambridge University Press
1971	*New American Standard Bible*	The Lockman Foundation
	The Living Bible	Tyndale House
1976	*The Good News Bible*	American Bible Society
1978	*The New International Version*	Zondervan Bible Publishers
1982	*The Holy Bible, New King James Version*	Thomas Nelson Publishers
1986	*The New Jerusalem Bible*	Darton, Longman & Todd, Ltd.
1989	*New Revised Standard Bible*	Thomas Nelson Publishers and others
	Revised English Bible	Oxford/Cambridge University Press
1995	*Contemporary English Version*	American Bible Society and Thomas Nelson Publishers
1996	*New Living Bible*	Tyndale Publishers

the French translation. The New Jerusalem Bible was published in 1986.

New International Version: This translation was produced in 1973 (New Testament) and 1978 (Old Testament) by a team of Protestant evangelical scholars mainly from the United States. They produced an updated, formal Bible in the tradition of earlier English versions.

New King James Version: The New Testament of the NKJV was published in 1979 by Thomas Nelson Publishers.

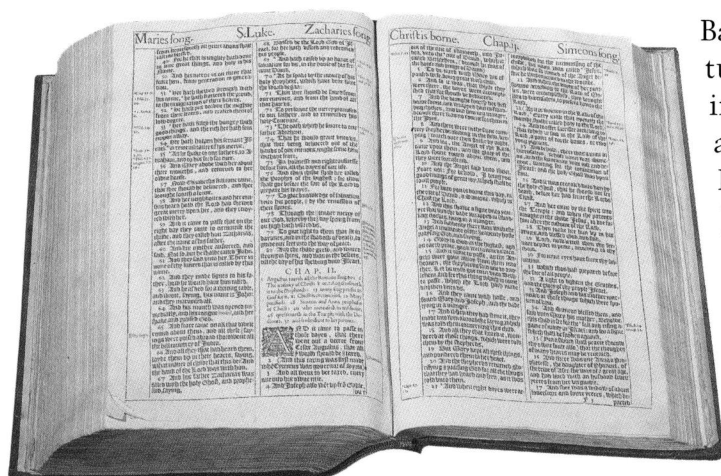

For more than three centuries, the King James Version of the Bible has had a stronger influence on the thought and literature of the English-speaking world than any other book. These pages from the popular translation represent Luke's account of the birth of Christ.

Based on the 1894 edition of the Textus Receptus, it both preserved the integrity of the text and eliminated archaic, difficult-to-read expressions. In 1982, the complete New King James Version was published by Thomas Nelson, and it became quite popular.

New Revised Standard Version: Responding to the need for a readable, accurate Bible—with gender-inclusive language—this new work was developed from the most ancient biblical texts available. Pioneered by Bruce M. Metzger and a stellar translation committee, the New RSV was published in 1989.

JEWISH TRANSLATIONS

The Holy Scriptures According to the Masoretic Text, A New Translation (put out in 1917), aimed to combine the heart of Jewish culture with the best of biblical scholarship. In 1955, the Jewish Publication Society appointed a committee to make a new Jewish translation of the Bible, the Tanakh. The New Jewish Version was published in 1962 (and revised in 1973).

THE WORK OF BIBLE TRANSLATORS

After the Middle Ages, the first translations of the Bible were made by Roman Catholics. By 1613, Jesuit missionar-

STATISTICS OF MODERN BIBLE TRANSLATION

Today, more than 5,440 languages are known to be spoken throughout the world. The work of Bible translation involves about 1,745 of these languages. However, of these, the entire Bible (or the New Testament) has been translated in under 600 languages:

Europe and the Middle East	46 languages
Asia-Pacific	285 languages
Africa	249 languages
Americas and the Caribbean	6 languages

There are also another 1,159 translations and revisions presently in progress:

Europe and the Middle East	12 languages
Asia-Pacific	465 languages
Africa	402 languages
Americas and the Caribbean	280 languages

ies had published the New Testament in Japanese. A Protestant version in Malay was then put together by workers of the Dutch East India Company. And the first entire Bible was translated in a complex American Indian language by John Eliot in 1633.

William Carey's work in India was a big step forward in this important task. Along with some colleagues and helpers, Carey spent 40 years working on translations of the Scriptures in 37 different languages or dialects, including Burmese and Chinese.

Amharic, the modern dialect of north-central Ethiopia, is related to ancient Hebrew of the Semitic family of languages. These finely decorated pages are from the Amharic Bible, Ethiopia, 1959.

In 1804, the British and Foreign Bible Society was founded. They put out the Hindustani New Testament in 1812 and the first modern African translation in 1816. Since the society began, there have been translations into approximately 480 African languages. Several other societies emerged decades ago and continued the work of Bible translation. These groups helped establish projects, they gave money where it was needed, and they had translations printed and distributed. In the case of the Netherlands Society, they trained their own linguists and sent them out as translators.

As the modern missionary movement grew, so did the work of translation. And although nationals were involved, the primary translators were usually missionaries. Thus, during the first half of the twentieth century, Bible translation moved along at a rapid pace.

Today, the largest missionary society in the world is the Wycliffe Bible Translators, founded in 1934. Their translators

THE HISTORY OF BIBLE TRANSLATION

B.C.	300	Greek
	200	
	100	
A.D.	100	Latin, Syriac
	200	Coptic
	300	Gothic, Georgian, Ethiopic
	400	Armenian
	500	Nubian
	600	Chinese
	700	Arabic, Anglo-Saxon
	800	German, Slavonic, Frankish
	900	
	1000	
	1100	French
	1200	Icelandic, Dutch, Spanish, Italian, Polish
	1300	English, Danish, Czech, Persian
	1400	
	1500	Swedish
	1600	Finnish
	1700	Portuguese, Tamil
	1800	Norwegian, Russian, Swahili, Hindi, Urdu, Bengali, Japanese
	1900	Hausa, Afrikaans, and more than 1,000 other languages

are thoroughly trained in linguistics before beginning the simplest task in figuring out a text. After months—or even years—of difficult translating work, the reward is to see the joy the translation brings to someone who is finally able to read the Scriptures in their local language for the very first time!

Another large group, the United Bible Societies, organizes more than 60 national societies all over the world. Both Protestants and Catholics are part of this work, which covers some of the major languages of the world—including Hindi, Chinese, and Arabic.

Today's translator is often a national—rather than a missionary— working to improve an existing translation developed by a foreigner. Translators often work together, sharing ideas, noting criticisms of the text, and drafting revisions. Bible society officers keep in close touch with translating projects throughout the world.

Besides Wycliffe Bible Translators and the United Bible Societies, there are several other translators at work today. However, there are still hundreds of language groups without an existing translation. Clearly, there is plenty of work to be done. And Bible society scholars estimate that as languages keep changing, a revision—if not a new translation—will be needed every 30 years for each language.

OPENING UP THE BIBLE

Why do millions of people the world over read the Bible on a regular basis? What appeal does this ancient book have for the average person today?

There are a number of reasons why people are fascinated by the Bible, and drawn to its stories and teachings. First, the

Bible is all about God and his dealings with humanity. The lives of biblical characters and their experiences with God reflect our personal stories, too. The spiritual journeys of those who have gone before give us insight and direction for our own lives.

Also, as we look at the history of humanity, it becomes evident that the Bible has played a central role in many cultures: shaping laws, politics, and religion—influencing human rights and the fabric of social life. This influence continues today in many parts of the world.

The foundation of the world: "In the beginning . . . God created the heavens and the earth . . . God saw everything that he had made, and indeed, it was very good." Gen 1:1, 31

GENESIS

Message: Genesis is about beginnings: the creation of the world, a new beginning after the great flood, and the beginning of the Jewish nation.

Key passages and events: The creation and corruption of the world (chapters 1–3); Cain kills his brother Abel (4); Noah and the flood (6–9); the Tower of Babel (11); the story of Abraham (12–25); the destruction of Sodom and Gomorrah (19); Jacob's story (27–35); Joseph's story (37–50)

God ordered Noah, his family, and animals of every kind into the ark for protection from the waters of judgment. This depiction is by 20th-century artist Andre Normil.

The deliverance of Israel at the Red Sea: "I will sing to the Lord, for he has triumphed gloriously; horse and rider he has thrown into the sea. The Lord is my strength and my might, and he has become my salvation . . ."
Ex 15:1–2

Setting: An area of the Middle East known as the "fertile crescent"
Time of events: About 2000–1650 B.C.
Author: Attributed to Moses

EXODUS

Message: Under Moses' leadership, God rescues his people from slavery in Egypt, and begins to show them how to live a new life.
Key passages and events: Moses in the reeds (chapters 1–2); the ten plagues (7–12); the Passover (12–15); crossing the Red Sea (14); the Ten Commandments and the Law (20–24); the tent of worship (tabernacle) (26)
Setting: The Nile Delta in Egypt and the Sinai peninsula
Time of events: About 1325–1225 B.C.
Author: Attributed to Moses

LEVITICUS

Message: An account of how to offer sacrifices and carry out ceremonial law, Leviticus concerns itself with the duties of the priests and Levites. It also describes the religious festivals that marked the year for the Israelites.
Key passages and events: Laws about offerings and sacrifices (chapters 1–7); Aaron and his sons ordained as priests (8–9); ritual health laws (11–15); the Day of Atonement (16); worship and the festivals (17–27)
Setting: The Sinai peninsula

TEN QUICK TITLES—BIBLES FOR CHILDREN

Children's Bibles are a popular item on the publishing market right now. Some of these Bibles are really adult translations with artwork for children. Other so-called Children's Bibles are, in fact, just Bible storybooks with nice pictures. However, a few publishers have taken existing Bible translations and simplified them for children. Here is a list of Bibles designed especially for children and young people:

1. The Bible For Children
2. Simplified Living Bible
3. Children's New Testament
4. Precious Moments Children's Bible
5. International Children's Bible
6. The Everyday Bible
7. The New Testament in Modern English
8. A Book about Jesus (contains passages from the four Gospels)
9. Good News Travels Fast: Acts of the Apostles
10. A Few Who Dared (portions of the Old Testament)

Time of events: Between 1325–1225 B.C.

Author: Attributed to Moses

NUMBERS

Message: The story of the clans of Israel living as nomads in the Sinai peninsula after escaping from Egypt.

Key passages and events: Life in the desert (chapters 1–14); Korah's rebellion (14); water pouring from the rock (20); the bronze snake (21); Balak and Balaam (24); the Promised Land, Canaan (34)

Setting: Mount Sinai and the Sinai peninsula

Time of events: Between 1325–1225 B.C.

Author: Attributed to Moses

In this stylized rendering of the battle of Jericho in Lincoln Cathedral, Lincoln, England, the priests blow the trumpets in obedience to Joshua's instructions from the Lord. The Book of Joshua recounts the unusual sequence of events that led to the fall of Jericho into the hands of the Israelites.

DEUTERONOMY

Message: The second record of God's laws, this book stresses obedience to God. As Israel is about to enter the Promised Land, Moses gives the people his final oration.

Key passages and events: Moses' reflections (chapters 1–4); obedience and God's laws (4–27); instructions for the new land (27–28); the covenant renewed (29); Joshua, the new leader (31); Moses' blessing (32–33); Moses' death (34)

Setting: The plain east of the River Jordan

Time of events: Approximately 1230 B.C.

Author: Attributed to Moses

JOSHUA

Message: The story of the Israelite invasion of Canaan, led by Joshua.

Key passages and events: Joshua commissioned as leader (chapter 1); Rahab and the spies (2); crossing the Jordan (3); the fall of Jericho (5–6); the conquest of Canaan (9–12); the land divided among the tribes (13–19); Joshua's farewell message and death (23–24)

Setting: The plain east of the River Jordan; Canaan

Time of events: About 1230–1200 B.C.

Author: Unknown

JUDGES

Message: In spite of Israel's disobedience, God provides national heroes to rescue his people during the time between Israel's taking of Canaan and the first kings.

Key passages and events: Deborah and Barak defeat the Canaanites (chapters 4–5); Gideon's fleece and the Midianites (6–7); Jephthah, his daughter, and the battle with the Ammonites (10–12); Samson's story (13–16)

Setting: Canaan, the land of Israel

Time of events: About 1200–1070 B.C.

Author: Uncertain (possibly Samuel)

Before he became Israel's greatest king, young David killed the Philistine champion, Goliath of Gath. David is seen here—Goliath's sword in hand—standing over his vanquished foe.

RUTH

Message: The story of Ruth is one of love, loyalty, and God's care for everyone who is faithful to him, whatever their nationality.

Key passages and events: Ruth's husband dies (chapter 1); Ruth goes to Moab with her mother-in-law, Naomi (1–2); Ruth and Boaz (3); Ruth marries Boaz and has a son (4)

Setting: Bethlehem and Moab

Time of events: 1375–1050 B.C.

Author: Unknown

1 AND 2 SAMUEL

Message: The history of Israel from the last of the judges, Eli and Samuel, and the first two kings, Saul and David.

Key passages and events: *1 Samuel:* Samuel's birth, call, and leadership (chapters 1–7); Saul becomes Israel's first king (8–15); God chooses David as Israel's future king (16); David kills Goliath (17); David and Jonathan (20); David outlawed (18–30); the deaths of Saul and Jonathan (31); *2 Samuel:* David mourns (1); David is crowned king (2–4); David conquers Jerusalem (5); David brings the Covenant to Jerusalem (6); David's adultery with Bathsheba and murder of Uriah (11–12); David's family troubles (13–20); David's song and final words (22–23)

Setting: Canaan, the land of Israel

Time of events: About 1200–1070 B.C.

Author: Unknown

Renowned for great wisdom and the building of the temple in Jerusalem, King Solomon, David's successor, led Israel into a period of great prosperity and peace. Nevertheless, his reign was marred by his ill-treatment of his subjects and by the idolatry of his foreign wives, which he embraced.

1 AND 2 KINGS

Message: The story of Israel's history from David's death, through the kingdom division following Solomon's death, to the fall of Jerusalem and destruction of the temple by the Babylonians.

Key passages and events: *1 Kings:* Solomon asks for wisdom (chapters 3–4); the building and dedication of the temple (5–8); the Queen of Sheba's visit (10); Solomon's failure and death (11); the kingdom is divided (12); Elijah's and Baal's contest (17–19); King Ahab and Naboth's vineyard (21); *2 Kings:* Elijah is taken to heaven (2); Elisha and his miracles (2–6); the curing of Naaman (5); Queen Athaliah and the boy king, Joash (11); Israel's capture by Assyria (17); King Hezekiah and the Assyrian threat (18); King Josiah's discovery (22–23); Jerusalem falls to Babylon (25)

Setting: The two kingdoms of Israel and Judah

Time of events: About 970–586 B.C.

Author: Uncertain (possibly Ezra, Ezekiel, or Jeremiah)

1 AND 2 CHRONICLES

Message: Chronicles tries to convince the Jews (now back home in Jerusalem after their exile in Babylon) that, in spite of their troubled history, they are still God's people. These books cover the same events as those in 2 Samuel and Kings.

Key passages and events: *1 Chronicles:* Family trees from Adam to the first kings (chapters 1–9); death of King Saul (10); the story of King David (11–21); David's preparations for building the temple and worship (22–29); *2 Chronicles:* King Solomon's story (1–9); the kings of Judah (10–36); last days and the fall of Jerusalem (36)

Setting: Israel and Judah

Time of events: About 1000—586 B.C.

Author: Uncertain (possibly Ezra)

EZRA

Message: The story of two groups of Jews who return to their homeland from exile in Babylon. They reconstruct the temple and, under the leadership of Ezra the priest, begin to observe the law.

Key passages and events: The first group returns to Jerusalem (chapters 1–2); in spite of opposition, the temple is rebuilt (3–6); the second group returns with Ezra (7–10)

Setting: Jerusalem

To godly Jews, Babylonian captivity was a sad period marked by deep longing for Jerusalem and the land promised to the children of Abraham. The people of God were unable to sing songs of joy in a strange land so they laid down their musical instruments by the waters of Kebar. In this painting by 19th-century German artist Eduard Bendemann, those in exile mourn their predicament.

Time of events: About 538–428 B.C.
Author: Uncertain (possibly Ezra)

NEHEMIAH

Message: Nehemiah, a Jewish exile and great leader, directs another group of exiles back to Jerusalem. He becomes governor of Judea, and initiates the rebuilding of the city walls. His reforms overlap Ezra's work.

Key passages and events: Nehemiah returns to Jerusalem and the walls are rebuilt (chapters 1–7); a list of the returned exiles (7); Ezra reads the law and the people repent (8–10); the dedication of the new walls (12); Nehemiah's reforms (12–13)

Setting: Jerusalem
Time of events: About 458–432 B.C.
Author: Nehemiah

ESTHER

Message: The beautiful Jewish girl, Esther, becomes queen to the Persian Emperor, Ahasuerus (Xerxes). With the help of her guardian, Mordecai, she thwarts a plot to have all Jews in the Emperor's kingdom exterminated.

Key passages and events: The emperor's wife, Vashti, is rejected (chapter 1); Esther is crowned queen (2); Haman's plot (3–4); the courage of Esther (5); the deliverance of the Jews (6–10)

Setting: Susa
Time of events: About 460 B.C.
Author: Unknown

JOB

Message: This dramatic poem deals with the problem of human suffering. It tells the story of Job, a good man, who loses everything yet still has deep faith in God.

Key passages and events: Job's disasters (chapters 1–2); the friends of Job (3–37); God reveals his greatness to Job (38–42); the deliverance of Job (42)

Setting: Unknown
Time of events: Unknown
Author: Unknown

This poignant portrayal of an afflicted and sorrowful Job—under the counsel and admonition of his three friends—is found in St. Mark's Church, St. Paul, Minnesota.

PSALMS

Message: A compilation of 150 hymns, prayers, and poems expressing the range of human emotions. The common thread throughout this collection is deep faith and love for the Lord.

Key themes and passages: Instruction (Psalms 1, 19, 39); praise (8, 29, 93, 100); thanksgiving (30, 65, 103, 107, 116); repentance (6, 32, 38, 51, 130); trust (3, 27, 31, 46, 56, 62, 86); distress (4, 13, 55, 64, 88); hope (42, 63, 80, 84, 137); history (78, 105)

Time of events: Collections of Psalms were made throughout Israel's history

Author: Different writers (many titles are linked to King David)

The faithfulness of God: "Praise the Lord, all you nations! Extol him, all you peoples! For great is his steadfast love toward us, and the faithfulness of the Lord endures forever. Praise the Lord!" Ps 117

PROVERBS

Message: A collection of wise sayings. The main theme is to discover and follow godly wisdom and apply it to everyday living.

Key themes: Wisdom and folly; the righteous and the wicked; how to speak wisely; wealth and poverty; hopes and fears; joys and sorrows; anger; hard work and laziness

Time of events: Wisdom literature flourished during and after Solomon's reign

Author: Solomon and other wisdom teachers

ECCLESIASTES

Message: Life is short, and there is nothing that lasts. The author trusts in God, but believes that we can never know what God's intentions are. Clearly, for this writer, the life of faith is difficult.

Key words: "For everything there is a season, and a time for every matter under heaven" (Ecc 3:1)

Time of events: Uncertain

Author: Solomon or a later Jewish sage

SONG OF SOLOMON

Message: A collection of six beautiful songs expressing the wonder of unselfish love between a husband and his wife.

Key themes and passages: Courtship (chapters 1–3); the wedding (3–5); growth in marriage (5–8); the nature and power of love (8)

Setting: The countryside in springtime

Time of events: About 971–931 B.C.

Author: Possibly Solomon

ISAIAH

Message: Isaiah the prophet is called by God to warn of judgment on all who turn away from him. The prophet's message is that Israel must depend on God alone. Along with Isaiah's prophecies, the book is full of promises about the coming Messiah and future restoration.

Key themes and passages: Isaiah's vision and call (chapter 6); God with us (7); the future king (9); the peaceful kingdom (11); the road of holiness (35); Isaiah and the Assyrian siege (36–37); comfort and the mighty God (40); the Lord's servant (42); a light to the nations (49); the suffering servant (52–53); God's invitation (55); future glory (60); deliverance (61)

Setting: Jerusalem

Time of events: About 790–722 B.C.

Author: Isaiah

JEREMIAH

Message: Jeremiah hated to bring bad news, but all of his prophecies came true. He spoke of coming judgment on Israel because of sin and idolatry.

Key themes and passages: God calls Jeremiah (chapter 1); God's word to his wayward people (2–6); captivity and destruction predicted (13–17, 25); the potter's house (18–19); the promise of restoration (30–33); the king destroys Jeremiah's scroll (36); Jeremiah in captivity (37–38); fall of Jerusalem (39, 52); messages to other nations (46–51)

Setting: Judah

Time of events: About 627–586 B.C.

Author: Jeremiah

LAMENTATIONS

Message: These five poems express the sorrow of the Jews at the destruction of Jerusalem by the Babylonians. Mostly written in an acrostic form (based on the letters of the Hebrew alphabet), these laments express fear that God has abandoned his people. However, the writer puts his faith in God's unfailing mercy.

Key passage: Hope (La 3:21–27)

Setting: Jerusalem

Time of events: Probably 586 B.C.

Author: Uncertain (attributed to Jeremiah)

EZEKIEL

Message: Much of Ezekiel's message is about sin and judgment. The prophet/priest proclaimed that God in his glory

Hannah's prayer of thanksgiving: "The Lord makes poor and makes rich; he brings low, he also exalts. He raises up the poor from the dust; he lifts the needy from the ash heap, to make them sit with princes and inherit a seat of honor." 1Sa 2:7, 8

The renewal of Israel: "I will remove from your body the heart of stone and give you a heart of flesh. I will put my spirit within you, and make you follow my statutes and be careful to observe my ordinances." Eze 36:26–27

and holiness could not tolerate impurity and idolatry. He predicted the fall of Jerusalem, but spoke of the hope of repentance, restoration, and renewed worship.

Key themes and passages: Ezekiel's vision (chapter 1); his call (2–3); Ezekiel dramatizes the siege of Jerusalem (4–5); God's glory leaves the temple (8–10); death of Ezekiel's wife (24); the valley of the dry bones (37); vision of a new temple (40–48)

Setting: Babylon

Time of events: About 593–571 B.C.

Author: Ezekiel

DANIEL

Message: Exiled in Babylon from boyhood, Daniel's story is one of uncompromising courage and faith in the midst of persecution. The Book of Daniel also includes visions of the future and a prayer.

Key themes and passages: Daniel in Babylon (chapters 1–6); the fiery furnace (3); Belshazzar's feast (5); Daniel escapes the lions (6); visions of four empires (7–8); Daniel's prayer (9); visions of future conflict (10–11); the time of the end (12)

Daniel, the wise Jewish counselor and administrator in Babylon, remains steadfast in the face of death, protected by the hand of God.

Setting: Babylon
Time of events : About 605–536 B.C.
Author: Daniel

HOSEA

Message: Compassionate Hosea speaks out against Israel's corrupt civic and religious life. His own experience with family problems makes the prophet sensitive to Israel's unfaithfulness. He warns Israel of destruction, and implores the people to return to God and enjoy his blessing.

Key themes and passages: Hosea's sorrow for his wife (chapter 1); unfaithful Israel (2); Hosea's wife returns (3); God loves his people but must judge their sin (4–13); promised restoration if Israel repents (14)

Setting: Northern kingdom of Israel
Time of events: About 790–715 B.C.
Author: Hosea

JOEL

Message: The image of locusts is used as a sign of the coming judgment day of the Lord. The prophet Joel calls for national repentance. He also looks forward to a time of rich blessing when God's Spirit will be poured out on everyone.

Key themes and passages: A plague of locusts (chapter 1); call to repentance (2); the gift of the Spirit (3); against the nations (3)

Setting: Judah
Time of events: Uncertain
Author: Attributed to Joel

Swarms of locusts plagued the biblical world, consuming food crops and causing famine. One of God's judgments on Egypt was a locust invasion. Yet, despite their destructive nature, locusts were good to eat, and were part of John the Baptist's diet in the wilderness.

AMOS

Message: The prophet speaks out against the unfairness, greed, and hypocrisy of Israel and other nations.

Key themes and passages: Prophecies against other nations (chapters 1–2); prophecies against Israel (2–6); five visions (7–9); a promise of restoration (9)

Setting: Northern kingdom of Israel
Time of events: About 790–722 B.C.
Author: Amos

OBADIAH

Message: In this short prophecy against the Edomites—a nation that had taken advantage of Jerusalem—Obadiah warns that God will destroy Edom. In the future, Obadiah declares, Israel will not only get back their land, but they will also get the land of the Edomites.

Setting: Jerusalem

Time of events: Uncertain

Author: Obadiah

JONAH

Message: Jonah dislikes the idea that God's mercy extends beyond Israel—particularly to one of their most violent enemies. In this riveting story, God sets out to transform Jonah's thinking.

Key themes and passages: Jonah's disobedience—the storm and the great fish (chapters 1–2); Jonah's obedience—the action and words of the Lord (3–4)

Setting: The Great Sea and Assyria

Time of events: 793–753 B.C.

Author: Jonah

The story of the prophet Jonah's deliverance from the belly of the great fish is dramatically depicted by Dutch painter, Pieter Lastman (1583–1633). After Jonah was spewed out upon dry land, the reluctant prophet went on to preach at Nineveh as the Lord commanded.

MICAH

Message: The prophet is appalled by the false sacrifices and empty worship of Israel. His central concerns are for social justice and true religion. His hope is in God's future peace and blessing.

Key themes and passages: Judgment will come (chapters 1–2); God's reign of peace (4); a king from Bethlehem (5); what God requires (6)

Setting: Israel and Judah

Time of events: 750–722 B.C.

Author: Micah

NAHUM

Message: This book is an oracle against Nineveh, capital of the cruel and powerful Assyrians. Nahum's message does include a call to repentance.

Key themes and passages: The certainty and description of God's judgment against Nineveh (chapters 1–2); the reasons for God's judgment (3)

Setting: Judah

Time of events: Around 612 B.C.

Author: Nahum

HABAKKUK

Message: The prophet faces the difficult question: How can God allow the wicked to prosper? Why is it that evil Babylonia overpowers weak, less evil nations? The prophet concludes that true faith will not be disappointed because God, who is in control, can be trusted.

Key themes and passages: Habakkuk's distress (chapter 1); a dirge from God: the "woes" of Habakkuk (2); Habakkuk's prayer for mercy and God's majestic presence (3)

Setting: Judah

Time of events: 612–597 B.C.

Author: Habakkuk

ZEPHANIAH

Message: The prophet predicts only doom for disobedient Jerusalem. But he believes that a remnant of the nation will survive and enjoy a great future.

Key themes and passages: The day of judgment (chapters 1–2); doom for the nations, and hope for the remnant (2–3)

Setting: Judah

Time of events: 640–609 B.C.

Author: Zephaniah

"But as for me, I will look to the Lord, I will wait for the God of my salvation; my God will hear me."
Mic 7:7

HAGGAI

Message: The prophet Haggai urges God's people who have returned from exile, to finish the job of rebuilding the temple. They had abandoned the project, and instead, built fine homes for themselves. The people respond to Haggai's challenge, and the work of rebuilding continues.

Key themes and passages: A command to rebuild the temple (chapter 1); God's blessing on the obedient (2); a word for Zerubbabel, the governor (2)

Setting: Jerusalem

Time of events: 520 B.C.

Author: Haggai

The coming ruler of God's people: "Lo, your king comes to you; triumphant and victorious is he, humble and riding on a donkey, on a colt, the foal of a donkey." Zec 9:9

ZECHARIAH

Message: The prophet declares that a new age is beginning. Zechariah speaks not only about the blessing and hope of Jerusalem, but of the whole world. Zechariah also speaks of the coming of a Messiah, a king of love and justice who will be sent by God.

Key themes and passages: A new age is starting (chapters 1–8); eight symbolic visions (1–6); a message of rejoicing (8); the nations surrounding Israel (9); the blessings of the Messiah (9); the redemption of Israel (12–13); the return of the King (14)

Setting: Jerusalem

Time of events: 520–515 B.C.

Author: Zechariah

MALACHI

Message: The prophet challenges Israel to keep God's commandments, and encourages the people to rely on him for future blessing.

Key themes and passages: God's love for Israel (chapter 1); broken promises and judgment (2); paying tithes (3); God's promise of mercy (3–4)

Setting: Jerusalem

Time of events: About 430 B.C.

Author: Malachi

Opposite page: *In his most renowned work, "The Battle of Issus" (1529), Albrecht Altdorfer displays in grand detail the battle in which Alexander the Great defeats the Persian king, Darius. The inscription hanging in the clouds describes the conquest.*

THE TIME BETWEEN THE TESTAMENTS

Ezra, Nehemiah, and Esther give us the last glimpse of the Jews in the Old Testament. After Malachi, and until the start of New Testament times, the biblical prophets were silent. What do we know about this period?

- Alexander the Great from Greece conquered Palestine and

ALEXANDER M. DARIVM VLT: SVPERAT
CÆSIS IN ACIE PERSAR: PEDIT: C.M. EQVIT
VERO X M. INTERFECTIS. MATRE QVOQVE
CONIVGE, LIBERIS DARII REG. CVM M. HAVD
AMPLIVS EQVITIB: FVGA DILAPSI, CAPTIS.

The tragedies of Tobit the Naphtalite, exiled in Nineveh, were remedied through the experiences of his son Tobias, and his daughter-in-law, Sarah—all under the supervision of the angel Raphael. Here, the angel Raphael takes leave of old Tobit and his son.

THE APOCRYPHA

Christians agree that the 39 books of the Hebrew Scriptures are the core of the Old Testament. Questions arise over the status of the books called *Apocrypha* (meaning "hidden") by Protestants and *Deuterocanonical* by Roman Catholics. The apocryphal books (written about 200 B.C.) were found and accepted by the early Christians when they took over the Septuagint as their Bible. Today, all Catholic Bibles contain the Deuterocanonical books (slightly different from the apocryphal collection). Some Protestant Bibles contain the Apocrypha. Many do not. And significant numbers of Christians believe that the apocryphal books are not part of the Scriptures, and therefore not authoritative.

The Apocrypha includes many types of literature, including wisdom, history, and visionary writing. There are even stories with startling supernatural details. In the book of Tobit, the liver and heart of a fish can—with the help of a guardian angel—drive away demons and cure blindness!

Apocryphal or Deuterocanonical Books

Tobit
Judith
Additions to Esther
Wisdom
Sirach (Ecclesiasticus)
Baruch
Letter of Jeremiah
Prayer of Azariah and the Song of the Three Jews
Susanna
Bel and the Dragon
1 Maccabees
2 Maccabees
1 Esdras
Prayer of Manasseh
Psalm 151
3 Maccabees
2 Esdras
4 Maccabees

the surrounding lands. He introduced Greek language and customs to Palestine (333–332 B.C.).

- When Alexander died, his empire went to four generals. Palestine was first conquered by the Egyptian kingdom, and then in turn, by the kingdom founded in Syria and Mesopotamia.
- Antiochus (one of the conquerors) tried to force the Jews to adopt Greek beliefs and ways of worship. In his zeal to destroy Jewish faith in God, he set up a statue of the Greek God Zeus in the temple at Jerusalem and even sacrificed a pig in the temple.
- The Jews revolted against Antiochus. The Maccabee family who led the revolt became the new rulers. However, Jewish independence did not last long.
- Palestine was then conquered by the expanding Roman empire. Jewish priests were killed, and the Jews were once again dominated by the rule of outsiders.
- Augustus Caesar became emperor of the Roman Empire in 27 B.C. By the time Jesus came, the Jews were under the rule of the Romans (who continued to encourage the Greek way of life).

Matthew

Message: This Gospel links the Old Testament and the New. It portrays Jesus as the Messiah, the one foretold by the prophets. Matthew emphasizes the concerns of Jewish Christians.

Great events: Jesus' birth (chapter 1); Jesus' baptism (3); the temptation of Jesus (4); the transfiguration (17); Jesus' entry into Jerusalem (21); trials and crucifixion (26–27); Jesus' resurrection (28)

Famous passages: Sermon on the Mount (5–7); the Lord's Prayer (6); the Great Commission (28)

Time of writing: 60–80 A.D.

Setting: Mainly Galilee

Author: Attributed to Matthew

Mark

Message: Jesus is depicted as a man of action. He is the "Son of man" (of Daniel's vision) who wants his identity kept hidden.

"He went up the mountain and called to him those whom he wanted, and they came to him. And he appointed twelve, whom he also named apostles, to be with him, and to be sent out to proclaim the message, and to have authority to cast out demons." (Mk 3:13-15)

Great events: John the Baptist prepares the way (chapter 1); Jesus' baptism (1); choosing 12 followers (3); feeding the 5,000 (6); the last supper (14); Jesus arrest, trial, and death (14–15); the resurrection (16)

Famous passages: Jesus and the children (9–10); casting out the money changers (11)

Time of writing: 60–70 A.D.

Setting: Mainly Galilee

Author: Attributed to John Mark

LUKE

Message: Jesus came first to the Jews, his chosen people, now salvation comes to everyone. However, salvation is for the needy, those without hope. Luke portrays Jesus as the Savior, a man of prayer, full of the Holy Spirit.

Great events: The angel's message and the birth of Jesus (chapters 1–2); Jesus' baptism and temptation (3–4); the transfiguration (9); Jesus' entry into Jerusalem (20); the last supper (22); trial and crucifixion (22–23); Jesus' resurrection (24)

Famous passages: The angel's message to Mary (1); Mary's song (1); the shepherds and the angels (2); the parable of the great feast (14); the parable of the prodigal son (15); a blind beggar (18); Jesus and Zacchaeus (19)

Time of writing: Between 60–85 A.D.

Setting: Mainly Galilee

Author: Attributed to Luke

The Word became flesh: "In the beginning was the Word, and the Word was with God, and the Word was God . . . All things came into being through him, and without him not one thing came into being. What has come into being in him was life, and the life was the light of all people." Jn 1:1–4

JOHN

Message: Jesus is the "Word of God" who desires to draw people to faith. John tells the story of Jesus' life in the framework of seven signs and seven sayings, and presents Jesus as light, life, and love.

Great events: Jesus at the wedding (chapter 2); the woman at the well (4); the raising of Lazarus (11); Jesus' anointing (12); the triumphal entry (12); the last supper (13); Jesus' arrest, trial, and death (18–19); the empty tomb (20); Jesus appears to Thomas (20)

Famous passages: The Word (1); God's great love (3); the light of the world (8); Jesus washes the disciples' feet (13); Jesus, the way, the truth, and the life (14); the coming Holy Spirit (16)

Time of writing: Between 60–100 A.D.

Setting: Mainly Jerusalem

Author: Attributed to the apostle John

ACTS OF THE APOSTLES

Message: Acts recounts the history of the early church from its small beginnings to its great expansion throughout the Roman Empire.

Great events: The ascension (chapter 1); the gift of the Holy Spirit (2); Saul's conversion (9); the voyage to Rome (27–28)

Famous passages: Peter's sermon (2); the jailer at Philippi (16); Paul before Agrippa (26)

Time of writing: About 60–85 A.D.

Setting: The Roman Empire

Author: Attributed to Luke

This painting by the great renaissance artist, El Greco (1541–1614), depicts the apostle Paul, a zealous Pharisee who—once converted—became the principal theologian of Christianity and a fervent missionary to the Gentiles.

ROMANS

Message: In his letter to the Romans, Paul reveals the message of the gospel step by step, and shows how a person's life is changed by believing the good news.

Key passage: Justification by faith (chapter 5)

Time of writing: Around 57 A.D.

Author: The apostle Paul

1 CORINTHIANS

Message: In his first letter to the Corinthians, Paul deals with social, moral, and spiritual issues confronting the young church.

Key Passage: Love comes first (chapter 13)

Time of writing: Between 54–57 A.D.

Author: Paul

2 CORINTHIANS

Message: Paul, in his second letter, sets out the essentials of being in Christian service.

Key passage: True spiritual service (chapters 2–4)

Time of writing: A year or two after the first letter to the Corinthians

Author: Paul

GALATIANS

Message: Paul wants his readers to know that a person does not need to keep the Law of Moses to be saved. Faith in Christ alone brings salvation.

Key passage: Living by faith (chapter 2)
Time of writing: Between 47–57 A.D.
Author: Paul

EPHESIANS

Message: Paul explains how vital the unity of all things in Christ is—in the church, between Jews and Gentiles, in marriage, and at the workplace.
Key passage: Practical Christian living (chapters 4–5)
Time of writing: Early 60s A.D.
Author: Attributed to Paul

PHILIPPIANS

Message: Paul expresses love and joy for the Christians at Philippi. He is grateful for the gift they sent him, and commends a coworker to them.
Key passage: Greeting, thanksgiving, and prayer (chapter 1)
Time of writing: Around 54 or early 60s A.D.
Author: Paul

"And you who were once estranged and hostile in mind, doing evil deeds, he has now reconciled in his fleshly body through death, so as to present you holy and blameless and irreproachable before him . . ."
Col 1:21–22

COLOSSIANS

Message: Paul tells the Christians at Colossae that in order to be reconciled to God, all they need is Jesus Christ.
Key passage: The supremacy of Christ (chapters 1–2)
Time of writing: Early 60s A.D.
Author: Attributed to Paul

1 THESSALONIANS

Message: Paul is encouraged by the faith of the Thessalonian Christians, and he wants to inspire them further. He advises them not to speculate on Christ's return but to live exemplary lives to the day of his coming.
Key passage: Be ready for Christ's return (chapters 4–5)
Time of writing: 50–51 A.D.
Author: Paul

2 THESSALONIANS

Message: Paul writes to clear up misunderstandings about Christ's second coming. The apostle stresses that what the believers should be most concerned with is the quality of their daily Christian lives.
Key passage: Warning against idleness (chapter 3)
Time of writing: Early 50s A.D.
Author: Attributed to Paul

Timothy, a Christian from Lystra who was a friend and helper of Paul, accompanied the apostle on his missionary journeys. Timothy in his early days is represented here by British artist, Henry Le Jeune (1819–1904).

1 TIMOTHY

Message: Paul writes to advise and encourage the young church leader, Timothy. Besides pastoral instruction, Paul tells Timothy how to deal with practical and spiritual problems in the congregation.

Key passage: Leadership in the church (chapter 3)

Time of writing: About 63–66 A.D.

Author: Attributed to Paul

2 TIMOTHY

Message: Paul uses his own life as an example to encourage Timothy to persevere in the faith.

Key passage: Hardships ahead (chapter 3)

Time of writing: About 67 A.D.

Author: Attributed to Paul

TITUS

Message: Paul instructs the leader of the church of Crete in what to teach, how to guide the believers, and in practical matters of church life.

Key passage: What to teach and how (chapter 2)

Time of writing: Unknown

Author: Attributed to Paul

The meaning of faith: "Now faith is the assurance of things hoped for, the conviction of things not seen." Heb 11:1

PHILEMON

Message: Paul asks Philemon to treat Onesimus not as a runaway slave, but as a beloved Christian brother.

Key passage: True brotherhood (vss. 13–16)

Time of writing: 62 A.D.

Author: Paul

HEBREWS

Message: This letter ties together the Old and New Testaments. Directed to Jewish Christians, the writer points out that Jesus has completed all that the Old Testament began. He argues powerfully against a return to Judaism and its institutions—the life of faith in Christ is what counts.

Key passage: Heroes of the faith (chapter 11)

Time of writing: Before 70 A.D.

Author: Unknown

JAMES

Message: True Christianity is faith and action, word and deed.

Key passage: Hearing and doing, faith and actions (chapters 1–2)

Time of writing: Possibly early first century A.D.

Author: James

1 PETER

Message: Peter writes to encourage Christians as they face coming persecution. He brings joy and hope, because he believes that faith is purified in struggle, and that persecution makes the union of Christians stronger.

Key passage: Suffering for doing right (chapters 3–4)

Time of writing: 64 A.D.

Author: Attributed to the apostle Peter

2 PETER

Message: Watch out for corrupt teaching, the writer warns his Christian readers; concentrate on true knowledge of God, and live as though awaiting the return of Christ.

Key passage: Knowledge of God and the truth (chapter 1)

Time of writing: Uncertain

Author: Attributed to the apostle Peter

1 JOHN

Message: This letter is written to Christians to confirm their faith.

Key passage: Walking in the light (chapter 1)

Time of writing: Early 60s A.D.

Author: Attributed to the apostle John

2 JOHN

Message: The major concerns of this short letter are truth and love in the body of Christ.

Key passage: Walking in love (vss. 5–6)

Time of writing: Early 60s A.D.

Author: Attributed to the apostle John

3 JOHN

Message: Written to Gaius, a church leader, commending him; this letter also warns against ambitious Diotrephes.

Key passage: Commendation for hospitality (vss. 5–8)

Time of writing: Early 60s A.D.

Author: Attributed to the apostle John

Along with Peter and James, John was a close follower of Jesus and called to be one of the 12 apostles. Known as the disciple whom Jesus loved, he was the author of the Gospel of John and other New Testament writings.

JUDE

Message: Beware of false teachers.

Key passage: Guidelines for avoiding apostasy (vss. 17–23)

Time of writing: Between 67–80 A.D.

Author: Jude

REVELATION

Message: The final victory of Jesus Christ over all forces that oppose God. Revelation's message is conveyed through a pattern of visions, and the book ends with a description of heaven, with God and his redeemed people at one— all evil and pain overcome forever.

Key passage: The victorious Christ (chapters 19–20)

Time of writing: 95 or 96 A.D.

Author: Attributed to the apostle John

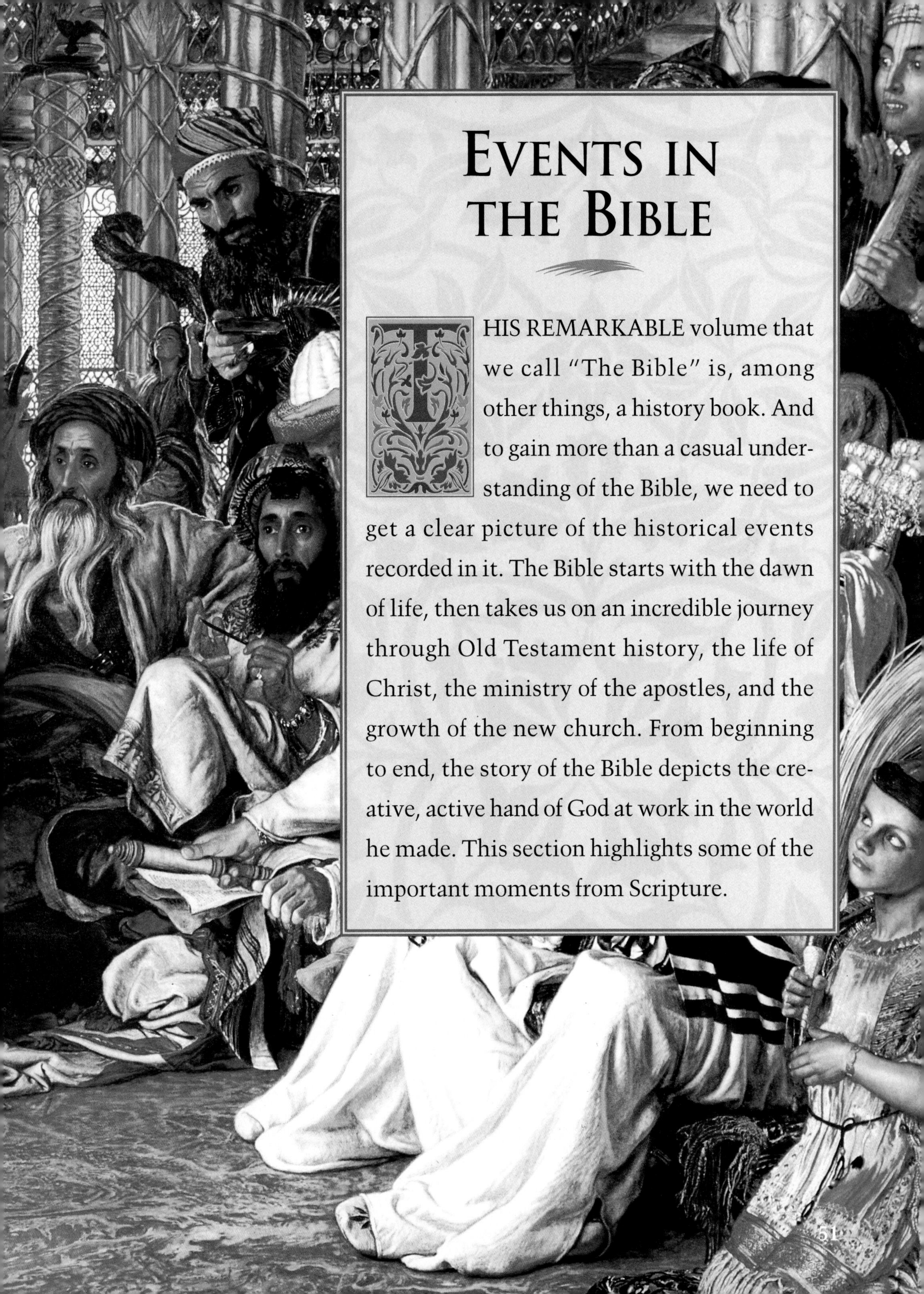

EVENTS IN THE BIBLE

THIS REMARKABLE volume that we call "The Bible" is, among other things, a history book. And to gain more than a casual understanding of the Bible, we need to get a clear picture of the historical events recorded in it. The Bible starts with the dawn of life, then takes us on an incredible journey through Old Testament history, the life of Christ, the ministry of the apostles, and the growth of the new church. From beginning to end, the story of the Bible depicts the creative, active hand of God at work in the world he made. This section highlights some of the important moments from Scripture.

This conception of the Tower of Babel, found in Ely Cathedral, Ely, England, depicts scenes from the story of Noah's descendants who decided to build a tower up to heaven to make a name for themselves. Their plans were thwarted by God when he confused the languages of the builders. Thus, the people of different language groups spread out, as God originally intended.

MAJOR MILESTONES IN THE BIBLE

The following is a roughly chronological list of significant biblical events. They have been divided into periods that start in the Old Testament and finish in the New Testament.

EVENTS FROM CREATION TO ABRAHAM

- God created all things, including the first human beings.
- The man and woman were put in charge of the earth. God provided them with rules to live by.
- Adam and the woman (Eve) disobeyed God. Sin entered the world.
- Adam and Eve had children. One of their sons, Cain, murdered his brother Abel.
- God gave Adam and Eve a third son, Seth. God promised to send the world a Redeemer; he would come from Seth's family.
- Rampant wrongdoing spread throughout the world.
- God sent a great Flood to punish sinful humanity. He preserved Noah, his family, and some animals, in an ark (a large wooden ship).
- After the Flood, God put a rainbow in the sky to remind everyone that he would never again destroy all humanity by water.
- Proud city-dwellers in Babel tried to build a tower to heaven. God put a stop to their arrogance by scattering the people and breaking them up into different language groups.

EVENTS FROM ABRAHAM TO MOSES

- Around 2000 B.C. God told Abraham to leave his homeland, Ur, and go to a new land.
- God promised Abraham a son through whom all nations on earth would be blessed.
- Abraham took matters into his own hands and secured an heir (Ishmael) for himself through Hagar, his wife Sarah's servant girl.

THE PATRIARCHS OF ISRAEL*

Abraham	2166 B.C.–1991 B.C.
Isaac	2066 B.C.–1886 B.C.
Jacob	2006 B.C.–1859 B.C.
Joseph	1915 B.C.–1446 B.C.

**Dates are approximate*

- 13 years after Ishmael's birth, the promised heir, Isaac, was born to Abraham and Sarah in their old age.
- Abraham's faith was tested when God told him to sacrifice Isaac. The boy's life was spared, and Abraham's trust in God and obedience to him grew.
- Isaac's second son, Jacob, lived about 1850 B.C. God chose Jacob to inherit the promises he had given to Isaac.
- Jacob stole the birthright (the right to succeed to Isaac's promises and blessings) from Esau, his brother. Because of this, Jacob left home to escape Esau's fury.
- After years of hard work and difficulties, Jacob had a family and became wealthy. He and his family returned to his father's home in Palestine. Jacob made peace with Esau.
- Jacob's sons, jealous of their younger brother Joseph, sold him into slavery to an Egyptian caravan.
- Joseph rose from slavery in Egypt to become second in command under the pharaoh.
- Joseph rescued his family from starving when a famine drove them to Egypt in search of food. He forgave his brothers, and Joseph's family settled in a rich part of Egypt.

Three special visitors attended Abraham as he sat by the oaks of Mamre. While enjoying his hospitality, the men promised Abraham that in due season, his wife Sarah would give birth to a child.

EVENTS FROM MOSES TO SAUL

- Jacob's descendants had many children. The pharaohs, afraid of an uprising, enslaved the Jews in Egypt.
- All Israelite boy babies were ordered killed.
- The pharaoh's daughter found an Israelite baby in a waterproof basket in the river. She named him Moses, and took him (along with his mother as nursemaid) to the Egyptian court to be brought up and educated.
- Moses lived from about 1526 to 1406 B.C.
- When he was about 40 years old, Moses killed an Egyptian for beating

THE WIVES AND SONS OF JACOB (ISRAEL)

Leah	**Rachel**	**Bilhah**	**Zilpah**
Reuben	Joseph	Dan	Gad
Simeon	Benjamin	Naphtali	Asher
Levi			
Judah			
Issachar			
Zebulun			

Each of these sons was the father of a large family (known as a "tribe" or "clan" in the Bible). Later on, Joseph's two sons, Ephraim and Manasseh, took their father's place as "children of Israel." About 400 years after Jacob (called Israel) died, the Israelites were brought out of Egypt to the land God had promised Abraham. In the new land, each clan was given its own area in which to live.

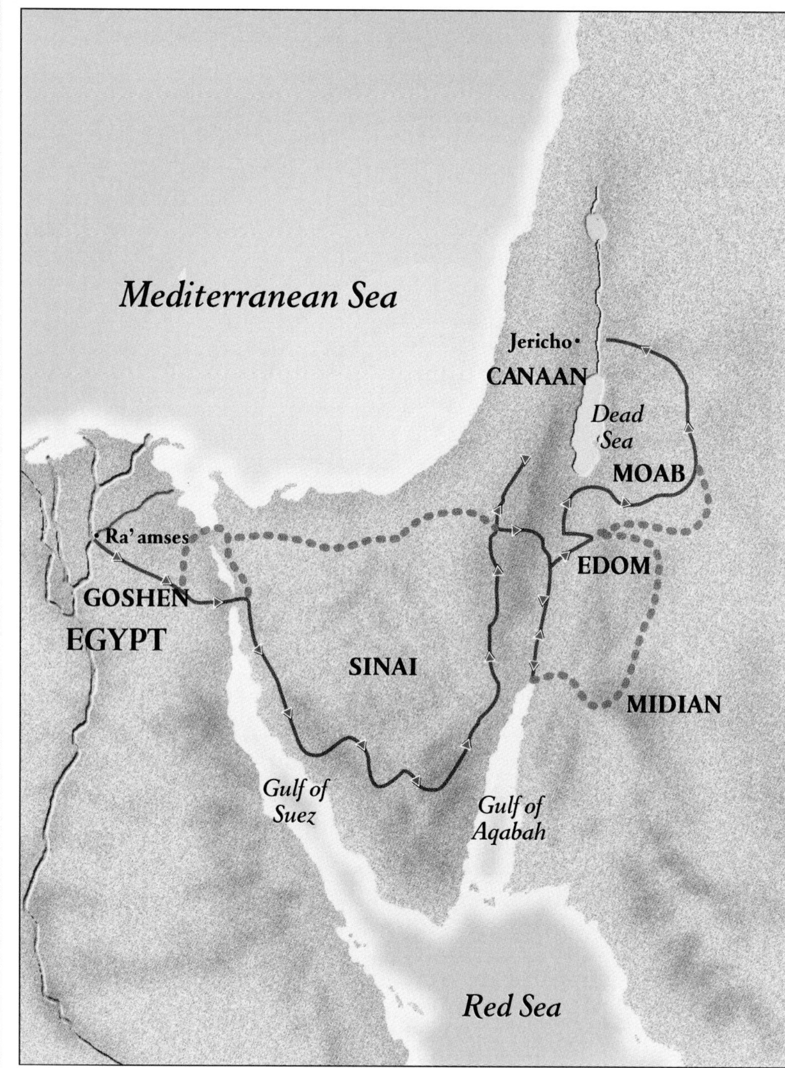

The solid line on this map represents the likely route of the Exodus from Egypt, including the wanderings through the wilderness region of the Sinai Peninsula, and on to Canaan. The dotted lines show possible alternate routes.

an Israelite. Afraid for his life, Moses disappeared into the Midian Desert.

- God spoke to Moses from a burning bush. He told Moses to go back to Egypt and lead the Israelites into Palestine, the land he had promised to Abraham.
- God sent Aaron, Moses' brother, along with him to speak for Moses.
- After Egypt experienced plagues, destruction, and death at the hand of God, the pharaoh agreed to let the Israelites go.
- Moses led the people out of Egypt, through the parted waters of the Red Sea, and on to Mount Sinai.
- At Mount Sinai, God gave Moses the laws (including the Ten Commandments) and social plans that would mold the Israelites into a holy nation.
- The Israelites complained, disobeyed God, and turned away from him. Because of their lack of trust, God condemned them to wander in the wilderness for 40 years.
- Moses spoke to the people for the last time on the plains of Moab. After his farewell address, God led him to the top of Mount Nebo to see the land the Israelites would enter. There Moses died.
- Joshua, one of the spies who had first looked at Canaan, the land promised to the Israelites, led the people in conquering and settling the new land.
- In all, Joshua and his troops conquered 31 kings in the new territory.
- Joshua divided the land among the Israelite tribes according to God's directions.
- After Joshua's death, the great leaders of this period were charismatic figures known as "judges." The most memo-

rable of these leaders were: Othniel, Deborah (the only woman judge), Gideon, Jephthah, Samson, Eli, and Samuel.

- When Samuel was just a boy, God spoke to him about his future role as Israel's prophet and judge.
- Samuel, Israel's first great prophet and last of the judges, anointed Saul to be the first king over Israel.
- Saul turned against David, the young, fearless shepherd who killed the giant Goliath, and who also served as Saul's court musician.
- God then chose David as the next king of Israel.
- After Saul's death, King David brought the ark of the covenant (the wooden box that held the stone tablets, on which was written the Ten Commandments) to Jerusalem, the capital city.
- David was a man of significant political and religious strength. The nation of Israel was more unified and stronger under David than it had ever been.
- David sinned against God: Among other things, he seduced Bathsheba, then had her husband killed; he took a census of the men of Israel because he lacked trust in God for military victory.
- David and the nation of Israel suffered because of David's great sin.
- David's son, Solomon, was Israel's next king.
- In spite of Solomon's legendary wisdom, Solomon often acted unwisely: His lavish lifestyle burdened the common people with high taxes; he made compromising trade agree-

Jephthah, the Israelite judge, is greeted by his daughter following his victory over the Ammonites. Before he went into battle, Jephthah vowed that if he was triumphant, he would sacrifice the first thing that emerged from his house. True to his word, the judge sacrificed his daughter, an only child.

THE TWELVE JUDGES

Name	Reference	Years of Rule (approximate)
Othniel	Jdg 3:7–11	1367–1327 B.C.
Ehud	Jdg 3:12–30	1304–1224 B.C.
Shamgar	Jdg 3:31	Uncertain
Deborah	Jdg 4–5	1224–1184 B.C.
Gideon	Jdg 6–8	1177–1137 B.C.
Tola	Jdg 10:1,2	1134–1089 B.C.
Jair	Jdg 10:3,5	1134–1089 B.C.
Jephthah	Jdg 11:1–12:7	1089–1083 B.C.
Ibzan, Elon, Abdon	Jdg 12:8–15	1083–1058 B.C.
Samson	Jdg 13–16	c. 1069 B.C.

ments; he put together a harem of foreign brides who encouraged him to worship pagan gods and introduce pagan worship rituals in Jerusalem.

- God still planned to raise a Redeemer from Abraham's family, through the House of David.
- When Solomon died, his sons and generals fought for the throne.
- Rehoboam took the southern half of the country and called it Judah. He claimed to be the chosen king.
- Jeroboam set up his government in the northern half of the country and kept the name of Israel. Jeroboam claimed to be the chosen king.
- Both kingdoms became pagan, fell to foreign powers, and God's people were carried away into exile.
- Elijah the prophet warned King Ahab that God would punish the people for their wickedness.
- Elijah, in a contest with the prophets of the pagan god Baal, asked God to end the drought. God sent a cloudburst, and the pagan prophets were killed.
- Elijah condemned King Ahab and his wife Jezebel for their sins.
- Elijah was carried away to heaven in a chariot. His mantle fell on Elisha, his successor.
- Elisha parted the waters of the Jordan River, brought rain in times of drought, increased food supplies, performed other miracles, pronounced judgment on kings, and destroyed enemies with supernatural powers.
- Elisha performed more miracles than any other prophet in the Old Testament.

The evil and pagan wife of King Ahab is seen here in Naboth's vineyard. When Naboth refused to sell his ancestral land to the king, Jezebel persuaded Ahab to have Naboth killed in order to get his desirable property. Later, the heartless queen herself was killed—thrown to her death.

- Isaiah, Jeremiah, Amos, Hosea, Micah, Ezekiel, and other prophets followed Elisha and warned Israel and Judah that God would punish their wickedness.
- While God's people were in exile, Isaiah and Ezekiel had words of consolation for them from God.

EVENTS FROM THE EXILE TO THE RETURN

- The Jews were taken into exile several times.
- "The Exile" refers to the 70-year Babylonian captivity of Judah.
- During the Exile, God used Ezekiel and Daniel to bring comfort and hope to the people.
- The Jews returned from the Exile to Palestine in two stages: One group was led by Sheshbazzar and Zerubbabel. The second was led by Ezra and Nehemiah.
- The Jews rebuilt the temple in Jerusalem. Zechariah and Haggai encouraged the people in their work.
- Toward the end of this time, Malachi reproached the Jews for slipping back into sinful patterns.

EVENTS BETWEEN THE TESTAMENTS

- 400 years elapsed between the writing of Malachi and the time of Jesus.
- Restored Israel came under the rule of Greek princes and generals, part of Alexander the Great's massive empire.
- The Seleucid king Antiochus III conquered Palestine in 198 B.C. The Roman legions defeated his army in 190 B.C.
- The Maccabee family began a civil war against the Seleucid governors and captured Jerusalem in 164 B.C.
- John Hyrcanus I of the Maccabee family established his own dynasty known as the Hasmoneans.
- The Hasmoneans ruled until 63 B.C., when Rome conquered Palestine. The Romans later installed the Herodian family as the new puppet government in Palestine.

The Maccabees (meaning "hammerer" or "exterminator") was the popular name for the Hasmonean family whose five brothers won a measure of independence for the Jews during the time between the Testaments. Four of the five brothers were killed in battle, and the fifth was eventually murdered by his son-in-law.

EVENTS DURING THE LIFE OF CHRIST

- Jesus was born in Bethlehem. Angels announced his birth and declared Jesus the long-promised Davidic king.
- Mysterious wise men from the east brought gifts to the Christ child.
- King Herod did not want the people to support an infant king so he ordered his soldiers to kill all boy babies in Bethlehem.
- Jesus's family escaped to Egypt to avoid the wicked decree.
- After Herod died, the family of Jesus returned to Palestine and settled in the town of Nazareth.

In this representation of Jesus in the temple at the age of 12, he is clearly the center of attention. His captive audience, the teachers of the law, are amazed at his questions and answers, and his understanding.

- At age 12 or 13, Jesus's knowledge of God astounded the Jewish religious leaders.
- John the Baptist urged people to prepare for the coming Messiah.
- John baptized Jesus, and God sent the Holy Spirit in the form of a dove that settled on Jesus.
- The Devil tempted Jesus in the wilderness. After Jesus sent the Devil away, angels came to comfort Jesus and provide him with food.
- At first, Jesus was very popular. He did amazing things, he taught, and he drew large crowds.
- Jesus healed the sick, cast out evil spirits, comforted the brokenhearted, and told people how to enter the kingdom of God.
- Jesus denounced the religious leaders of the day because of their hypocritical faith.
- Jesus told his hearers that the only way to God the Father was through faith in himself.
- Jesus fed thousands of people with a few loaves of bread and two fish.

The Life and Ministry of Jesus

Between 6 and 4 B.C.	Birth
Between 6 and 8 A.D.	Visit to the Temple
Between 26 and 27 A.D.	Beginning of Ministry
28–29 A.D.	Galilean Ministry
29 A.D.	Training of Disciples
29 A.D.	Later Ministry: Judea and Perea
Between 30 and 33 A.D.	Death

- The Pharisees and other leaders rejected Jesus' claims and teaching.
- Jesus trained his twelve disciples to continue his ministry. He told them about his coming death and resurrection.
- The religious leaders plotted to kill Jesus.
- Judas Iscariot, one of the 12 disciples, betrayed Jesus to the hostile leaders in Jerusalem.
- Jesus was nailed to a wooden cross to die among criminals.
- Jesus rose from the grave and appeared before many of his followers.
- As the disciples watched Jesus ascend into heaven, an angel appeared and told them that they would see him return in the same way.

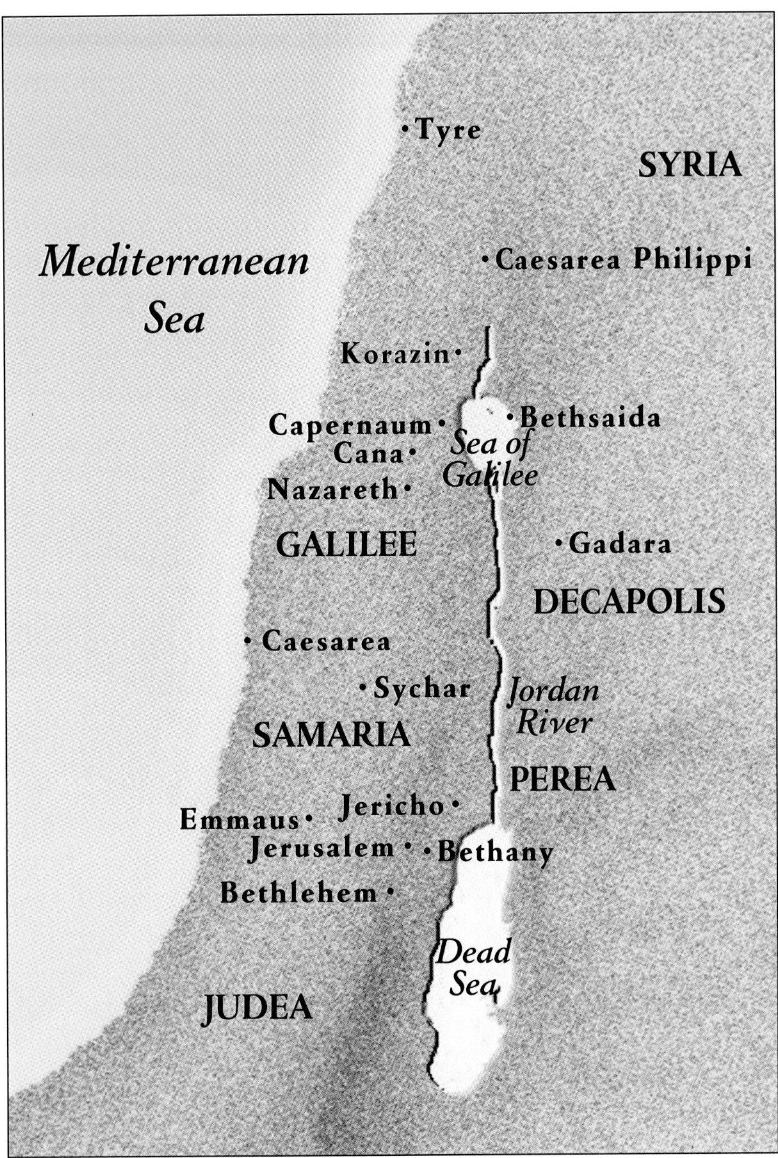

Most of Jesus' ministry took place in the Galilee region. He also journeyed to Jerusalem and Judea, often taking a route through Samaria.

EVENTS DURING THE MINISTRY OF THE APOSTLES

- After Jesus' ascension, his disciples replaced Judas (who had killed himself after betraying Jesus) with Matthias to round out the group of 12.
- On the Day of Pentecost, the risen Christ sent the Holy Spirit to the church to equip them for their worldwide task of spreading the good news of salvation.
- The young church lived in close community. They shared everything they had with each other, and took care of the poor among them.
- A couple in the church, Ananias and Sapphira, tried to deceive the community of believers about the proceeds from a property they had sold. God struck them dead for lying.
- The apostles and early Christian leaders were persecuted for their faith.

This painting captures both the horror and hope experienced by Stephen, a saint of the church and the first Christian martyr. After a brave speech of faith, the outspoken Christian was stoned to death. But even as he died, he asked God to forgive his murderers.

- Stephen, an ordained deacon in the early church, was stoned to death because of his preaching.
- Philip, another of the apostles' helpers, explained the good news to an Ethiopian diplomat, who became a Christian and took the gospel to his homeland.
- Before his conversion, Saul of Tarsus was an aggressive enemy of the church. On his way to Damascus to attack Christians there, God confronted him. As a result, Saul gave himself to Christ, beginning a new life as a Christian.
- Filled with the Holy Spirit, Paul began to preach about Jesus in the Jewish synagogue. The Jewish leaders drove him out of Damascus.
- Peter was the primary leader of the apostles. He performed many miracles, he was a great preacher of the gospel of Christ, and God used Peter to bring salvation to the Gentiles.
- James, one of the apostles, was martyred in Jerusalem.
- Peter was miraculously delivered from prison.
- The Holy Spirit called Paul and Barnabas to be missionaries, and the church ordained them for this work of preaching, teaching, and healing.
- The church expanded from Antioch to Rome through Paul's missionary journeys. Along the way, Paul was stoned, imprisoned, and shipwrecked. He faced conflict, hostility, and death. He also saw the church grow and mature because of his ministry. He witnessed the conversion of many.
- At the end of his third missionary journey, Paul was imprisoned in Jerusalem because of a speech he made there.
- On the way to Rome to stand trial, the ship carrying Paul wrecked on the island of Malta. Paul was bitten by a poisonous snake there but was not harmed.
- Once in Rome, Paul lived for two years in a rented house, preaching the gospel to leading Jews and whoever visited him.
- At this point, the church was becoming a distinct organization. Starting in Jerusalem, it had grown and expanded all the way to Rome.

BIBLE CHRONOLOGY: FROM CREATION TO THE TIME OF CHRIST

The Beginning: Creation

1056 years after Creation	Noah and the Flood
2166 B.C.	Abraham and the beginning of a nation
1915	Joseph
1450	The Exodus
1399	Joshua and the Promised Land
1069	Samson
1043	Saul*
1000	David
960	Solomon
931	The Kingdom divides
722	Kingdom of Israel destroyed
720	Hezekiah
610	Josiah
605	Daniel
586	The destruction of Jerusalem
458	Return from captivity

(400 years of silence)

5 B.C.	Birth of Jesus

**Dates prior to Saul are approximate.*

100 IMPORTANT EVENTS IN THE BIBLE

Event	Reference
1. The Creation	Gen 1
2. The Fall of humanity	Gen 3
3. The first murder: Cain kills his brother Abel	Gen 4
4. Noah and the Flood	Gen 6–8
5. The Tower of Babel	Gen 11
6. The call of Abram (Abraham)	Gen 12
7. Selling Joseph into slavery	Gen 37
8. Israelites enslaved in Egypt	Ex 1
9. Moses in the bulrushes	Ex 1–2
10. The call of Moses	Ex 3
11. The ten plagues	Ex 7–12
12. The Passover	Ex 12–15
13. The Exodus from Egypt: Crossing the Red Sea	Ex 12–15
14. The institution of the Sabbath	Ex 16

This depiction of Moses and his people crossing the Red Sea, is found in Gloucester Cathedral, Gloucester, England. It is a reminder of the parting of the waters, the crossing to safety, and the final escape of the Israelites from Egyptian slavery as recorded in the Book of Exodus.

In this magnificent portrayal of Gideon, the mighty leader is seen holding a fleece of wool, the object he twice put to the test to make sure that the call to defeat the Midianites was from God.

15. Giving the Ten Commandments and the law	Ex 20–24
16. Completing the tabernacle (tent of worship)	Ex 40
17. The anointing of Aaron as first high priest	Lev 8
18. The Israelites: 40 years of wandering	Nu 14
19. Korah's rebellion	Nu 16
20. Water from the rock	Nu 20
21. The bronze snake	Nu 21
22. Moses' farewell	Dt 32–34
23. Joshua commissioned as leader	Jos 1
24. Rahab and the spies	Jos 2
25. Crossing the Jordan River into Palestine	Jos 3
26. The fall of Jericho	Jos 6
27. Achan's sin	Jos 7
28. Defeat at Ai	Jos 8
29. The conquest of Canaan	Jos 10–12
30. The land divided among the tribes	Jos 13–19
31. Joshua's farewell	Jos 23–24
32. Deborah and Barak defeat the Canaanites	Jdg 4–5
33. Gideon's fleece	Jdg 6–7
34. Samson and his strength	Jdg 13–16
35. The marriage of Ruth to Boaz	Ru 4
36. The call of Samuel	1Sa 3
37. Saul becomes king and is rejected	1Sa 10–15
38. Samuel anoints David as future king	1Sa 16
39. David kills Goliath	1Sa 17
40. The friendship of David and Jonathan	1Sa 20
41. The deaths of Saul and Jonathan	1Sa 31
42. David is crowned king	2Sa 2
43. David conquers Jerusalem and recovers the Ark of the Covenant	2Sa 5–6
44. David's adultery with Bathsheba and murder of Uriah	2Sa 11
45. David's song of praise and last words	2Sa 22–23
46. The anointing of Solomon	1Ki 1

47. The building and dedication of the Temple	1Ki 5–6, 8
48. Visit of the Queen of Sheba	1Ki 10
49. Israel is divided into two kingdoms: Israel (north) and Judah (south)	1Ki 12
50. Elijah and the prophets of Baal	1Ki 18
51. Elijah is taken up to heaven in a chariot	2Ki 2
52. Joash is delivered from Queen Athaliah	2Ki 11
53. Israel captured by Assyria	2Ki 17
54. King Josiah's discovery of the Book of the Law	2Ki 22–23
55. The destruction of the Temple	2Ki 25
56. The Babylonian captivity of the southern kingdom	2Ki 25
57. The return of the captives under Cyrus's decree	Ezr 1
58. The completion of the new temple under Zerubbabel	Ezr 6
59. Celebrating the rebuilding of Jerusalem's city walls	Ne 12

As depicted here in vivid imagery, the prophet Elijah's eventful life ended in dramatic fashion. According to the second Book of Kings, the prominent prophet was swept up to heaven in a whirlwind, with the chariots of Israel and its horsemen, leaving his prophet's mantle for Elisha.

Event	Reference
60. Esther, Mordecai, and the deliverance of the Jews	Est 4–7
61. Daniel in the den of lions	Da 6
62. Jonah and the large fish	Jnh 1–2
63. Birth of John the Baptist	Lk 1
64. Birth of Christ	Lk 2; Mt 1
65. Escape into Egypt	Mt 2
66. Jesus visits the temple	Lk 2
67. Jesus' baptism	Mt 3
68. The temptation of Jesus	Mt 4
69. Call of the 12 disciples	Mt 10
70. The Sermon on the Mount	Mt 5
71. The raising of Lazarus	Jn 11
72. Death of John the Baptist	Mk 6
73. Peter's confession of faith	Mt 16
74. The Transfiguration	Mt 17
75. Triumphal entry into Jerusalem	Mt 21; Mk 11; Lk 19; Jn 12
76. Passover/Last Supper	Mt 26; Mk 14; Lk 22; Jn 13–14
77. Jesus in Gethsemane	Mt 26; Mk 14; Lk 22–23; Jn 18
78. Jesus' arrest and trial	Mt 26–27; Mk 14–15; Lk 22–23; Jn 18–19
79. Jesus crucified and buried	Mt 27; Mk 15; Lk 23; Jn 19
80. Resurrection and appearances	Mt 28; Mk 16; Lk 24; Jn 20
81. Giving the Great Commission	Mt 28
82. Jesus' Ascension	Ac 1
83. The coming of the Holy Spirit (Pentecost)	Ac 2
84. Peter and John heal a crippled beggar	Ac 3
85. Martyrdom of Stephen	Ac 7
86. Severe persecution of the church in Jerusalem	Ac 8
87. Philip baptizes the Ethiopian convert	Ac 8
88. Conversion of Saul (Paul)	Ac 9

A contemporary of Jesus, the bold prophet John prepared the way for the Messiah by preaching repentance and announcing that God's kingdom was near. John introduced baptism as an outward sign of confession and repentance.

THE AGE OF THE APOSTLES

EVENT	DATE
The coming of the Spirit at Pentecost	30 A.D.
Death of Ananias and Sapphira	31
The murder of Stephen	32 or 33
Conversion of Saul (Paul)	33 or 34
Conversion of Cornelius	40
Paul and Barnabas in Antioch	42
Martyrdom of the apostle James	44
Paul's first missionary journey	47–49
The Council at Jerusalem	49
Paul's second missionary journey	50–52
Paul's third missionary journey	53–57
Arrest of Paul in Jerusalem	57
Paul's trial before Festus	57
Paul's trial before Agrippa	59
The voyage to Rome	59
Paul's arrival in Rome	60
Paul's first Roman imprisonment	60–62
Martyrdom of James, Jesus' brother	62
Final Roman imprisonment of Paul	66
Jewish revolt against Rome	66
Destruction of Jerusalem by Romans	70

89. Peter's vision	Ac 10
90. Establishing the church at Antioch	Ac 11
91. The death of James	Ac 12
92. The deliverance of Peter	Ac 12
93. Paul's first missionary journey	Ac 13–14
94. The Jerusalem Council	Ac 15
95. Paul's second missionary journey	Ac 15–18
96. Paul and Silas in prison	Ac 16
97. Paul's third missionary journey	Ac 18–21
98. Arrest of Paul, trials, and shipwreck	Ac 21–28
99. Paul's house arrest in Rome	Ac 28
100. The visions of John the apostle on Patmos	Rev 1

The Jewish historian Josephus records that James, a leader in the church in Jerusalem and probable writer of the Letter of James, was martyred in 62 A.D.

POPULAR BIBLICAL EVENTS

Abraham's Test of Faith (Gen 22): When Abraham's son Isaac was a young man, God did an extraordinary thing. He asked Abraham to offer up Isaac as a sacrifice. At that time, human sacrifice was practiced among some groups of people in the region—but never was permitted among God's people.

Captured in this dramatic painting is the Old Testament story of Abraham, his son Isaac, and an extraordinary test of faith. Told by God to sacrifice his son, Abraham was on the brink of obeying, when an angel of God stayed his hand, sparing the life of Isaac.

Abraham set off with Isaac to do as the Lord asked. As they came to the place of sacrifice, Isaac noted that they had fire and wood, but not the lamb of offering. With a heavy heart, Abraham told Isaac that God would provide the lamb.

As Abraham raised the knife to kill his son, God's angel stopped him in the nick of time. Instead of Isaac, a substitute offering was found—a ram in a thicket, caught by its horns. Abraham offered it as a sacrifice, Isaac's life was spared, and Abraham discovered that he was prepared to trust God absolutely.

Belshazzar's Feast (Da 5): Belshazzar, the spineless and self-indulgent monarch of Babylon, decided to host a great festival. During the course of the extravagant gala at the palace, Belshazzar ordered that sacred vessels from the Jewish temple be brought in so that he and his guests could drink from them.

As soon as he did this profane act, a disembodied hand appeared and wrote a message on the royal wall. Deathly afraid, Belshazzar demanded an interpretation of the strange words from his enchanters and diviners.

However, only Daniel the prophet could interpret the message, which was from God and directed to the king. Daniel told Belshazzar that his days were numbered, he had been weighed and found wanting, and that his kingdom would soon be divided.

That very night Belshazzar was killed.

Crossing the Red Sea (Ex 14): As soon as the vast group of Israelites left Egypt, Pharaoh immediately regretted his decision to let his slaves go. He sent an army to bring them back. When the Israelites saw the approaching Egyptian horses and chariots, they were terrified. How could they escape with an army at their heels and the way ahead blocked by water?

Moses told the people not to be afraid and to trust the deliverance of the Lord. As God commanded, Moses stretched out his hand over the sea. A strong east wind blew back the water into two walls, and the Israelites walked across on dry land.

When they were safely on the other side, God told Moses to bring the waters back together. When Moses stretched out his hand over the sea, the waters flowed together again, drowning the pursuing Egyptian army.

That day the people of Israel celebrated the great deliverance God had given them.

David Kills Goliath (1Sa 17): David left tending his father's sheep and made his way to the encampment where his three brothers were in King Saul's army. Battle lines were drawn between the Israelite and the Philistine armies. Goliath, the giant champion of the Philistine army, challenged the Israelite army to settle the dispute in single combat. The Israelites cringed at the sight of the warrior.

David volunteered to fight the giant. Instead of protective armor and the usual weaponry, the young shepherd chose a few stones and a sling to face the bold predator. Goliath was incredulous that David was the one sent to fight him. Undaunted by the giant's mockery, David hurled a stone and struck the Philistine on his forehead. Goliath fell to the ground. David ran to him, took the huge man's own sword and

It was a frightening moment when strange writing appeared on the wall of Belshazzar's banquet hall. The ruler of Babylon had Daniel decipher the words—a message of judgment from God. In this scene, Daniel delivers the ominous prophecy to the king. That night Belshazzar lost his kingdom and his life.

cut off his head. The courageous shepherd knew that the Lord had given him the victory.

Dismayed by the death of their hero, the frightened Philistine troops fled in disarray, chased by the soldiers of Israel and Judah.

Elijah's Contest (1Ki 18): Elijah told King Ahab to call the people of Israel to Mount Carmel to witness a contest between God and the 450 prophets of Baal (Queen Jezebel's pagan god). In this showdown, both sides would prepare an altar, then the deity who could call down fire to burn the waiting sacrifice would prove himself the true God.

The prophets of Baal went first. They prayed, danced, shouted, cut themselves with knives and swords, but nothing happened. They kept this up all day, but to no avail.

When evening came, it was Elijah's turn. He called the people to come close. He prepared the altar and doused it with water to make a miracle more difficult. Then Elijah called on the Lord. Fire came down and consumed the sacrifice and licked up all the water.

Amazed at the miracle, the people acknowledged the God of Israel as the true God.

Then Gideon said to God, "Do not let your anger burn against me, let me speak one more time; let me, please, make trial with the fleece just once more. . . ."
Jdg 6:39

Felix, the Compromising Governor (Ac 23–24): Felix, the Roman governor of Judea, was corrupt and easily bribed. When the apostle Paul was falsely accused of breaking temple laws, he came before Felix to be judged. Without making a decision about Paul's case, Felix kept Paul in custody for the last two years of his governorship, hoping to be offered a bribe for the apostle's release!

Gideon's Fleece (Jdg 6): God called Gideon to rescue Israel from Midianite oppression. Gideon started by destroying the pagan altar, and building instead an altar to God. Then Gideon pulled together an army to follow him. However, this meek farmer turned judge still had doubts. Had God really called him? Would he be victorious?

To be certain, Gideon told God that he would put a wool fleece on the threshing floor overnight, and if it gathered dew while the floor remained dry, this would be a sign from God of Israel's deliverance. When Gideon got up the next morning, he squeezed enough water from the fleece to fill a bowl! However, not quite satisfied, Gideon asked the Lord to perform one more test. This time, Gideon requested that the fleece remain dry and that the floor be wet with dew.

Next morning when Gideon checked the fleece and the floor, the Lord had done exactly as the uncertain judge had asked.

The first Book of Samuel tells of Hannah, the wife of Elkanah, and the longed-for birth of her son, Samuel. Here, Hannah gives her young boy to Eli, the priest at Shiloh, to be his helper and understudy. Samuel grew up to be the last great judge of Israel and one of its first prophets.

Hannah's Hope (1Sa 1–3): Hannah longed for a child. She was taunted by her husband's second wife because she had no children, and—to make matters worse—Hannah's culture considered childlessness a form of punishment for hidden sin.

For several years, during annual visits to the worship center at Shiloh, Hannah pleaded with God for a son. She promised that she would dedicate him to the Lord. During one visit, Eli the priest observed Hannah's emotionalism in the temple and thought she was drunk. Hannah explained her behavior and the needs of her heart to the listening priest. He told her that her request for a son would be granted by the God of Israel. Hannah left in peace.

God heard her prayer, and Hannah and Elkanah had a son whom they named Samuel. When he was weaned, true to her vow, Hannah brought the young boy back to Shiloh to be dedicated to the Lord's service. There Samuel lived with Eli and learned from him.

Isaac's Favoritism (Gen 27): Isaac and Rebekah had twin sons, Esau and Jacob. He favored Esau, while Rebekah preferred Jacob. This division of love produced such fierce competition that Jacob managed to take his brother's birthright. Aided by Rebekah, Jacob tricked an elderly, blind Isaac by dressing as Esau. Isaac then blessed Jacob with the birthright intended for Esau.

Jericho's Fall (Jos 5–6): Although now an embattled city, Jericho would not easily fall to the Israelites. God told Joshua to follow an unusual ritual in order to conquer besieged Jericho. For six successive days the Israelite troops were to march around the city, blowing trumpets and carrying the Ark of the Covenant with them. The soldiers were commanded not to speak or shout. On the seventh day, the procession was to march seven times around the city. When the priests sounded

Several people witnessed the miracle of Jesus raising Lazarus from the dead. From the account in the Book of John, it was clear to many onlookers that Jesus loved his friend as he wept at the tomb along with Mary and Martha, the sisters of Lazarus. After the miracle was performed, many believed that Jesus was the Messiah.

one long note on their trumpets, the soldiers were to shout with all their might.

Joshua put these strange commands into action, and as the soldiers gave their final vigorous shout on the seventh day, the city walls collapsed. The troops were able to walk right in and take Jericho.

Korah's Rebellion (Nu 16): Korah, a Levite, and his group of dissidents confronted Moses and Aaron. They accused the Israelite leaders of exalting themselves above the people. Korah's complaint was without merit and did not disguise his greed for power. Moses challenged Korah and his followers, charging them with rebelling against the Lord.

Korah and his company continued to dispute Moses' authority, and the rebellion was so serious that he and all his cohorts were killed by an act of God. They were all buried and burned alive—by earthquake and fire. However, Korah's own clan was spared.

Lazarus' New Life (Jn 11): Lazarus and his sisters, Mary and Martha, were friends of Jesus. When Lazarus became seriously ill, his sisters sent for Jesus. Surprisingly, Jesus waited until Lazarus was dead before going to Bethany to visit his friends' household. The grieving sisters wondered why Jesus had not come sooner. (Lazarus had died four days earlier.) Jesus assured Martha that Lazarus would rise again. Martha took this as a reference to the final resurrection on the day of judgment. Jesus then identified his power over life and death. In a strong show of faith in the Gospel, Martha declared Jesus the Messiah and Son of God.

Going to Lazarus' tomb with the group of mourners, Jesus ordered the stone rolled away from the door. With deep emotion, Jesus prayed, and shouted for Lazarus to come out.

Lazarus emerged, still wrapped in his burial cloths. Jesus told the people to loosen his cloths and let him go.

Mary's Visit by Gabriel (Lk 1): Mary, the young virgin, was engaged to Joseph, a descendant of Abraham and David. The angel Gabriel visited Mary, startling her. The angel told Mary not to be afraid and announced to her that she would become pregnant; she would have a child who would be called Son of the Most High, and he would inherit the throne of King David and reign forever. Mary wondered how it could happen since she was a virgin. Gabriel explained that Mary would become pregnant by the power of the Holy Spirit. Mary believed and accepted the unusual tidings that would inevitably transform her life.

Naboth's Vineyard (1Ki 21): Naboth's family plot adjoined King Ahab's winter palace, and the king wanted the vineyard for his garden. Naboth refused to sell the land of his ancestors to King Ahab, so Queen Jezebel schemed to acquire the land for her husband. She had Naboth falsely accused of blasphemy, and the consequence of that was murder. Thus Naboth was taken outside the city and stoned to death. Through Jezebel's treachery, the land became the property of the crown.

Obadiah the Hero (1Ki 18): Jezebel, the pagan wife of King Ahab began killing off priests of the Hebrew God. This was part of her strategy to promote Baal worship in Israel. Obadiah, the head of the royal household of King Ahab of Israel—and a godly man—decided to do something about the horrifying massacre. He risked his life by safely hiding 100 priests in caves to keep Jezebel from killing them.

Another time, Obadiah again took his life into his hands when he agreed to take a message from the prophet Elijah to King Ahab. Elijah had a price on his head and all who protected him were to be killed as well. Once again Obadiah's courage paid off: The king agreed to meet with Elijah, and Obadiah was not harmed.

Phoebe's Helpfulness (Ro 16): The apostle Paul spoke of Phoebe in glowing terms. In his letter to the Roman church, he commended her and asked the believers there to welcome her with open arms. Phoebe was a deacon or church worker in the port of Cenchreae, a village on Corinth's east harbor.

Obadiah's prophetic message was that Edom would be destroyed for refusing to help God's people when they were in need. The prophet lived in the sixth or fifth century B.C.

She was a woman of some means and social position in the community, and was known for her helpfulness to Paul and to the church as a whole. No wonder Paul asked the Roman church to take care of "our sister Phoebe."

Queen of Sheba's Royal Visit (1Ki 10): In Solomon's time, the rich kingdom of Sheba was ruled by a queen. She was fascinated by reports of Solomon's legendary wisdom, and Israel's growing power and wealth. No doubt she thought it useful to establish ties with this burgeoning kingdom. She decided to pay King Solomon a visit.

The Queen of Sheba and her entourage set out by camel caravan for the long and arduous trek across deserts and mountains. Solomon graciously received the queen, who was amazed by the luxury of his surroundings. The Queen of Sheba asked the king many hard questions and cunning riddles, and found him easily able to answer them all. Impressed by his great wisdom, she presented him with lavish gifts—gold, precious gems, and spices. In return, Solomon made the queen gifts from the royal treasury, and a satisfied queen set out once more on the long journey home to her domain.

So she [the Queen of Sheba] said to the king, "The report was true that I heard in my own land of your accomplishments and of your wisdom, but I did not believe the reports until I came and my own eyes had seen it." 1Ki 10:6–7

Rahab and the Spies (Jos 2): Rahab the prostitute lived along the city wall of Jericho. When Joshua sent spies there to explore the territory, Rahab hid the Israelites in her home and protected their whereabouts from the soldiers. She had heard all about the Israelite God and was convinced that he was the true God.

Certain that Jericho would later be taken by the Israelites, Rahab asked the spies to reward her for helping them by sparing her family when the city was overthrown. The spies promised her safety if she tied a crimson cord in her window and had all her relatives in the house at the time of the attack. Rahab promised to do as they asked.

When the Israelites destroyed Jericho, they rescued Rahab and her family before destroying the city. Rahab became known as a great spiritual hero.

Saul's Conversion (Ac 9): Saul, a brilliant Jew educated in Greek culture and born a Roman citizen, set out to get rid of Christians. He voted for Stephen's death and watched while he was murdered. He organized house-to-house searches and arrests, and when some Christians escaped, he had orders to find them in Damascus and bring them to Jerusalem for trial.

On his way to Damascus, a blinding light from heaven stopped him in his tracks. Saul fell to the ground, and Jesus confronted him in a vision. In a moment, Saul's anger and enmity subsided and he gave himself over to the authority of the Lord.

Opposite page: *In the elegant style of Mannerism, Parmigianino (1503–1540) depicts the conversion of the apostle Paul recorded in the Book of Acts. On his way to Damascus to persecute believers, Paul was dramatically intercepted by the Lord and was subsequently converted to Christianity.*

Blinded by the vision, Saul had to be led into Damascus where he remained for three days without food or drink. God led the disciple Ananias to Saul and he laid hands on the new convert: Saul's sight returned, he received the Holy Spirit, and was baptized. Saul was also known in Greek as Paul.

This colorful scene reflects the first miracle Jesus performed as recorded in the Gospels. Fermented grape juice was an important product in Palestine, and it was served at celebrations. Jesus gave his blessing by turning water into wine at a wedding in Galilee.

Turning Water to Wine (Jn 2): Jesus was at a wedding in Cana when they ran out of wine. His mother asked him to do something about it. Jesus may have been reluctant at first, but finally he agreed. Standing there were six large water pots. Each held 20 or 30 gallons. Jesus told the servants to fill the pots with water. When Jesus commanded them to dip water out, it had already turned to wine.

Uriah's Untimely Death (2Sa 11): Uriah the Hittite was a leading soldier in King David's army. While Uriah was away in battle, David committed adultery with Uriah's wife, Bathsheba. When she became pregnant, David sent for Uriah hoping that he would have relations with his wife and think that he was the father of the child. This plan failed. David then sent Uriah back to the scene of battle, and commanded that he be placed in an unprotected position at the forefront of the battle. David wanted to make sure that Uriah would die. After Uriah was killed, David married Bathsheba. Later, God punished David for this crime.

Vashti's Refusal (Est 1–2): The beautiful Queen Vashti of Persia was ordered by her husband to appear before him. King Ahasuerus was having a feast and he wanted to show off his wife's beauty to his guests. The queen boldly refused. As a punishment for her disobedience—and as a warning to other women in the kingdom—the king divorced her and started a search for a new wife!

Wise Men from Afar (Mt 2): Some time after Jesus was born, sages from the east followed a star and came to where the child was in Bethlehem. These Gentile astrologers recognized Jesus as the Messiah, and they wanted to worship him. They brought him rich gifts of gold, frankincense, and myrrh.

Before arriving in Bethlehem, the wise men stopped in Jerusalem and asked for the whereabouts of the young king. Herod told the sages to go and search for the child and then bring word to him so that he, too, could go and worship. (Secretly, the cruel and suspicious ruler planned to murder the young boy.) After the wise men had paid homage to Jesus, they were warned in a dream not to go back to Herod, so they went back to their country another way. And the life of Jesus was spared.

Xerxes 1 and the Feast of Purim (Est 3–10): Xerxes 1 (King Ahasuerus) ruled over a vast Persian empire. After divorcing his first wife, he married Esther, the Jewish adopted daughter of Mordecai. Soon thereafter, Haman—the king's prime minister—hatched a plot to persecute the Jews in the region. However, influenced by Esther and Mordecai, an enlightened king later executed Haman and granted political freedom for the Jews—an event still celebrated as the Feast of Purim.

Young Jesus in the Temple (Lk 2): When the Passover festival in Jerusalem was over, the family of Jesus started on their way back to Nazareth. After a day's journey, Mary and Joseph realized that their 12-year-old son, Jesus, was not with them. So they returned to Jerusalem to look for him.

After a three-day search they discovered him in the temple among the religious leaders and teachers, who were amazed at his wisdom and understanding, and the depth of his questions.

The astonished parents quizzed Jesus about his behavior and whereabouts. "Child, why have you treated us like this?" they wanted to know. Jesus told them that he had to be in the temple of God.

Jesus then returned to Nazareth with his parents, and Mary treasured these early experiences with her godly son.

Zacchaeus—a New Man! (Lk 19): Zacchaeus, chief Jewish tax collector for the Romans at Jericho, wanted to see Jesus when he came to the city. Being a short man, Zacchaeus had to climb a tree to get a glimpse of Jesus through the crowd. When Jesus passed by, he looked up and told Zacchaeus to host him at his house. The crowd, who viewed Zacchaeus as a traitor assisting the Roman oppressors, was outraged. Why would Jesus go to the house of a despised and dishonest tax collector?

After his encounter with Jesus, Zacchaeus was a changed man. He vowed to repay the poor and all those he had defrauded. Jesus underscored the tax collector's conversion by telling the crowd that salvation had come to a son of Abraham and his household that day.

"These days should be remembered and kept throughout every generation . . . and these days of Purim should never fall into disuse among the Jews, nor should the commemoration of these days cease among their descendants."
Est 9:28

The Language and Literature of the Bible

WE ALL KNOW the Bible is a powerful religious document that describes God's relationship with humanity throughout history; but the Bible can also be seen as an equally impressive work of literature. It is, after all, a collection of books, encompassing many authors and many different writing styles. The Scriptures have been passed down from generation to generation over thousands of years! And much can be learned about the people described in the Bible—their beliefs, values, and customs—by examining its words.

ARCHAEOLOGY AND THE BIBLE

When we read the Bible, we form some kind of idea about the people, objects, and ideas that are mentioned. However, introducing our modern minds to the world of the Bible has its problems.

What kind of clothing did Abraham really wear? Was he dressed like a Bedouin Arab as some illustrations suggest? How about big Goliath? Many of us imagine a medieval warrior hidden within a chunky suit of armor. And what about Jesus? For many, the image of Jesus is influenced by European art rather than a clear understanding of how people who lived in Bible lands looked.

By approaching the Bible with accurate pictures in our minds, the people, places, events, and ideas will come alive. The language and literature of the Bible will resonate richly when we understand the people and places in which its timeless message is firmly rooted.

This is where the value of archaeology comes in. Archaeologists are people who study the past. They excavate, or dig up, ancient sites and study what they find buried there. They examine houses, implements, grave sites, and other artifacts. They carefully decipher inscriptions, evaluate the language,

An aerial view of the excavated mound of Megiddo, a powerful and battle-weary city in ancient times because of its strategic geographical location between Egypt and Syria. Excavations at this site have uncovered settlements from 3500 B.C. through the time of Israel's kingdoms.

literature, monuments, art, and other aspects of human life. Their work is painstaking and time-consuming. Many years may pass from the time an archaeologist first digs into a ruin-mound (called a tell), studies the artifacts, and actually publishes the findings.

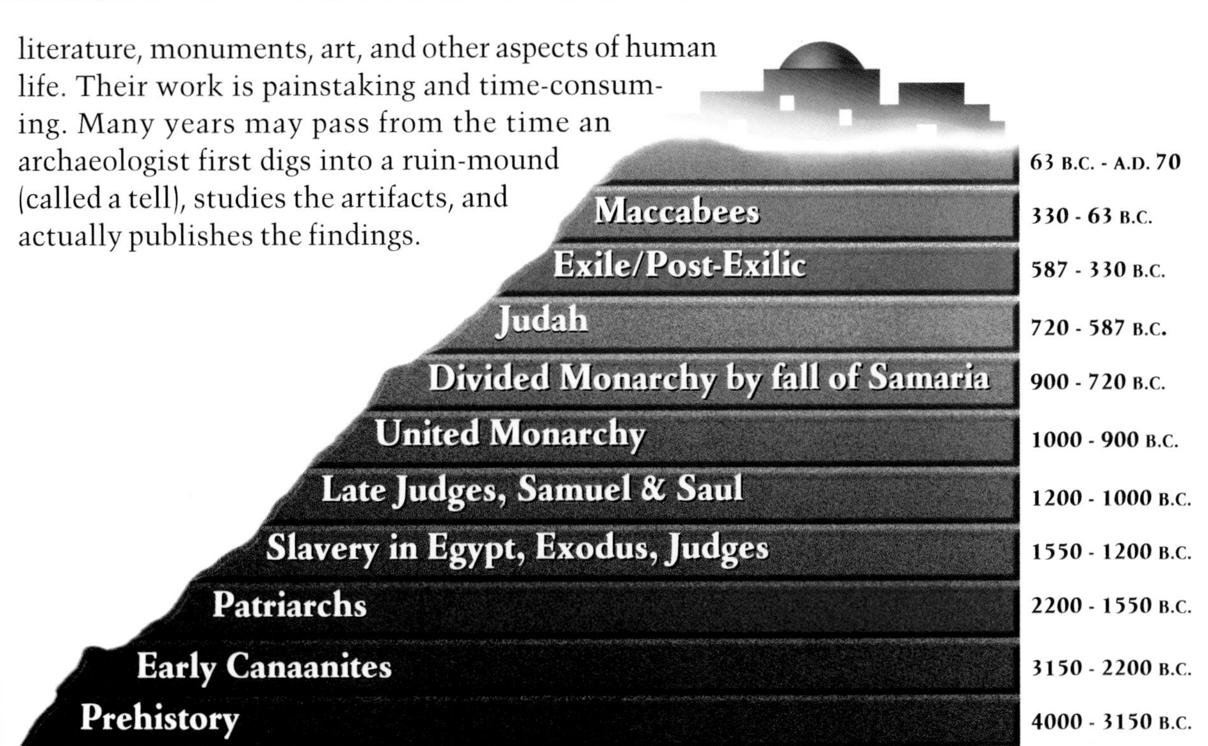

An archeological term for a mound or hill, this diagram of a tell marks the site of ancient settlements dating from prehistory to the time of the New Testament.

By examining the results of the excavator's careful work, we can satisfy our curiosity about life in Bible times, and gain a better understanding of the Bible itself. Fragments of ancient oil lamps can be glued together to give us an idea of what they looked like. And, for example, by uncovering ruined towns of the ninth century B.C., we may not only discover the style of the lamp used by Elisha's hostess (see 2Kings 4:8), but we may also find a great deal of information about the kind of town the prophet visited:

> *One day Elisha was passing through Shunem, where a wealthy woman lived. She urged him to have a meal. So whenever he passed that way, he would stop there to eat. She said to her husband, "Look, I am sure that this man who regularly passes our way is a holy man of God. Let us make a small roof chamber with walls, and put there for him a bed, a table, a chair, and a lamp, so that he can stay there whenever he comes to us."*
>
> *2Ki 4:8–10*

The tombs of kings and warriors provide valuable information about the lifestyles of ancient people. Graves in Jericho dating from about 1600 B.C. had grain and seeds left in them, giving us valuable evidence about the dietary habits of

Workers carefully remove and examine the dirt surrounding an ancient artifact. Every item found is charted, photographed, and labeled as it is removed. A large find such as this may take hundreds of hours of digging by hand to uncover completely.

the time. Occasionally, a discovery may relate directly to a passage of the Bible. Excavators may find an object or building mentioned in the text.

Archaeological research of the Near East is fairly recent. In 1865, the Palestine Exploration Fund was established to finance excavations. So far, only a few hundred mounds have been examined. They have provided valuable information, but much of the Palestinian ruins still wait to be explored. Although the hub of biblical archaeology is in Palestine and Israel (Canaan), it fans out from there to the Mesopotamian Valley, Egypt, Persia (modern Iran), and Asia Minor.

Although there is still much work to be done, current findings give us a better knowledge of the biblical world.

IMPORTANT DISCOVERIES AND THE WORLD OF THE BIBLE

- During excavations at Ur in 1929, Sir Leonard Woolley came across a thick layer of water-laid clay. He believed that he had found silt left by the Flood.
- Early Egyptian texts specify the quotas of bricks to be made by groups of laborers. One from the reign of Ramses II mentions a group called Apiru; this group may have included the Israelites.
- The law-code of Hammurabi, king of Babylon (about 1750 B.C.), is similar to the laws concerning social life found in the Book of Exodus.
- Examples of shrines found in the tomb of Tutankhamen are similar to the tent-shrine (tabernacle) that Israel used in the Sinai Desert for the worship of God.

TEN QUICK FINDS: IMPORTANT EXCAVATIONS IN PALESTINE

Sites	Dates
Jerusalem	1867–70
Megiddo	1925–39
Jericho	1930–36
Lachish	1932–36
Qumran, Dead Sea Caves	1949–1967
Jericho	1952–58
Shechem	1956–73
Megiddo	1960, 1965–67
Ashdod	1962–
Ai	1964–72

- Fragments of city walls and gateways at three cities have been identified from Solomon's time. They are Gezer, Hazor, and Megiddo. The style of pottery found in the ruins supports the dating.
- Extensive stables dating to the tenth century B.C. were uncovered at Megiddo. Some archaeologists believe that they were built by Solomon and used by succeeding generations.
- The Moabite Stone, discovered in Transjordan in 1868, revealed the inscription YHWH (the name of Israel's God). Mesha, king of Moab, had this monument inscribed and set up at Dibon about 840 B.C.
- The monument known as the Black Obelisk of Shalmaneser lists Ahab (874–853 B.C.) and other kings of the northern kingdom.
- Pottery fragments (known as "ostraca") with writing listing payments of oil and wine as revenue were found at the excavation of Samaria. The fall of Samaria is described in the archaeological records of Sargon, king of Samaria.
- Clay tablets found near the Ishtar Gate in Babylon illuminates the last days of the southern kingdom (just before and after 600 B.C.). These tablets record the rations given by the king of Babylon to captive King Jehoiachin (2Ki 25:27–30).
- Tablets excavated at Nippur record evidence of the exiles in Babylonia and Egypt.
- A clay cylinder of Cyrus was discovered on which the edict of Cyrus and the return from Exile is recorded. The inscrip-

The detailed work of the dig requires a skilled team of workers. Archaeologists excavate the site of Ashdod, one of five fortified Philistine towns mentioned in the Old Testament. In the prophet Isaiah's day, Ashdod was captured by King Uzziah of Judah.

A number of ancient writing materials are mentioned in the Bible or have been discovered by archaeologists. Ink made out of soot was applied with brushes. This is an example of an early ink pot.

tion concerns his sending displaced and captive people back to their original dwelling places.

- From the close of the Old Testament (425–400 B.C.) to the time of the New Testament, the rise of Alexander the Great and the spread of Greek culture are well documented in discoveries from practically every excavation of this period.
- Greek documents excavated in Egypt show that the New Testament was written in the Greek of everyday life, not classical Greek. One papyrus document reveals that the word "daily" is at the head of a food shopping list— a list of food "just for the day."
- Recent discoveries in Jerusalem have revealed the wealthy lifestyle of some households at the time the city fell to the Romans in 70 A.D.
- Excavations made by Israeli scholars since 1967 show the richness of King Herod's palace.
- An inscribed stone found in the Roman theater at Caesarea names Pilate "Prefect of Judaea." The Gospels and Acts represent that title in Greek.
- The names of the dead were often scratched or written on the burial-chests found in the tombs of New Testament times. Many chests bear names that are familiar to us in the New Testament. These names are written in Hebrew, Aramaic, and Greek.

EGYPTIAN WASTE PAPER

Archeological discoveries of throwaway papyrus documents from Egypt are extremely important for New Testament study. During the nineteenth century they were discovered in houses and rubbish dumps and sold to museums in large numbers.

The papyri cover all sorts of records, from tax receipts to books. The Greek language and alphabet were used for most of these documents, and the style of Greek is identical with the language of the New Testament. Consequently, the way language is used in the New Testament can be understood much better with the help of the papyri. For example, orders from government to local officials instruct them to get ready for the visit of a ruler. The word for the visit is "parousia," the same word used in the New Testament for the second coming of Christ. Readers would have readily pictured the coming of royalty.

Among the papyri are Egyptian census records that help illustrate Luke's account of the birth of Jesus. The documents also reflect the unpopular view of tax collectors depicted in the Gospels. Copies of famous Greek books have been found among the papyri. Similarly, Old Testament copies in Greek (the Septuagint) and copies of New Testament books have been recovered. A small recovered fragment belongs to a page of John's Gospel, copied about 130 A.D. This is the oldest known piece of a New Testament manuscript to survive.

THE SCRIBES

Professional scribes were important figures in biblical times. They had training, power, and authority in ancient Jewish society. The profession was not hereditary and was open to anyone who completed the training. The scribes came into existence when the nation developed a central government. Besides being writers of documents (for example, copyists of the Bible: Jeremiah dictated his prophecies to the scribe Baruch), they could be counselors, secretaries of state, and tax officials of the king's court.

Scribes formed professional guilds, and they had special quarters in the temple or palace. They carried a special writing case attached to their girdle (an article of clothing), probably sitting in public places to read or write documents for the majority of people, who were illiterate.

After the Exile, scribes took on new functions. Increasingly they studied civil and religious law and decided how it should be applied. Their decisions became the oral law—the "tradition of the elders" spoken of in the Gospels. In fact, their opinions and decisions were considered to have equal power and authority with the written law of God by the Pharisees.

By the first century A.D., the scribes were a powerful group of Jewish leaders, and they—along with the Pharisees—were the target of some of the most critical words of Jesus.

THE DEAD SEA SCROLLS

Mohammed was a shepherd boy who took care of goats in the valley of the Dead Sea. By chance he discovered a number of clay jars in one of many caves in the area. Inside the jars were wads of cloth covered with pitch (a tarlike substance). These cloths were wrapped around manuscripts. This discovery was made in 1947.

One of the most important excavations in Palestine was at Qumran, 1949–67. Many scholars uncovered the carefully hidden manuscripts known as the Dead Sea Scrolls. These fragments from the ancient collection are written in ancient Hebrew.

Not knowing what the scrolls were, the boy sold them for next to nothing. Several years later, the true value of the discovery was realized. Archaeologists and shepherds searched the almost inaccessible caves. By the time they were finished, they had discovered more than 400 scrolls or books.

The books, mostly written in Hebrew or Aramaic, include copies of all Old Testament books (except Esther). The Isaiah scroll—dating from about 100 B.C.—was 1,000 years older than any other known manuscript of the Old Testament. The scrolls belonged to the library of a strict Jewish religious sect (probably the Essenes) at Qumran on the edge of the Dead Sea. The owners had placed their valuable manuscripts in jars and hidden them in caves when the Roman army invaded the area in 68 A.D. Fortunately, the dry heat of that location preserved the historic collection.

These important copies of the Scriptures provide valuable information concerning the text. The scrolls also tell us a lot about Jewish religious and political life in the New Testament period.

READERS AND WRITERS

Besides scribes, there were others in ancient Israel who could read and write. Many inscribed objects found in Israel and Judah, especially from 750 B.C. and later, make it clear that it was not difficult to find ordinary people who were readers and writers. The discovery of alphabet letters written in order on potsherds and seal-stones seems to suggest the work of those learning to write. Teaching basic literacy skills was likely done in small groups in private homes.

The typical Jewish boy could read and write Hebrew (and perhaps Aramaic, as well). The ability to read and write in Greek was not as widespread. By New Testament times, it is probable that more children received a basic education in a school attached to the synagogue.

In ancient times, scribes fashioned pens from reeds and rushes for writing on papyrus and leather. In this photograph, a scribe corrects a Torah scroll.

WRITTEN LANGUAGES OF BIBLE LANDS

In an era of printouts and e-mail, it is hard to imagine what written communication was like in Bible times. Written materials were limited, and writing surfaces were different from what we know today. Papyrus and leather scrolls, as well as wooden and clay tablets, were used for permanent or important records. Bits of pottery, stone, clay, and metal were used for names, short messages, and texts. Kings everywhere would have their deeds carved on stone monuments and on the walls of buildings, and inscriptions were often engraved on tombs.

When Jesus stood before his hometown synagogue in Nazareth, he unrolled the scroll of Isaiah—very much like this example—and read from chapter 61. Documents were not put together in book form until after New Testament times.

The discovery of written information is quite valuable. It provides us with the names of places, leaders, and other important people. We learn of invasions, wars, social life, and religious beliefs. Once the alphabet was invented, any aspect of human life could be kept on record—reading and writing was brought within the reach of everyone.

It is also clear that several ancient languages provided the basic framework for the Scriptures. Understanding the development of Semetic languages will help give us a better understanding of the people who used them.

Sumerian: Writing was invented in Babylonia between 3500 and 3000 B.C. The first language to be written down seems to have been Sumerian. Archaeologists discovered

tablets with this language at the ancient city of Sumer. Sumerian used wedge-shaped picture symbols (cuneiform) to represent words.

Akkadian: The oldest northeast Semitic language is called Akkadian. Akkadian texts from 2300 B.C. contain many Sumerian words and forms. The Akkadian language has helped Bible scholars understand the structure and historical variations in other Semitic languages.

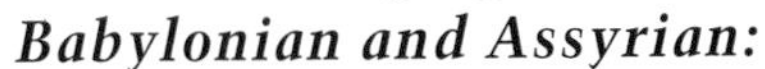

Babylonian and Assyrian: These two dialects of Akkadian were written in a more simplified script. The stories of many Old Testament kings were written in these languages. The history and ideas of these ancient cultures are also preserved in these languages.

Eblaite and Amorite: Both of these languages are in direct line behind biblical Hebrew. And though archaeologists have uncovered thousands of tablets that contain material in these languages, research is still in the early stages. Scholars report that many names of places in Genesis appear on these texts (written in cuneiform).

Egyptian: The idea of writing was carried from Babylonia to Egypt. Egyptian clerks made up their own system of pic-

Believed to be the first language ever written down, ancient Sumerian used picture symbols to represent words. This clay tablet impressed with wedge-shaped cuneiform signs was likely written with a pen made of bone for writing cuneiform.

Soon after it was invented, writing was carried from Babylon to Egypt. The Egyptians created their own system of picture word-signs, which are known as hieroglyphics. This system of picture forms was used for inscriptions on buildings and monuments until the fifth century A.D.

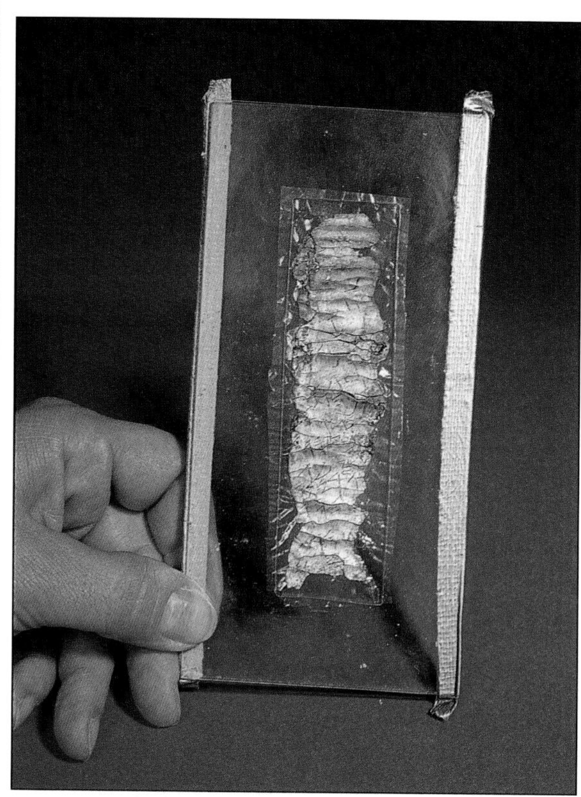

The oldest surviving inscription from the Old Testament, this silver scroll was rolled up and used as an amulet. The scroll contains Numbers 6:24, Israel's priestly blessing, written in Hebrew.

ture word-signs known as *hieroglyphs*. Egyptians used this writing system for inscriptions on buildings and other monuments until the fifth century A.D. After that, simpler handwriting forms were developed.

Ugaritic: The west Semitic language of the Canaanites, Ugaritic contains many words and expressions that are identical with those in the earlier parts of the Hebrew Bible.

Hebrew: This language has been written down since at least 1500 B.C. A dialect of Hebrew is still spoken and written today. Hebrew belonged to the Semitic group of languages, and was written in a script from right to left. The word order in a typical Hebrew sentence is very different from English.

Over the centuries there were different dialects of Hebrew, and all of them have affected the copying of Old Testament manuscripts. For example, Genesis contains many Egyptian expressions as well as some Akkadianisms. Numbers, Joshua, Judges, and Ruth include very early Canaanite expressions, and some of the oldest Hebrew in the Old Testament. Some books reflect Aramaic and Babylonian influences and language patterns.

Aramaic: Aramaic words, phrases, and sometimes entire passages (Da 2–7; Ezr 4–7) appear in the Old Testament. Of all the Semitic languages, Aramaic was most like Hebrew. The

Classical Greek, which was prominent in the fifth century B.C., was a complex and sophisticated language in which a single verb might have many separate forms. On the other hand, the everyday Greek of the New Testament was written in a simple language to communicate with everyone.

HOW BIBLE ALPHABETS COMPARE TO OURS

English: ABCDEFGHIJKLMNOPQRSTUVWXYZ
Hebrew: אבגדהוזחטיכךלמםנןסעפףצץקרששת
Greek: ΑΒΓΔΕΖΗΘΙΚΛΜΝΞΟΠΡΣΤΥΦΧΨΩ

primary works of Jewish religious tradition, the Talmud and its other writings, were written in a dialect of Aramaic.

Aramaic became the common language of the Jews after the Exile. From that time, they began translating the Old Testament into Aramaic. These translations are called the Targums. In the New Testament several Aramaic words and expressions may be found. Aramaic was the language of Jesus and his disciples.

Greek: The written form of Greek has been around for nearly 3,600 years. The first written Greek was developed by the Mycenaeans. They derived their written language from the Hittite hieroglyphs. However, by 1000 B.C. the Greeks had adapted the simpler form of the West Semite script to their language and added all-important vowels—something missing from all Semitic scripts. Thus the Greeks were the first to have a written language based on an alphabet system. This revolutionized communication.

One of the most important archaeological finds in history, the Rosetta Stone was found accidentally at Fort St. Julien on the Nile, near the city of Rosetta, in 1799. The monument, set up in 196 B.C., was in honor of Ptolemy V Epiphanes with an identical inscription in three parts: hieroglyphic, demotic, and Greek.

The conquest of Alexander the Great spread a simple dialect of Greek (called *koine*) to the Mediterranean countries. This form of Greek was the language of the Greek Old Testament (the *Septuagint*) and the Greek New Testament. After the writing of the Greek New Testament, the language continued to change. Today, modern Greek is different from the text of the New Testament.

Latin: As Rome became the hub of the ancient world, Latin spread to influence generations of Europeans. By 50

B.C., it was spoken, written, and understood from the coast of England to the Baltic Sea. Latin has influenced many languages, particularly English. It was the common language of western Christianity from 400 A.D. until the 1800s. Jerome's Latin version of the Scriptures (the Vulgate) has influenced the thinking of the church, and all of the significant modern translations of the Bible.

THE BIBLE—A LIBRARY OF BOOKS

The Bible is not just one book. It is a collection—a library—of 66 books written over many centuries by more than 40 different writers. There are books of law, history, prophecy, poetry, wisdom, letters, and apocalyptic literature—written in a variety of literary styles.

THE PENTATEUCH

The first five books of the Bible are known as the Pentateuch. (The Jewish name for this grouping is the *Torah,* which means instruction or teaching.) These are the books of God's Law. God told Moses how the people of Israel should live, and Moses recorded these commands in the Pentateuch. A few scholars believe that there are four distinct strands to the writings of the Pentateuch. One writer used the name Yahweh for God, another used the term Elohim; there were also two other groups of writers—compilers who used their own skills, traditions, and purposes in compiling the books. Exactly when these writers lived is uncertain. Some parts of the five books are extremely old and seem to date to oral or written records of Moses himself.

The common Hebrew word for "law," torah occurs more than 200 times in the Old Testament. Meaning direction and guidance from God, the Torah encompasses the Old Testament in all its aspects. Seen here, each Torah scroll is encased and placed in a special alcove in the synagogue.

BOOKS OF THE PENTATEUCH

- Genesis
- Exodus
- Leviticus
- Numbers
- Deuteronomy

When the Jews in the Persian empire faced destruction, Queen Esther, at the risk of her life, went before King Ahasuerus to plead for her people. In her honor, the Book of Esther is read every year at the Feast of Purim.

Although the five books are very different, they all tell the story of God at work, not just in creating the world, but in calling out individuals and a nation to obey him and to bless the whole world.

OLD TESTAMENT HISTORY

A large series of books (from Joshua to Esther) records what happened to the people of Israel, beginning with the time they conquered and settled the Promised Land, through the period of judges and kings, to the time of exile. This section spans approximately 800 years of Jewish history (from about 1200 B.C. to 400 B.C.). Ezra and Nehemiah describe the return of the Israelites from captivity. The Book of Esther tells the story of a Jewish queen and how she saved her people from destruction.

The primary purpose in providing this history was to show how God fulfilled his intentions for Israel. Thus the writers faithfully recorded disasters as well

BOOKS OF OLD TESTAMENT HISTORY

Joshua	1 and 2 Samuel	Ezra
Judges	1 and 2 Kings	Nehemiah
Ruth	1 and 2 Chronicles	Esther

as blessings, the stories of good and bad kings, the actions and attitudes of obedience and disobedience by God's people.

THE WISDOM BOOKS

Job, Proverbs, and Ecclesiastes are known as books of Wisdom. This type of writing also appears elsewhere in the Old Testament, particularly in the Book of Psalms. Wisdom literature is also found in the writings of some of Israel's neighbors.

The three Wisdom books are quite different from each other in subject matter. Job focuses on the meaning of suffering, Ecclesiastes dwells on the apparent meaninglessness of life, and Proverbs is a series of sayings—practical advice on how to behave in everyday life. All three books, however, do have aspects in common. God is the central figure within each book, but he is in the home rather than in the temple. A core teaching in the wisdom poems of all three books is that we find true knowledge when we obey God and his laws.

Remember your creator in the days of your youth, before the days of trouble come, and the years draw near when you will say, "I have no pleasure in them";... Ecc 12:1

BOOKS OF WISDOM		
Job	Proverbs	Ecclesiastes

BOOKS OF POETRY

Psalms, the Song of Solomon, and Lamentations are known as the poetic books of the Bible. Besides poetry, this body of literature includes hymns, prayers, and songs. The Book of Psalms is the largest collection of Old Testament poetry. Jewish scholars put this book in a section of the Bible they call the "Writings."

The song poems contained in Psalms express profound emotion—from great ecstasy to utter despair. Recurrent themes are lifting praises to God, warning Israel of the consequences of sin, personal spiritual struggles, and prophetic words. After the Exile, the Psalms became Israel's Psalter.

The theme of the Song of Solomon is the delightful expression of love between a young husband and his bride. This collection of six songs is in the form of a dialogue between the man and the woman, and is set in the countryside in spring.

Jewish scholars also include Lamentations in the "Writings." The book is made up of five poems, four of which are written as acrostics based on the letters of the Hebrew alphabet. The writer expresses personal laments over the fall of Jerusalem. The book also voices the nation's collective despair concerning the collapse of their holy city. The writer holds out a thread of hope to those who put their faith in God's unfailing mercy. The Book of Lamentations, written in a beautiful style, reflects a long tradition of ancient Near Eastern lament poetry.

BOOKS OF POETRY

Psalms Song of Solomon Lamentations

THE PROPHETIC BOOKS

This last section of the Old Testament consists of 16 books. All are called by the name of the prophet whose words they contain. Isaiah, Jeremiah, Ezekiel, and Daniel are known as "major prophets." The other 12 are called the "minor prophets." The prophets were good interpreters of history. Their words reflect the social and religious conditions of their age. God told the prophets to be his servants; they were to take his words to the people, and they were given special abilities to carry out their tasks.

Biblical prophetic literature consists of four categories: First, the prophets communicated messages of faith, advising God's people to trust in God alone. Second, they urged people to know and practice God's word. These prophets based their teachings on the law of Moses, and they emphasized messages of obedience. Third, the prophets gave messages of hope, encouraging faithful ones about the future. Fourth, God's messengers taught the people that Yahweh was Lord of all creation. The prophets proclaimed messages on the lordship of God.

Jeremiah wore his prophetic mantle with great heaviness. His sorrow over the impending destruction of Jerusalem is poignantly captured in Rembrandt's painting of the prophet. Jeremiah was known for his outspoken preaching and laments.

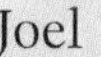

BOOKS OF THE PROPHETS

Isaiah	Amos	Habakkuk
Jeremiah	Obadiah	Zephaniah
Ezekiel	Jonah	Haggai
Daniel	Micah	Zechariah
Hosea	Nahum	Malachi
Joel		

Before his call to be one of Jesus' select group of 12, the apostle Matthew, seen here, was a tax collector who also went by the name Levi. Saint Matthew is also traditionally accepted as the author of the Gospel bearing his name.

NEW TESTAMENT HISTORY

The four Gospels are more than biographies of Jesus. They do not tell us much about his early years, but they do focus on the last week of his life and what happened in the days following his death. The word "gospel" means "good news," and these four books (Matthew, Mark, Luke, and John) concentrate on telling the good news—that Jesus, the promised Redeemer, had come to bring salvation to all who would put their trust in him.

For 30 years after Jesus' ascension, the apostles spread the good news about him. Simultaneously, stories, records, sayings, and word-of-mouth memories about Jesus were being collected. Eventually they were written down by the Gospel writers. The first three books have a considerable amount of material in common. (The fourth Gospel, written by Jesus' disciple John, uses a different approach.) The four

Besides being the author of the Gospel of Luke and the Book of Acts, Luke was a physician and missionary who accompanied the apostle Paul on his journeys.

I too decided, after investigating everything carefully from the very first, to write an orderly account for you . . . so that you may know the truth concerning the things about which you have been instructed.
Lk 1:3–4

Gospels give us a comprehensive picture of Jesus and his ministry. Each account has something unique to bring to the whole.

The Acts of the Apostles completes New Testament history. The author, Luke, writes in a careful, detailed manner, with the touch of an accurate historian. He tells the story starting with Jesus' ascension into heaven, the coming of the Holy Spirit, and the growth of the Christian movement from a group of two hundred to a great community of believers that spread across the Roman Empire.

BOOKS OF NEW TESTAMENT HISTORY				
Matthew	Mark	Luke	John	Acts

I thank my God every time I remember you.... Php 1:3

THE LETTERS

Much of the New Testament consists of letters that we call "epistles"—a common form of writing among ancient Greeks. The New Testament letters provide penetrating insight into the faith and life of the early church.

The apostle Paul wrote several epistles, and they are unique compared to letter styles found outside biblical literature. Paul's letters include proclamation and exhortation, which turns them into written sermons. Before launching into the main part of his letters, Paul bestows a rich blessing on his readers. Usually the body of his epistles focuses on practical and spiritual matters in the life of the church. Paul closes each letter with notes of greeting, a doxology (expression of praise), and a benediction (blessing).

The Book of Hebrews, included among the epistles, is part letter, theological essay, and sermon combined. This epistle, the author of which is not known, refers to the Old Testament, and applies Old Testament passages to main doctrinal points.

Besides Paul, other followers of Jesus wrote general letters to the churches scattered throughout the Roman empire. Each writer had a particular style and emphasis, and sometimes, the words were directed to a particular church or group of Christians.

BOOKS OF LETTERS

Romans	1 and 2 Corinthians	Galatians
Ephesians	Philippians	Colossians
1 and 2 Thessalonians	1 and 2 Timothy	Titus
Philemon	Hebrews	James
1 and 2 Peter	1, 2, and 3 John	Jude

APOCALYPTIC LITERATURE

This type of writing includes religious works that abound in visions of God or revelations from God concerning the depravity of the present age. Throughout the Old Testament there are certain passages that are apocalyptic in nature, for example sections in Joel, Amos, Zechariah, and Daniel 7–12.

In the Book of Daniel, the prophet presents God and evil opposing each other. In the end, God will triumph, and in the future age, the righteous will be resurrected and the wicked will be judged. Daniel sets forth his themes through visions, revelations, and symbols; this symbolism makes the literature difficult to interpret.

This dramatic painting depicts the Four Horsemen, the ominous precursors of disaster, that the Book of Revelation associates with the end of the world.

In the New Testament, apocalyptic writing is found in Matthew, 1 Thessalonians, and the Revelation to John. Revelation highlights the Son of Man, the second coming of Christ, the final glory of the kingdom of God, and the last judgment. The literary style of Revelation is similar to the writing of Old Testament prophets, and the apocalyptic works of the intertestamental period.

APOCALYPTIC WRITING—BETWEEN THE TESTAMENTS

Apocalyptic literature between the two testaments was passive: it encouraged readers not to struggle against the forces of evil but let God deal with them. In contrast, the Old Testament writers encouraged God's people to fight against, or flee from the forces of evil. The intertestament apocryphal book, 2 Esdras, contains some visions and revelations of the early Jewish rabbis, and includes chapters that predict the rejection of the Jews. It speaks of a Jewish book of visions of the future ascribed to Ezra.

The Dead Sea Scrolls also contain apocalyptic material from this period.

Apocalyptic writing was designed to reveal its message to insiders in terms that an outsider could not understand. Writers of this genre could encourage readers to stand against pagan governments, and predict destruction without fear of reprisal.

Revelation emphasizes contrasts as to conflict, actions, location, and time: God is pitted against Satan; a new Jerusalem will be established and Babylon will be destroyed. The writer speaks of heaven and earth, land and sea; there is a distinction between time and eternity. These contrasts express the sense that good and evil vie for supremacy in this world, and we cannot hope for peace until the day of Christ's triumph.

SIGNIFICANT BIBLE THEMES

The language and literature of the Bible are the means to express its unique teachings and major themes. From Genesis to Revelation significant topics, ideas, and images on the life of faith are presented and underscored. Some are very familiar, others are less well known—and all are found within the pages of Scripture:

A depiction of the Passover meal shared by Jewish families and celebrated in the first month of the Hebrew calendar. Moses established this rite as a reminder to all Jews that God spared his people and released them.

1. God's covenant with Abraham (Ge 12:2–3; 15:18; 17:1–8)
2. The Passover (Ex 12:11–14)
3. The Ten Commandments (Ex 20; Dt 5)
4. The Day of Atonement (Lev 16; Heb 7–9)
5. The Day of the Lord (Isa 2:12; Jer 30:7; Eze 7:19; Ob 15; Zec 14:1; Rev 16:14)
6. The "I am" claims of Jesus (Jn 6:35; 8:12; 10:7; 10:11; 11:25; 14:6; 15:1)
7. The Sermon on the Mount (Mt 5; Lk 6)
8. The Beatitudes (Mt 5; Lk 6)
9. The Lord's Prayer (Mt 6:9–13; Lk 11:2–4)
10. The Parables of Jesus (Mk 12:1–9; Lk 10:25–37; Lk 15:11–32)
11. The Kingdom of God (Mic 4:6–7; Mt 5:1–20; Lk 7:18–23)
12. The Miracles of Jesus (Mt 8:2–3; Mk 5:1–15; Lk 18:35–43; Jn 6:19–21)
13. The Lord's Supper (Lk 22:19)
14. The Fruit of the Spirit (Gal 5)

The events of the Lord's Supper are described in three of the four Gospels. It was at this Passover seder, the night before the crucifixion of Jesus, that the celebration of communion was instituted.

POPULAR BIBLE VERSES

Besides many well-known Scripture passages such as the Lord's Prayer, the Ten Commandments, and the 23rd Psalm, many of us have a favorite Bible verse or two. In childhood we may have memorized a few on our own, or learned them in Sunday school or Vacation Bible School, or from some other religious influence in our lives. Here is a list of the top ten familiar and well-liked Bible verses.

1. "For God so loved the world that he gave his only Son, so that everyone who believes in him may not perish but may have eternal life."
   Jn 3:16
2. Trust in the Lord with all your heart, and do not rely on your own insight. In all your ways acknowledge him, and he will make straight your paths.
   Pr 3:5–6
3. . . . all have sinned and fall short of the glory of God. . . .
   Ro 3:23
4. Cast all your anxiety on him, because he cares for you.
   1Pe 5:7
5. We know that all things work together for good for those who love God, who are called according to his purpose.
   Ro 8:28

6. If we confess our sins, he who is faithful and just will forgive us our sins and cleanse us from all unrighteousness.
1Jn 1:9

7. "Let the little children come to me, and do not stop them; for it is to such as these that the kingdom of heaven belongs."
Mt 19:14

8. "I hereby command you: Be strong and courageous; do not be frightened or dismayed, for the Lord your God is with you wherever you go."
Jos 1:9

9. There is no longer Jew or Greek, there is no longer slave or free, there is no longer male and female; for all of you are one in Christ Jesus.
Gal 3:28

10. For surely I know the plans I have for you, says the Lord, plans for your welfare and not for harm, to give you a future with hope.
Jer 29:11

WRITING STYLES OF THE BIBLE

Pious King Hezekiah of Judah made extensive religious reforms during his reign, including restoring the temple of Jerusalem and abolishing pagan practices in Judah.

Within this general framework of unique themes, the Bible is noted for its profound prayers, poems and hymns, wise sayings, warm greetings, farewells, and blessings. These samples portray deep content and expressive language.

Prayers: The Bible is filled with many eloquent examples of prayer. The act of prayer involves confession of sin, petition to the Lord, thanksgiving, and worship. When King Hezekiah prays to God, he speaks openly and simply. He is seriously ill and wants to live, so he begs God for help:

"Remember now, O Lord, I implore you, how I have walked before you in faithfulness with a whole heart, and have done what is good in your sight." (2Ki 20:3)

Concerned for Israel's sins, Nehemiah approaches God in grand tones, appealing to his power and faithfulness:

"O Lord God of heaven, the great and awesome God who keeps covenant and steadfast love with those who love him and keep his commandments; let your ear be attentive and your eyes open to hear the prayer of your servant that I now pray before you day and night for your servants, the people of Israel,. . . " (Ne 1:5–6)

Biblical Poetry: The songs and poems of the Hebrews reflect the whole range of human feelings. Rhythms and word patterns are flexible, and the thoughts are drawn from the depths of experience. In the Psalms we find the writers pouring out their hearts to God—at times deep in sorrow, at others with unfettered joy:

Psalm 117
Praise the Lord, all you
nations!
Extol him, all you peoples!
For great is his steadfast love toward us,
and the faithfulness of the Lord endures forever.
Praise the Lord! (Ps 117)

Many of the Psalms were probably used as hymns in worship. And some psalms have a call and response pattern as if they were used in a liturgy. Psalm 24 is an example of a liturgical psalm with its call:

Who is this king of glory?
and the response:
The Lord, strong and mighty,
the Lord mighty in battle. . .
The Lord of hosts,
he is the king of glory. (Ps 24:8, 10)

TEN QUICK FACTS ABOUT BIBLE LITERATURE

- Three ancient sources—the Rosetta Stone, the Behistun Rock, and the clay tablets of Ugarit—have helped to make clear the ancient languages of Bible times.
- Hebrew wisdom literature centered on almighty God.
- Wisdom for the Egyptians centered on the individual.
- Some Bible books existed in spoken form long before they were written down.
- The shorter prophetic books in the Old Testament are called "minor" only because of their length, not because they are less important than the "major" prophetic books.
- Like authors everywhere, the Bible writers had their own perspective, and the way they pass on a story tells us a lot about their point of view.
- The chiasm was one of the writing styles of the Bible. It worked like this: the writer recorded each idea in sequence, in ascending order. Then the ideas were presented again in inverted form, in descending order , for example:

  For my thoughts are not your thoughts,
  nor are your ways my ways, says the Lord.
  For as the heavens are higher than earth,
  so are my ways higher than your ways
  and my thoughts than your thoughts.

  ISA 55:8–9
- Jesus told parables to help ordinary people understand what God's kingdom was like.
- Poetry is not limited to the Old Testament. The Gospels and Letters contain flowing, poetic language. For example, Mary's Magnificat (Lk 1:46–55) is steeped in Old Testament imagery, and there are many poetic fragments in Paul's writing.
- Miracle stories are prominent in the Gospels.

A beautiful depiction of the young Jewish virgin who was chosen by God to bear the Messiah, Jesus Christ. Mary, at prayer in this portrait, is presented in the Bible as a humble and willing servant of God.

Biblical Songs: Songs of praise are recorded throughout the Bible. Moses and his sister Miriam broke into song and danced when God preserved the Israelites from the Egyptians. Deborah the judge sang a triumphant song after victory over Sisera. Perhaps one of the best known songs of Scripture is Mary's canticle of praise known as the "Magnificat":

"My soul magnifies the Lord,
and my spirit rejoices in God my Savior,
for he has looked with favor on the lowliness of his servant.
Surely, from now on all generations will call me blessed;
for the Mighty One has done great things for me,
and holy is his name.
His mercy is for those who fear him from generation to generation.
He has shown strength with his arm;
he has scattered the proud in the thoughts of their hearts.
He has brought down the powerful from their thrones,
and lifted up the lowly;
he has filled the hungry with good things,
and sent the rich away empty.
He has helped his servant Israel,
in remembrance of his mercy,
according to the promise he made to our ancestors,
to Abraham and to his descendants forever."
(Lk 1:47–55)

Biblical Wisdom: The wisdom literature of the Bible is godliness applied to everyday experience. Its pithy sayings and wise proverbs are as varied as life itself. Underneath all the good advice is the belief that the first step in wisdom is reverence for God, and that true wisdom is a gift from God:

The fear of the Lord is the beginning of wisdom,
and the knowledge of the Holy One is insight. (Pr 9:10)

Proverbs includes a wealth of instruction on life at home:

Better is a dry morsel with quiet
than a house full of feasting with strife. (Pr 17:1)

Train children in the right way,
and when old, they will not stray. (Pr 22:6)

Proverbs also has much to say about neighbors and friends, and places high value on friendship:

Some friends play at friendship
but a true friend sticks closer than one's nearest kin. (Pr 18:24)

Well meant are the wounds a friend inflicts,
but profuse are the kisses of an enemy. (Pr 27:6)

In the poetry and wisdom of Ecclesiastes, there is a sense of the futility of life without God. But though there is a gloomy tone throughout the book, the writer inserts an optimistic note:

This is what I have found out: the best thing anyone can do is to eat and drink and enjoy what he has worked for during the short life that God has given. (Ecc 5:18)

As depicted in this striking portrayal, the apostle Paul was a prolific writer. As he traveled from place to place, Paul wrote teaching letters to the early churches of the Christian faith. These letters were copied and passed on to other churches, and eventually they became part of the New Testament.

Greetings: During the apostle Paul's day, there was a well-known Greek letter form that was similar in some ways to the structure of the New Testament epistles. In the popular Greek form, the standard greeting was ordinary and colorless. In his letters, Paul created a rich new salutation:

Grace to you and peace from God our Father and the Lord Jesus Christ. (Eph 1:2)

In his short letter, Jude varies the wording of his greeting:

May mercy, peace, and love be yours in abundance. (Jude 2)

Farewells: Closing greetings are another unique characteristic of New Testament letters. In typical Greek letters, the farewell was usually a single word but Paul expanded his into notes of greeting, a doxology, and a benediction:

Greet every saint in Christ Jesus. The friends who are with me greet you. All the saints greet you, especially those of the emperor's household.

The grace of the Lord Jesus Christ be with your spirit. (Php 4:23)

Greet one another with a holy kiss. All the saints greet you.

The grace of the Lord Jesus Christ, the love of God, and the communion of the Holy Spirit be with all of you. (2Co 13:12–13)

Jude's closing has become a popular doxology in many church services:

Now to him who is able to keep you from falling, and to make you stand without blemish in the presence of his glory with rejoicing, to the only God our Savior, through Jesus Christ our Lord, be glory, majesty, power, and authority, before all time and now and forever. Amen. (Jude 24–25)

Blessings: Besides benedictions, the Bible is known for its remarkable blessings. Prophetic blessings were often bestowed on individuals, family members, or the nation as a

With the establishment of the tabernacle, Aaron and his sons (depicted here in James J. Tissot's painting) were consecrated to the priesthood. Aaron became the high priest and was put in charge of Jewish national worship.

whole. Aaron and the priests pronounced this special blessing on the Israelites. It is a benediction that is familiar to many:

The Lord bless you and keep you;
the Lord make his face to shine upon you, and be gracious to you;
the Lord lift up his countenance upon you, and give you peace. (Nu 6:24–26)

Before he died, Moses blessed the clans of Israel. They were about to enter the Promised Land without him. Their valiant, departing leader set before them God's covenant promises, and he reminded them to be obedient to God in order to experience his blessing:

Happy are you, O Israel! Who is like you,
a people saved by the Lord,
the shield of your help,
and the sword of your triumph!
Your enemies shall come fawning to you,
and you shall tread on their backs. (Dt 33:29)

Curses and Judgments: Included within biblical literature are several solemn and searing pronouncements on sin and disobedience. Curses are the reverse of "blessings," and on the human level wish harm or calamity. On the divine, they call for the imposition of God's holy judgment against wrongdoing. Quite unlike today's common practice of cursing—that is, using profane language freely and loosely—biblical curses embodied powerful consequences, and were expressed in somber, exact terms:

"... those blessed by the Lord shall inherit the land, but those cursed by him shall be cut off." Ps 37:22

Upon the serpent:
The Lord God said to the serpent,
"Because you have done this,
cursed are you among all animals
and among all wild creatures;
upon your belly you shall go,
and dust you shall eat
all the days of your life.
I will put enmity between you and the woman,
and between your offspring and hers;
he will strike your head,
and you will strike his heel." (Gen 3:14–15)

Upon the ground:
And to the man he said,

"Because you have listened to the voice of your wife,
and have eaten of the tree
about which I commanded you,
'You shall not eat of it,'
cursed is the ground because of you;
in toil you shall eat of it all the days of your life;
thorns and thistles it shall bring forth for you;
and you shall eat the plants of the field.
By the sweat of your face
you shall eat bread
until you return to the ground,
for out of it you were taken;
you are dust,
and to dust you shall return." (Gen 3:17–19)

Abel offered God a lamb from his flock, and God was pleased with this first sacrifice. At the same time, Cain's bloodless sacrifice was rejected by the Lord. Disconsolate and angry, Cain murdered his younger brother, and God placed divine judgment on Cain for choosing to do evil rather than good.

Upon Cain:

And now you are cursed from the ground, which has opened its mouth to receive your brother's blood from your hand. When you till the ground, it will no longer yield to you its strength; you will be a fugitive and a wanderer on the earth. (Gen 4:11–12)

Upon Israel:

But if you will not obey the Lord your God by diligently observing all his commandments and decrees, which I am commanding you today, then all these curses shall come upon you and overtake you:

Cursed shall you be in the city and cursed shall you be in the field.

Cursed shall be your basket and your kneading bowl.

Cursed shall be the fruit of your womb, the fruit of your ground, the increase of your cattle and the issue of your flock.

Cursed shall you be when you come in, and cursed shall you be when you go out.

(Dt 28:15–19)

Upon false teachers:

But even if we or an angel from heaven should proclaim to you a gospel contrary to what we proclaimed to you, let that one be accursed! (Gal 1:8)

Upon the law:

Christ redeemed us from the curse of the law by becoming a curse for us—for it is written, "Cursed is everyone who hangs on a tree"—in order that in Christ Jesus the blessing of Abraham might come to the Gentiles, so that we might receive the promise of the Spirit through faith. (Gal 3:13–14)

FASCINATING FACTS FROM ALEPH TO TAW

What do aleph-taw, alpha-omega, and A-Z have in common? They are all the first and last letters of the alphabet in three languages—Hebrew, Greek, and English respectively. Here are 20 other intriguing and factual stories from the world of biblical language, writing, and literature.

A is for Ox: Very early alphabets used pictures of everyday objects to represent the sounds of the first letters of these words. The first letter of the Hebrew alphabet is aleph, derived from alpu "ox," and so the Hebrew "A" was a line drawing of an ox head.

Blessings from A to Z: In Jewish tradition, God blesses Israel from "aleph to taw." These Hebrew letters are the first and last in the Hebrew alphabet, so the expression means that God blesses Israel completely. By striking coincidence, the list of blessings found in Leviticus 26:3–13 begins with aleph and ends with taw.

Codes, Commands, and Covenants: The Mosaic Law contains 613 specific commandments that regulate most aspects of people's lives and worship—from circumcision to food laws. The concept of covenant was familiar to people living in the time of Moses. Archaeologists have discovered records of Hittite covenants dating from 1400 to 1200 B.C.

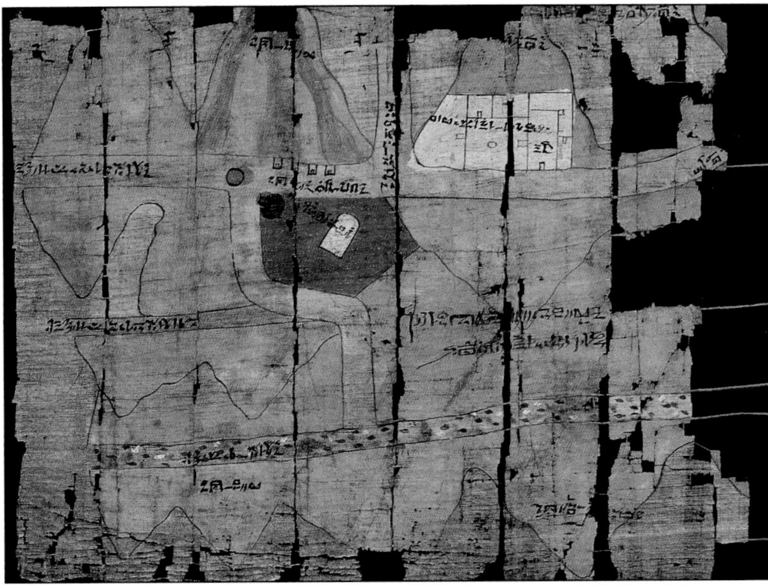

Papyrus, a durable reedlike plant, grew in marshy areas along the upper Nile. In biblical times, the plant was used in the construction of boats, for making medicines, and most importantly, to make the paper used in ancient times. The papyrus fragment shown here is from a map of the gold mines in the Sinai, 20th dynasty.

Did Adam Speak Hebrew?: Adam's words recorded in the Scriptures are in Hebrew, but he likely did not speak this language. Although Hebrew goes back beyond 2000 B.C., we cannot trace its roots all the way to early Bible people such as Adam, Noah, or Abraham.

Early Paper: Our word "paper" comes from papyrus—an early, inexpensive material used as a writing surface. Papyrus was made by stripping long papyrus reeds of their bark, laying them next to each other in rows. Another layer was laid crosswise across the top. The two layers were soaked with glue and water, then pounded into one sheet. It was finally smoothed with pumice.

Familiar Greek Words: Many English words have their roots in Greek words used in the New testament. *Theos* (God) and *logos* (word, study) give us theology (the study of God). *Anthropos* (man) gives us anthropology (the study of humanity). Other words include *angelos* (angel) and *ethnosis* (nation).

God's Writing: The Bible tells us that the Ten Commandments were "written with the finger of God" (Ex 31:18). In fact, this is emphasized later when the writer says: "The tablets were the work of God, and the writing was the writing of God, engraved upon the tablets." (Ex 32:16)

How to Write on Clay: In ancient times, even before Abraham, clay was a popular writing surface. Wet clay was touched with the tip of a sharp pointed reed to make impressions. Soft clay tablets were used for writing, and afterward baked hard. Broken fragments of pottery (shards) might also be used. Assyrian and Babylonian scribes used a wedge-shaped stylus to make cuneiform characters on their clay documents. Thousands of these artifacts have survived, providing scholars with valuable information about people in Bible lands.

Hammurabi's law code, inscribed on a grand stele of black diorite, was discovered at Susa in 1902. The 282 laws are engraved in cuneiform characters in 51 columns of text. Above them, Hammurabi is shown at the top of the stele.

It's Carved in Stone!: The most important documents in ancient times were laboriously carved into stone so they would remain permanently on record. The Ten Commandments were written on two stone tablets. Hammurabi's Law Code was engraved on a stele (a type of stone marker) eight feet high. At the top, Babylon's King Hammurabi is shown receiving the symbols of authority from the god Marduk.

Joseph's Robe: There have been many stories, plays, and even a Broadway musical about Joseph and his famous coat. It is usually depicted in gorgeous colors and fancy design. Indeed, Joseph's gift from his father Jacob has taken on a legendary life of its own. Yet the best Bible translations simply describe the garment this way: ". . . and he [Jacob] had made him a long robe with sleeves." (Gen 37:3)

King Mesha's Inscription: Moabite king Mesha carved a message on a large black basalt stone. It had 34 lines of text and dates to 830 B.C. It tells of his conflicts with the Israelite kings Omri and Ahab. Mesha says of Omri:

"As for Omri, king of Israel, he humbled Moab many years, for Chemosh [the Moabite god] was angry with his land."

Leviathan and Behemoth: Although people are fascinated by these mysterious creatures of the Bible, they disagree on the true meaning of leviathan and behemoth (Job 40:15–24; 41). Some think they refer to imaginary monstrous creatures, or ancient animals that are now extinct. Others think that behemoth was either an elephant or a hippopotamus, and that leviathan was a whale or a crocodile. Although scholars cannot agree on the identity of these creatures, they are wonderfully described in the Scriptures!

mrhdlttllmb: This is the nursery rhyme "Mary had a little lamb," written without any vowels, word divisions, or punctuation. The Old Testament was originally written without any of these, and readers had to supply these themselves to make sense of the text.

Not All the Old Testament Is in Hebrew: While most of the Old Testament was written in Hebrew, several chapters in Ezra and Daniel (and even one verse in Jeremiah) were written in Aramaic.

Old Hebrew Inscription: The earliest object with a Hebrew text written on it is a limestone tablet containing a farmer's calendar. It was use in Gezer, a biblical city, almost 3,000 years ago. It reads in part:

"His two months are (olive) harvest,
His two months are planting (grain)."

Psalm 119—Poetic and Precise: Psalm 119 is the longest psalm—176 verses in all, consisting of 22 eight-verse sec-

The Book of Job speaks of behemoth, a large beast possibly similar to a hippopotamus or water buffalo, and leviathan—probably the crocodile. In biblical poetic passages, sea monsters are often associated with the mythology of paganism.

tions. Each section begins with a successive letter of the Hebrew alphabet, and each verse within that section begins with the same letter. In this stylized, formal psalm, the writer expresses delight in God's law.

Q and the Synoptics: Matthew, Mark, and Luke are sometimes called the synoptic Gospels. The word "synoptic" means "able to be seen together." It is possible to look at these three books side by side and compare their contents. Much of the material is shared and seems to come from a common source.

Q is the first letter of the German word for source (Quelle). It is the name given to the unknown document from which scholars think Matthew and Luke took their sayings of Jesus (which do not appear in the Book of Mark). Q may have been written in Aramaic in about 50 A.D.

"I will sing to the Lord as long as I live; I will sing praise to my God while I have being. May my meditation be pleasing to him, for I rejoice in the Lord." Ps 104: 33–34

Revival of a Language: Hebrew began to die out as a spoken language toward the end of the Old Testament period. Nehemiah was distressed to find Jews who had married foreign women and whose children could not even speak "the language of Judah" (Hebrew).

After that, Hebrew was kept alive only among the rabbis in the synagogues for more than 2,000 years. Then—about 100 years ago—Eliezer Ben-Yehuda, a Lithuanian Jew, proposed and worked tirelessly for its revival as a spoken language. Modern Hebrew is based upon biblical Hebrew and Talmudic Aramaic, and it has traces of Yiddish, German, and Russian.

Strange Meditations: The Hebrew word for "meditation" (hagah) is also used to describe the coo of a dove, the growl of a lion, the plotting of evil rulers, and the reading of the Bible. These things are all something done audibly. Thus, when Jews were instructed to meditate on God's word (Psalm 1:2), this meant that they should recite it aloud to themselves.

Tablets of Clay: More than 4,000 clay tablets were discovered in the 1920s at ancient Nuzi, east of the Tigris River. These date to the middle of the second millennium B.C. The texts give a wide-ranging picture of everyday life at that time, including things such as land ownership, the position of slaves and women, prices and sales of goods, legal customs, and family law. Many intriguing parallels are found between Genesis and the Nuzi documents.

BIBLE STATISTICS

	Old Testament	New Testament
1. Books	39	27
2. Chapters	929	260
3. Verses	23,214	7,959
4. Longest book	Psalms	Acts
5. Shortest book	Obadiah	3 John

FUN FACTS FROM GENESIS TO REVELATION

There are many fascinating figures and facts about the books, chapters, verses, and authors of the Bible. Bible readers everywhere are curious about Bible statistics. Commonly asked questions include: Which are the longest books in the Bible? What are some best-loved Bible passages? Who are the Bible authors? What is the significance of numbers in the Bible? This section will answer some of these questions.

20 IMPORTANT CHAPTERS

1. God's covenant with Abram	Gen 15
2. The Ten Commandments	Ex 20
3. God's faithfulness	Jos 15
4. The friendship of David and Jonathan	1Sa 20
5. The heavenly shepherd	Ps 23
6. Confession of sin	Ps 51
7. Thanksgiving for God's goodness	Ps 103
8. The virtues of God's Law	Ps 119
9. Wisdom	Pr 8
10. An ode to a capable wife	Pr 31
11. The majesty of God	Isa 40
12. An invitation to abundant life	Isa 55
13. The Beatitudes	Mt 5
14. The Lord's Prayer	Mt 6
15. Pentecost	Ac 2
16. Justification	Ro 5
17. Directions about marriage	1Co 7
18. The gift of love	1Co 13
19. The meaning of faith	He 11
20. Hearing and doing the Word	Jas 1

The bond between David and Jonathon (portrayed in this painting by Rembrandt) was established when David entered Saul's service. The loyalty and commitment between the two withstood the threats, plottings, and vendettas of Saul against the popular young courtier. David finally had to flee for his life from the king, but not before he and Jonathan reaffirmed their sworn oath of friendship.

AUTHORS OF THE BOOKS OF THE BIBLE

Author	Book
1. Moses	Genesis, Exodus, Leviticus, Numbers, Deuteronomy
2. Possibly Joshua, Phineas, Eleazer, Samuel, Jeremiah, or one of Joshua's elders	Joshua

3. Uncertain	Judges
4. Uncertain	Ruth
5. Samuel likely wrote only part of 1 Samuel	1 and 2 Samuel
6. Possibly Ezra, Ezekiel, or Jeremiah	1 and 2 Kings
7. Possibly Ezra	1 and 2 Chronicles
8. Possibly Ezra	Ezra
9. Nehemiah	Nehemiah
10. Attributed to Mordecai (by Josephus)	Esther
11. Uncertain	Job
12. Attributed to many authors: David, Solomon, Asaph, and the sons of Korah among them	Psalms
13. Solomon and other wisdom writers	Proverbs
14. Solomon or a Jewish sage	Ecclesiastes
15. Possibly Solomon	Song of Solomon
16. Isaiah	Isaiah
17. Jeremiah	Jeremiah
18. Attributed to Jeremiah	Lamentations
19. Ezekiel	Ezekiel
20. Daniel	Daniel
21. Hosea	Hosea
22. Attributed to Joel	Joel
23. Amos	Amos
24. Obadiah	Obadiah
25. Attributed to Jonah	Jonah
26. Micah	Micah
27. Nahum	Nahum
28. Habakkuk	Habakkuk
29. Zephaniah	Zephaniah
30. Haggai	Haggai
31. Zechariah	Zechariah
32. Malachi	Malachi
33. The apostle Matthew	Matthew
34. John Mark	Mark
35. Luke	Luke, Acts

Early tradition holds that the Gospel of Mark was written in Rome between 65–70 A.D. by John Mark, the apostle. The author (pictured here in a 15th-century Book of Hours detail) is the same John Mark often mentioned in the New Testament. He accompanied Paul and Barnabas on the first missionary journey.

36. The apostle John	John
37. The apostle Paul	Romans, 1 and 2 Corinthians, Galatians, Ephesians, Philippians, 1 and 2 Thessalonians, Philemon, Colossians, 1 and 2 Timothy, Titus
38. Unknown	Hebrews
39. James, the brother of Christ	James
40. The apostle Peter	1 and 2 Peter
41. The apostle John	1, 2, and 3 John and Revelation
42. Jude	Jude

NUMBERS: SIGNS AND SYMBOLS IN THE BIBLE

Number **Meaning and Reference**

One Unity and absolute singleness:
"There is one body and one Spirit . . . one Lord, one faith, one baptism, one God and Father of all, who is above all and through all and in all." (Eph 4:4–6)

Two Witness, work, and support:
a) *"After this the Lord appointed 70 others and sent them on ahead of him in pairs to every town and place where he himself intended to go."* (Lk 10:1)
b) *"Two are better than one, because they have a good reward for their toil. For if they fall, one will lift up the other; but woe to one who is alone and falls and does not have another to help."* (Ecc 4:9–10)

Three Accomplishment, power, and emphasis:
a) *"Jesus answered them, 'Destroy this temple, and in three days I will raise it up.' "* (Jn 2:19)
b) *"Go therefore and make disciples of all nations, baptizing them in the name of the Father and of the Son and of the Holy Spirit, . . . "* (Mt 28:19)
c) *"A ruin, a ruin, a ruin—I will make it!"* (Eze 21:27)

Four Related to the earth:
"I, Daniel, saw in my vision by night the four winds of heaven stirring up the great sea, and four great beasts came up out of the sea, different from one another." (Da 7:2–3)

"Three times in the year you shall hold a festival for me. . . . Three times in the year all your males shall appear before the Lord God." Ex 23:14, 17

When Jesus fed the multitudes in a miraculous way, Matthew's gospel recounts that he divided only five loaves of bread and fed the entire crowd.

Opposite page: *In this 15th-century painting, Jesus stands in the temple surrounded by his 12 disciples. The number 12 was often identified with the divine purposes of God in the Bible.*

Five An expression of grace:
a) *"Taking the five loaves and the two fish, he looked up to heaven, and blessed and broke the loaves, and gave them to the disciples, and the disciples gave them to the crowds. And all ate and were filled; . . . "* (Mt 14:19–20)
b) *". . . and five were wise."* (Mt 25: 2)

Six The number of humanity:
a) *"God saw everything that he had made, and indeed, it was very good. And there was evening and there was morning, the sixth day."* (Ge 1:31)
b) *"And there came out from the camp of the Philistines a champion named Goliath, of Gath, whose height was six cubits and a span."* (1Sa 17:4)

Seven Divine perfection:
a) *"And on the seventh day God finished the work that he had done, and he rested on the seventh day . . . God blessed the seventh day and hallowed it, . . . "* (Gen 2:2–3)
b) *"The promises of the Lord are promises that are pure, silver refined in a furnace on the ground, purified seven times."* (Ps 12:6)

Eight A new beginning:
". . . and it shall be a sign of the covenant between me and you . . . every male among you shall be circumcised when he is eight days old, . . . " (Gen 17:11–12)

Nine The number of blessing:
". . . the fruit of the Spirit is love, joy, peace, patience, kindness, generosity, faithfulness, gentleness, and self-control . . . " (Gal 5:22)

Ten Law, human government:
"He declared to you his covenant, which he charged you to observe, that is, the ten commandments; . . . " (Dt 4:13)

Twelve Divine government:
a) *"Then Jesus summoned his twelve disciples and gave them authority . . . "* (Mt 10:1)
b) *"It [the holy city Jerusalem] has a great, high wall with twelve gates, and at the gates twelve angels, and on the gates are inscribed the names of the twelve tribes of the Israelites. . . . And the wall of the city has twelve foundations, and on them are the twelve names of the twelve apostles of the Lamb."* (Rev 21:12, 14)

Thirty Associated with sorrow:
"The Israelites wept for Moses in the plains of Moab thirty days; then the period of mourning for Moses was ended." (Dt 34:8)

Angels hover over the soggy land, surveying the aftermath of the Great Flood in this painting by 19-century American artist Washington Alston. According to the Bible, the flood lasted 40 days and nights—a number associated with testing and trial.

Forty The number of testing and trial:
a) "*. . . I will send rain on the earth for forty days and forty nights; . . .* " (Gen 7:4)
b) "*And your children shall be shepherds in the wilderness for forty years, and shall suffer for your faithlessness, . . .* " (Nu 14:33)
c) "*Then Jesus was led up by the Spirit into the wilderness to be tempted by the devil. He fasted forty days and forty nights, and afterwards he was famished.*" (Mt 4:1–2)

Fifty Celebration and ceremony:
a) "*And you shall hallow the fiftieth year and you shall proclaim liberty throughout the land to all its inhabitants. It shall be a jubilee for you: . . .* " (Lev 25:10)
b) "*After this Absalom got himself a chariot and horses, and fifty men to run ahead of him.*" (2Sa 15:1)

Seventy The number associated with committees and judgment:
a) "*So the Lord said to Moses, 'Gather for me seventy of the elders of Israel, whom you know to be the elders of the people and officers over them; bring them to the tent of meeting, and have them take their place there with you. I will come down and talk with you there; and I will take some of the spirit that is on you and put it on them; and they shall bear the burden of the people along with you so that you will not bear it all by yourself.'*" (Nu 11:16–17)

b) *"Seventy weeks are decreed for your people and your holy city: to finish the transgression, to put an end to sin, and to atone for iniquity, to bring in everlasting righteousness, to seal both vision and prophet, and to anoint a most holy place. . . . "* (Da 9:24)
c) *"For thus says the Lord: 'Only when Babylon's seventy years are completed will I visit you, and I will fulfill to you my promise and bring you back to this place....' "* (Jer 29:10)
d) *"After this the Lord appointed seventy others and sent them on ahead of him. . . . "* (Lk 10:1)

POPULAR BIBLE PHRASES

We may not be aware that some expressions that we regularly use actually come from the Bible! Many well-known Bible phrases are part of church liturgy, Christian hymns, songs, and inspirational material.

1. Vanity of vanities, says the Teacher; **all is vanity**. (Ecc 12:8)
2. Is there no **balm in Gilead**? (Jer 8:22)
3. **Blessed are the peacemakers**, for they will be called children of God. (Mt 5:9)
4. But to all who received him, who believed in his name, he gave power to become **children of God.** (Jn 1:12)
5. Do not give what is holy to dogs; and **do not throw your pearls before swine**, or they will trample them under foot and turn and maul you. (Mt 7:6)
6. If any harm follows, then you shall give life for life, **eye for eye, tooth for tooth**. . . (Ex 21:24)
7. And now **faith, hope, and love abide,** these three; and the greatest of these is love. (1Co 13:13)
8. **Fight the good fight** of the faith; take hold of the eternal life, to which you were called and for which you made the good confession in the presence of many witnesses. (1Ti 6:12)
9. **For everything there is a season** and a time for every matter under heaven; . . . (Ecc 3:1)
10. And he said to the woman, "Your faith has saved you; **go in peace**." (Lk 7:50)
11. **God is love**, and those who abide in love abide in God, and God abides in them. (1Jn 4:16)
12. Each of you must give as you have made up your mind, not reluctantly or under compulsion, for **God loves a cheerful giver.** (2Co 9:7)

"For God so loved the world that he gave his only Son, so that everyone who believes in him may not perish but may have eternal life." Jn 3:16

13. Jesus said to him, "**I am the way, and the truth, and the life**." (Jn 14:6)
14. But strive first for the **kingdom of God** and his righteousness, and all these things will be given to you as well. (Mt. 6:33)
15. "Here is the **Lamb of God** who takes away the sin of the world! . . . "(Jn 1:29)
16. But **let justice roll down like waters** and righteousness like an ever-flowing stream. (Am 5:24)
17. But I say to you, **Love your enemies** and pray for those who persecute you . . . (Mt 5:44)
18. **Out of the mouths of babes and infants** you have found a bulwark because of your foes, to silence the enemy and the avenger. (Ps 8:2)
19. Jesus came and stood among them and said, "**Peace be with you.**" (Jn 20:19)
20. "In the wilderness **prepare the way of the Lord,** make straight in the desert a highway for our God. . . . " Isa 40:3
21. **Pride goes before destruction**, and a haughty spirit before a fall. (Pr 16:18)
22. "You are the **salt of the earth**; but if salt has lost its taste, how can its saltiness be restored? . . . "(Mt 5:13)
23. . . . and you show that you are a letter of Christ, prepared by us, written not with ink but with the **Spirit of the living God . . .** (2Co 3:3)
24. **Trust in the Lord** with all your heart, and do not rely on your own insight. (Pr 3:5)
25. But if God so clothes the grass of the field, which is alive today and tomorrow is thrown into the oven, will he not much more clothe you—**you of little faith?** (Mt 6:30)

IT'S NOT IN THE BIBLE

People attribute all manner of sayings, numbers, and things to the Bible that are not found anywhere in it. Here's a chance to get the facts straight:

1. The Bible does not say Eve sinned by eating an apple. It says that the woman ate a fruit from the forbidden tree.
2. All animals did not come to Noah in twos. Some came in sevens.
3. The Bible does not say that Jonah was swallowed by a whale. It says a large fish.

Opposite page: *When Jesus approached John the Baptist, the forerunner of Christ declared, "Here is the Lamb of God who takes away the sin of the world!" (Jn 1:29) In this first-century Italian mosaic, the Lamb of God forms the central motif, surrounded by angelic figures.*

This German painting by Johann Friedrich Overbeck (1789–1869) depicts the three wise men of popular tradition visiting the young Christ child. However, the actual number of wise men is not given in the Scriptures.

4. The Bible does not say that there were three wise men who visited the child Jesus. It only names the three gifts that they brought, and does not number the men.
5. Jesus did not just feed five thousand with the loaves and fish. The Bible says that besides about five thousand men, there were women and children who also ate.
6. The Bible does not say that money is the root of all evil. It says the love of money is a root of all types of evil.
7. Hezekiah is not a book in the Bible. He was, however, a king of Judah for 29 years.
8. The maxim "God helps those who help themselves" is not found anywhere in the Bible.

BIBLE TRIVIA

The wonderful literary world of the Bible is filled with unusual bits of information, strange expressions, and curious trivia. As you travel through this section, you will find out who Belial was, how to say Shibboleth, and what's not new under the sun.

Heavenly Books: In many passages, the Bible refers to books kept in heaven. Moses pleads with God to blot him out of the "book that you have written" (Ex 32:32) for the sake of Israel's forgiveness. The books of Daniel and Revelation both speak of the day that "the books were opened" (Da 7:10 and Rev 20:12). Malachi speaks of a "book of remembrance" written about those who feared the Lord (Mal 3:16).

Book Burning in the Bible: King Jehoiakim of Judah burned the Book of Jeremiah strip by strip as it was read to him (Jer 36:23). On another occasion, a number of magicians at Ephesus—who were newly converted as a result of Paul's preaching—brought their books of magic together and burned them publicly (Ac 19:19).

What's a Parbar? Many words in the Bible occur only once or twice, and scholars have no real idea what they mean. Parbar is one. The word is used in 1 Chronicles 26:18, and it probably means "colonnade" or "court."

Can you say Shibboleth? How do you say shibboleth? If you were an Ephraimite, you couldn't pronounce the first h, so you would say "Sibboleth." And you would be seized by the Gileadites and killed immediately! This is what happened to 42,000 Ephraimites at the fords of the Jordan. There the men of Gilead determined who were Ephraimites by the way they said this tricky word—which, incidentally, is pronounced SHIB-uh-leth (Jdg 12:1–6).

Aramaic, the Language of Diplomats: Aramaic was the language of trade and diplomacy during the time of Israel's monarchy. Assyrian King Sennacherib's emissaries insulted King Hezekiah's envoys during the siege of Jerusalem by issuing demands in Hebrew, the local language, in full hearing of everyone. This occurred despite the envoys' request that negotiations be conducted in Aramaic—for secrecy's sake (2Ki 18:26–35).

Under the Sun: The author of Ecclesiastes uses the phrase "under the sun" more than 25 times as he expresses a weariness with life. He says:

What has been is
what will be, and
what has been done
is what will be done;
there is nothing new
under the sun.

(Ecc 1:9)

The powerful Assyrian Empire took hold of the Middle East from 911–609 B.C. This Assyrian relief depicts Sennacherib, one of Assyria's most ambitious rulers.

Who Was Belial? Belial (or Beliar) was not originally a name, but it developed into a name for Satan in Jewish literature between the Testaments. The apostle Paul used the word in this way when he asked "What agreement does Christ have with Belial?" (2Co 6:15)

Stroke of a Letter: Jesus affirmed the importance of the Old Testament law when he said, "not one letter, not one stroke of a letter, will pass from the law until all is accomplished." (Mt 5:18)

Eat Your Words: On two occasions, Bible characters ate a scroll that contained God's words. The prophet Ezekiel (Eze 2:8–3:2) and also the apostle John (Rev 10:9–10). They both said that God's words tasted as "sweet as honey."

The Land of the Bible

F WE TAKE a close look at the lands of the Bible, we catch a fresh glimpse of the people who lived there. This has always been a difficult environment, filled with many challenges. It is home to lush farmland, but also barren deserts, sweltering heat, freezing rain, and the Dead Sea. Though it is masked today in places by modern cities and conveniences, the basic geography and temperament has changed little since the days when Jesus walked the earth. When we get a feel for the hills and valleys, the rivers and lakes, the rainy seasons and the hot dry periods, we begin to understand how these natural elements affected the way people lived their lives.

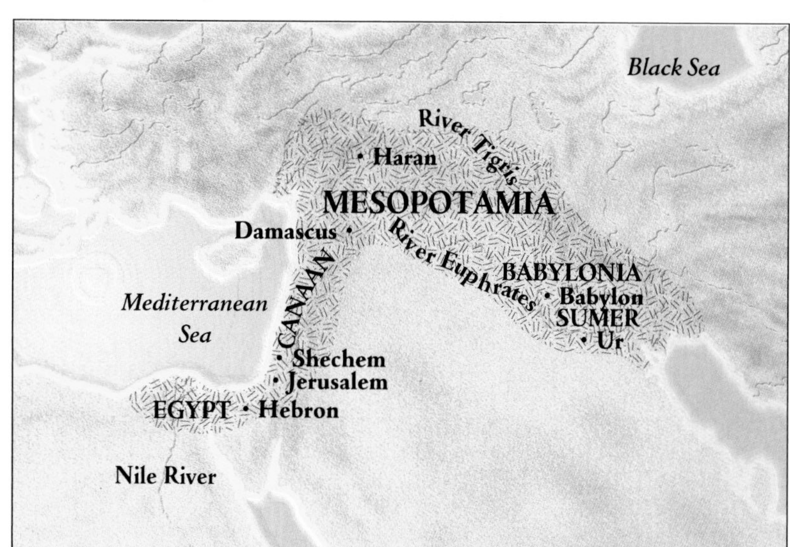

The earliest stories of the Bible, including the journeys of Abraham, all take place in this semi-circular region known as the Fertile Crescent, located in the Middle East.

GEOGRAPHY OF THE REGION

Surprisingly, the story of the Bible took place in a relatively small area. Palestine lies in the middle of a region called the Fertile Crescent, the name given to a belt of lush lands that includes Egypt (and the River Nile) to the south, and Mesopotamia (with its Tigris as well as Euphrates river systems) to the east. The Fertile Crescent is sandwiched between the vast arid world of the Arabian desert on one side, and the Mediterranean Sea on the other.

From early times, the people of God lived squarely in this corridor, which was well-traveled because of its strategic location. Back then, Egypt and Mesopotamia were major civilizations and they developed important trade routes right through the heart of Israel. International routes such as the Transjordanian King's Highway intersected Palestine, making it a crucial point of cultural and trade interchange. Because of its position on the map, Palestine became not only an important crossroads, but a place that powerful nations vied for as they tried to dominate the Near East. Several important geological features mark this area.

The Coastal Plain: When Israel captured the Promised Land, the coast lands were controlled by the Philistines. This

Covered in spring flowers, the Shephelah region is a narrow strip of land 8 by 40 miles. It lies between Palestine's coastal plain and the Judean hill country, and it was a heavily populated area during Bible times.

area is made up of stretches of sand dunes in front of forests, lagoons, and swamps. This part of the Mediterranean coast was not particularly desirable during Old Testament times, and there was no major port in this area until King Herod the Great built an artificial harbor at Caesarea just before Jesus was born.

The Shephelah or Piedmont: Between the coastal plain and the central hill country is an area of low foothills that used to be covered by sycamore trees. In Old Testament times, there were several skirmishes between the Philistines and the Israelites in this area. Today, much of the Shephelah is under cultivation.

The Central Hill Country: In Bible times, the capitals of the northern and southern kingdoms of Israel were both in this location. These highlands rise to just over 3,280 feet at the highest point, near Hebron. The western slope to the coast is gradual, while the east drops sharply into the Jordan Valley. Most of the region is composed of limestone, and the soil that exists is of poor quality. Cultivation is done on a small scale, and much of the area is used for raising livestock.

Even though this region contains Jerusalem, the only major highway is the one connecting the holy city with Hebron and Nablus (Shechem). Most of the main roads through Palestine lie to the north of these hills, or run parallel with them along the coast.

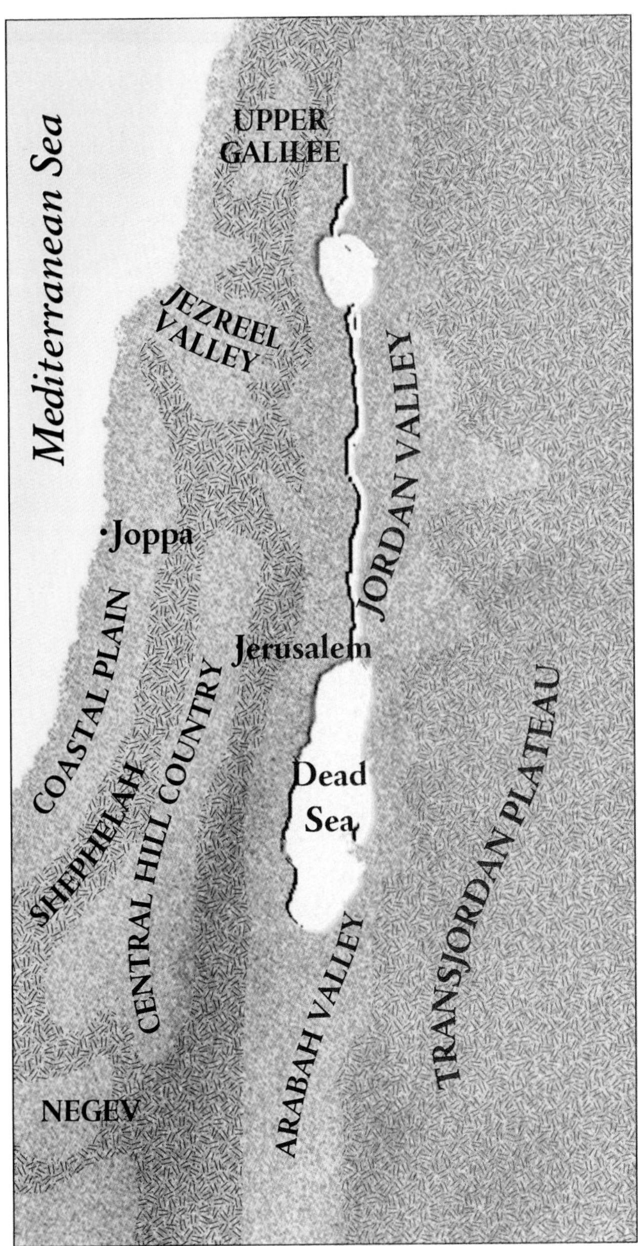

Geographical regions of Palestine.

The Jordan Valley: The River Jordan originates near Mt. Hermon and flows south into the Sea of Galilee. At the southern tip of the sea, the river enters a deep gorge that is filled with dense vegetation. As the river then winds its way south, the water becomes increasingly salty as it meanders closer to the Dead Sea. This affects the type of crops that are planted along its banks. Wheat is planted in the north, and the salt resistant barley is planted in the south. By the time the Jordan River reaches the Dead Sea, the water is so brack-

ish that vegetation along its banks is limited to the poplar and tamarisk trees.

The Jordan Valley is part of a large geological rift or fissure which runs from just above the Sea of Galilee down to Africa. The valley is extremely deep and temperatures in the heart of this area (known as the Ghor) are oppressively hot. People are glad to travel as quickly as possible from the mountains on one side of the Ghor to the mountains on the other side.

The Transjordan: The uplands of this area are higher than those to the west and provide good pasture for the vast numbers of sheep and cattle raised on these lands. This is a well-watered fertile area that stands between the dry valley and the Arabian Desert. In Bible times, people living in this region were fairly protected from invaders because it was difficult to move into the Transjordan from the east or the west.

The Nabateans, an Arabian tribe mentioned in the Apocrypha, took over the city of Petra in 312 B.C. One of the main curiosities of this ancient city is the rock-hewn temples, tombs, and other buildings, such as the treasury shown here, carved into the rock cliffs surrounding the town.

TEN QUICK GEOGRAPHY FACTS

- Most of the land surface in Palestine is made up of limestone and chalk.
- The water sinks through the limestone rocks to underground streams, where it can be recovered by sinking wells.
- There are many limestone caves in this region.
- Wind and water erosion transform desert rocks into fantastic shapes!
- Flash floods can fill a dry valley several feet deep with water in a short space of time.
- The Galilee area of Palestine enjoys the highest annual rainfall and the richest soil in the region.
- Rainfall declines from east to west because the hill country blocks the storms that move in from the Mediterranean.
- An arid area known as the Judean wilderness is so barren it has always been associated with pain, trial, and death.
- The Judean wilderness and the Negeb desert have the most severe environments in Palestine.
- Jerusalem is 2,500 feet above sea level. Fifteen miles to the east, however, Jericho is 1,275 feet below sea level!

RAINFALL AND CLIMATE

In Christ's day, Judea was a small area, partly hilly and partly arid desert. There were no major trade routes in the district, and most of the population lived in the Jerusalem section of Judea.

The climate of the Mediterranean lands is somewhere between temperate and tropical. Winters are wet and cool; summers are hot and dry. Because coastal areas lie in such close proximity to mountains and deserts, snow will blanket the tops of coastal mountains while fruit trees flourish in the plain.

The lowlands receive less rainfall than the mountain areas, and the latter tend to block rain-bearing winds from flowing inland. Going south, the annual rainfall lessens until arid desert conditions prevail. There can be great variations in annual rainfall from place to place, and the constantly moving desert margin overtakes certain areas from time to time, plunging them into drought and famine. The Bible speaks frequently about these extreme conditions. We read of dry years and famine, flooding rains, and years of plenty.

The Bible and the apocryphal books mention several times the importance of dew in the lives of Bible people. And

FAMINES—A CONSTANT THREAT

In Bible times, famines occurred for a number of reasons: lack of seasonal rainfall; destructive hailstorms; crops destroyed by locusts and caterpillars; war; the erosion of the land by the encroaching desert; and judgment by God because of sin. The Bible records several famines and what people did when food was scarce.

- Famine in Palestine caused Abraham to go to Egypt to find food (Gen 12:10).
- Isaac went down to Gerar because of famine in Palestine (Gen 26:1–3).
- Famine in Palestine caused Jacob's sons to look for food in Egypt (Gen 42:1–5).
- Famine in Palestine caused Naomi to go into Moab (Ruth 1:1).
- God allowed a three-year famine in David's time because of Saul's sins (2Sa 21:1).
- Famine in Elijah's day was caused by the sins of Ahab and Israel (1Ki 17:1).
- There were three famines recorded in Elisha's time (2Ki 4; 6; 8).
- The famine in Jerusalem was caused by Nebuchadnezzar's siege (2Ki 25:2).
- During the famine in Nehemiah's day, the prophet preached a sermon and there was a revival among the people (Ne 5).
- Christians outside of Judea sent help to the believers there because they were suffering from a famine (Ac 11:28).

as we look at the region, we discover that many areas with low rainfall rely on dew to water the land. Most of the areas with heavy dewfall are on the coast. Some areas may have dew on as many as 200 nights each year.

There are great contrasts in the temperature range in the Near East. It may be a hot summer's day by the Dead Sea (100 degrees Farenheit), but a hundred miles away in Galilee, a cool rain may be falling. Winter can be miserably wet and cold in the highlands, but the lowlands experience some extreme weather as well. Summer weather on the coast and in the mountains average a mild 75 degrees. Temperate winds from the Mediterranean blow onshore to relieve some of the heat. However, there is a searing wind—known as the *hamsin*—which blows in from the south, and its effect can be felt all the way to the coast. Jesus even referred to the hamsin when he mentioned the scorching south wind:

> *He also said to the crowds, "When you see a cloud rising in the west, you immediately say, 'It is going to rain'; and so it happens. And when you see the south wind blowing, you say, 'There will be scorching heat'; and it happens."*
>
> Lk 12:54–55

The pomegranate was a popular fruit in Bible times, and its juice was a refreshing drink that was also made into a sweet wine. This seed-filled fruit was a symbol of Canaan's abundance (Nu 13:23), and its motif was used in the high priest's garments (Ex 28:33), and included in the ornamentation of Solomon's temple (1 Ki 7:18–20).

BIBLE PLANTS

The natural plant life of Bible lands was important to the everyday life of the people. Leaves, bark, stems, and gum from various plants were used to make medicines,

BIBLE PLANTS

Plant	Description	Reference
Aloe	a succulent plant used for cleansing the bodies of the dead	*Ps 45:8*
Balm	an evergreen shrub used for medicinal purposes	*Gen 37:25*
Bulrush	a type of reed whose stems were used to make paper	*Ex 2:3*
Cumin	used to flavor meat, and in eye medicine	*Mt 23:23*
Dill (anise)	used to flavor bread or cakes	*Mt 23:23*
Flaxstem	fibers used to make linen,string nets, and lamp wicks	*Ex 9:31*
Hyssop	this bushy plant was used for sprinkling blood and other purification rites in the Old Testament; on the cross, Jesus was given a sponge filled with vinegar on a bunch of hyssop	*Ex 12:22; Jn 19:29*
Lilies of the field	may refer to a variety of wild flowers: anemone, crocus, poppy, narcissus, and yellow chrysanthemum	*Mt 6:28*
Mustard	a tiny seed that produces a great plant; Jesus likely referred to the black mustard used for oil as well as flavoring	*Mt 13:31–32*
Myrrh	light-yellow gum from a shrub grown in north Africa; used as a spice, medicine, holy oil, and embalming treatment	*Mt 2:11*
Pomegranate	a wild shrub with a red fruit, used for medicine and food	*Ex 28:31–34*
Reed	a tall plant with purple flowers, used to make pens and measuring devices	*Eze 40:3*
Rose	the "rose" in the Bible is probably the narcissus or the mountain tulip	*SS 2:1*
Rush	used to make chair seats, baskets, and other items	*Isa 35:7*
Tares, thistles, thorns	these destructive weeds abound in the dry areas of Palestine, often choking the growth of young grain plants	*Mt 13:24–30; Gen 3:18; Mt 7:16*
Wormwood and gall	a bitter-tasting plant, wormwood and gall (possibly the juice of the opium poppy) are associated with sorrow and bitterness in the Bible	*Mt 27:34*

oils, and cosmetics. A variety of reeds were useful for making paper and pens. Crops were grown for food, for making cloth, and for religious purposes. Dyes were extracted from some plants. And other plants were merely enjoyed for their beautiful blossoms!

BIBLE TREES

Trees were crucial to the Bible world. They affected climate and soil erosion, and on a practical level, their everyday value was immeasurable. People depended on trees for food, shelter, fuel, and building materials. There are more than 300 references to trees and wood in the Bible, and more than 25 different kinds of trees have been identified as having

BIBLE TREES AND SHRUBS

Tree or Shrub	Description	Reference
Acacia (shittim)	one of the few trees to grow in the Sinai desert, the ark of the covenant was made from this wood	*Ex 25:10*
Almond	a favorite food, the nut also produced oil; Aaron's famous rod, which budded overnight and bore ripe fruit, was from this tree!	*Nu 17:8*
Cedar	the famous cedars of Lebanon are legend; today only a few of these trees remain, high in the mountains; the durable red wood was used to panel Solomon's temple and palace	*1Ki 6–7*
Cypress	this hard, durable red-toned wood is believed to have been used to construct Noah's ark	*Gen 6:14*
Fig	these slow-growing trees bear fruit most of the year; the fig was a popular fruit in Bible times	*Jdg 9:10–11*
Fir and pine	the wood was used for building the temple, ship building, and making musical instruments	*Eze 27:5*
Frankincense	the gum collected from this tree (native to Arabia) was used as incense	*Mt 2:11*
Gourd	a large, fast-growing bush, this castor bean plant may have grown up overnight to shade Jonah from the sun	*Jnh 4:6*
Myrtle	a large, evergreen, sweet-smelling shrub used for wreaths and for making festival booths	*Isa 41:19*
Oak	there are many types of oak trees in Israel, some are evergreen; wood was used for oars and statues; black dye was obtained from the acorn cups of the Valonia oak	*2Sa 18:9–10*
Olive	an evergreen, one tree could supply an entire family with fats; olive oil was used for cooking, as oil for lamps, and as a skin lotion; it was also used to anoint kings and priests; carvings and decorative work were made from the wood	*Dt 24:20*
Palm (date)	a tall tree topped by a crown of huge leaves, the valuable fruit grew in clusters below the leaves; leaves were woven into mats, and the sap was fermented to make liquor or vinegar	*Jn 12:13*
Poplar	this fast-growing tree found in the hills of Palestine provides dense shade; the "willows" of Babylon, where the exiles mourned, were probably a type of poplar	*Gen 30:37*
Sycamore	a type of fig tree, the sycamore is known for its durability; Zacchaeus climbed this type of tree to get a better view of Jesus	*Lk 19:4*
Terebinth	this spreading tree is common in the warm, dry hilly places of Israel	*Isa 6:13*
Vine	one of the earliest cultivated plants in biblical history, the vine produced one of the most important fruit crops in Israel; after the grapes were harvested, time was set aside for joyous festivities	*Dt 8:8*
Willow	These trees are found in thickets along the margins or streams or rivers from Syria to Palestine	*Job 40:22*

grown in Palestine. Today, most of the wooded parts of this area have been cut down.

In Bible times, trees that were identified with holy places were allowed to flourish. In some pagan cultures, people believed that their gods inhabited the trees, and sacrifices were often offered under trees. According to the Law, however, the Hebrews were forbidden to plant a tree near an altar to the Lord:

You shall not plant any tree as a sacred pole beside the altar that you make for the Lord your God; nor shall you set up a stone pillar—things that the Lord your God hates.

Dt 16:21

Wood of the acacia tree, still common in the Sinai and Israel's southern desert area, was used in the construction of Israel's tabernacle and its furnishings in Old Testament times. The wood is hard, durable, fine-grained, and yellowish-brown in color.

BIBLE ANIMALS AND BIRDS

A look at the animals and birds of the Bible lands gives us an idea of the kinds of creatures that thrived in this environment, their place in the natural habitat, and their importance to the lives of the people of the region. The Bible makes reference to a variety of animals, and birds are mentioned in 45 books of the Bible and 19 times in the apocryphal books. The animals and birds listed on the following pages are those most often mentioned in the Bible—and the most important ones.

WILD ANIMALS

Bear: The Syrian brown bear lived in the hills and woods of Israel in Bible times. David had to protect his flocks against them, and two she-bears once attacked a group of boys who were ridiculing the prophet Elisha (1Sa 17:34–36).

Fox and jackal: Both of these scavengers damaged crops. Jackals hunted in packs at night, and the fox went after grapes hanging on low vines (Jdg 15:4).

Leopard: The prophets Isaiah and Jeremiah mention this wild animal that was clearly around in Bible times (Isa 11:6; Jer 13:23).

Lion: Mentioned several times in the Bible, lions lived in the thickets of the Jordan Valley and were dangerous to flocks and people (Da 6:16–24).

Wolf: These savage hunters would feed on smaller animals but would sometimes attack and kill deer, sheep, and even cattle (2Esd 5:18).

Deer and gazelle: These wild animals were a major source of meat (Dt 12:15).

Badger: This bashful creature lived in colonies in rocky regions (Pr 30:26).

An invaluable animal, the one-humped camel was the most common beast of burden in Bible times. Traveling 8 to 10 miles per hour, caravans of camels (each carrying about 400 pounds) plodded over well-worn, ancient trade routes transporting spices and other goods from one place to another.

WORKING ANIMALS

Camel: The Arabian camel was valuable to desert nomads, travelers, and merchants. It could live on poor food and go for several days without drinking. The camel could carry a load of about 400 pounds—as well as the rider. These beasts of burden are mentioned in the stories of Abraham, Jacob, and Job (Gen 12:16; 30:43; Job 1:3).

Donkey and mule: These were the most common pack animals in Bible times. Sure-footed and dependable, they also provided transportation for rich and poor alike. It was on a donkey that Jesus rode into Jerusalem on Palm Sunday (Mt 21:1–11).

Horse: In Bible times, horses were owned by the rich, and first came to Israel during David's reign. They were primarily used in war (Jos 11:4).

FLOCKS AND HERDS

Cattle: Herds of cattle were kept to provide milk, meat, and leather. Oxen were used to pull the plough, threshing-sledge, wagons, and carts. Cattle were also offered as temple sacrifices. Wealth was reckoned by the number of cattle and sheep a man owned. Bashan, east of Jordan, was known for its cattle (Gen 13:2).

Sheep and goat: From ancient times, these animals were an important part of the lives of Bible people, many of whom depended on them for milk, cheese, meat, and clothing. Goatskins were used to make a variety of coverings—from water bottles to tents. Wool from sheep was used to make cloaks and tunics. Sheep and goats were also used in temple sacrifices. These animals were well suited to the craggy hill pasture areas of Palestine (Gen 27:9; Jn 10:1–12).

At one time, the ibex, a type of mountain goat, was abundant in Palestine's rocky areas. Today this shy animal, mentioned only three times in the Old Testament, is protected on reserves.

BIRDS OF PREY

The raven was considered unclean, according to Old Testament law, and therefore could not be sacrificed or eaten. Yet, God used this lowly creature to show his providential care when he sent ravens with food to the prophet Elijah (1Ki 17).

Eagle and vulture: These large, hawklike birds were similar to one another. The eagle had a powerful beak, talons, and a wing spread of more than four feet. Mentioned often in the Bible, the eagle was a symbol of swiftness and strength. The vulture, wide ranging in its soaring, would feed on the carcasses of dead animals. Both the eagle and vulture were listed as unclean birds in Leviticus (Lev 11).

Owl: Pictured in the Bible as inhabiting ruined and desolate places, many varieties of owls are known in Israel today (Isa 34:15).

Raven: After the flood, Noah sent out this black, flesh-eating bird to see if the land was dry (Gen 8:6–7).

BIRDS FOR FOOD AND SACRIFICE

Dove and pigeon: Common in Israel, these birds were an important food source and were offered for sacrifice by the

Called the 'lapwing' in the King James Version of the Bible, the hoopoe of ancient times was an insect-eating bird known for its decorative plumage. Hoopoes depicted in old Egyptian art look just like the hoopoes seen in Bible regions today.

poor. After the Flood, it was a dove that brought back the first green leaf to Noah (Gen 8:8–12).

Partridge: The eggs and flesh of this bird made a good meal (1Sa 26:20).

Quail: These birds provided the Israelites with meat as they journeyed from Egypt during the time of the Exodus (Ex 16:13).

Sparrow: Often used in reference to any small bird suitable for eating, it refers specifically to the hedge sparrow (Mt 10:29–31).

MIGRATORY BIRDS

Crane: The prophet Jeremiah spoke of this large gray bird that is still a regular visitor to Israel. It feeds on seeds and leaves (Jer 8:7).

Peacock: The peacock was imported into Israel by King Solomon, who used the graceful creatures to decorate his palace (1Ki 10:22).

Stork: Black and white storks pass through Israel every year as they fly north from Arabia and Africa. They feed on small animal life—snakes, fish, mice, worms, and insects (Jer 8:7).

WATER—A SCARCE RESOURCE

For us in the western world, fresh water is easily accessible at the turn of a tap. Many of us take this resource for granted, both using and wasting it freely. But for the average Israelite in Bible times, dealing with water was a daily struggle. It had to be found, saved, and carried from one place to another for personal use, for their animals, and for their crops. It is no wonder that abundant, clear water was a strong symbol of God's blessing in Bible times. Back then, people were grateful for a shower of rain, a clear brook, or a family well with a ready supply of water.

Constantly menaced by the desert at its door and limited winter rainfall, Israel has always had to conserve water. The Jordan is the only major river in this territory, and it empties into the Dead Sea, where water evaporates at the rate of 60 inches a year. Fortunately, the Jordan flows year round. Many smaller rivers and streams flow during the rainy season but have dry beds the rest of the year. Given the situation, how then did people in Bible times actually deal with their water problems?

Wells: Any family that owned a well was fortunate. Water was available right outside the home and it was likely to be less polluted than the water from a stream or storage cistern.

Throughout Palestine, wells were important as a source of water for people and for herds of animals. For safety as well as permanence, a well—a deep pit or hole dug in the earth down to the water table—was often surrounded by a wall of stone.

The great river Nile was viewed by the ancient Egyptians as the source of their life and their economy. Every year in spring, the river overflowed its banks, providing rich new soil for abundant crops. The Nile was also Egypt's highway, supplying ready transportation by boat north and south.

RIVERS OF BIBLE LANDS

Name of River	Location	Reference
Pishon	flows out of Eden around the land of Havilah	*Gen 2:11*
Gihon	flows out of Eden around the land of Cush	*Gen 2:13*
Tigris	flows out of Eden and east of Assyria	*Gen 2:14*
Euphrates	flows out of Eden and through the Taurus mountains	*Gen 2:14*
Nile	Egypt	*Gen 15:18*
Jabbok	east of the Jordan, about halfway between the Dead Sea and the Sea of Galilee	*Gen 32:22–30*
Arnon	boundary river between Israel and Moab	*Nu 21:13*
Kishon	near the town of Megiddo	*Jdg 5:21*
Ahava	Babylonia	*Ez 8:21*
Chebar	Babylonia (the land of the Chaldeans)	*Eze 1:1*
Abana and Pharpar	rivers of Damascus	*2Ki 5:12*
Jordan	the principal river in Palestine	*Jos 3:13–17*
Yarmuk	six miles to the southeast of the Sea of Galilee, marked the southern boundary of ancient Bashan. It is an important river, though there is no biblical reference to the name "Yarmuk"	

"Lot looked about him, and saw that the plain of the Jordan was well watered everywhere like the garden of the Lord, like the land of Egypt, . . ." Gen 13:10

FAMOUS WELLS

Location	Description	Reference
Kadesh wilderness	where God spoke to Hagar	*Gen 16:14*
Beersheba	where Abraham made a covenant with Abimilech	*Gen 21:30*
Nahor	where Abraham's servant found Rebekah	*Gen 24:11–20*
Gerar	dug by Isaac	*Gen 26:18*
Haran	where Jacob met Rachel	*Gen 29:1–12*
Midian	where Moses met Zipporah	*Ex 2:15–21*
Sinai wilderness	dug by the Israelites	*Nu 21:16–18*
Bahurim	where two of David's spies hid from Absalom	*2Sa 17:18–19*
Ramah	where Saul looked for David	*1Sa 19:18–24*
Bethlehem	where David longed for a drink	*2Sa 23:15*
Samaria	where Jesus conversed with the Samaritan woman	*Jn 4:6–26*

A spiral stone staircase (with 93 steps) winds down into the landmark cistern at Gibeon (present day El-Jib). During times of siege, the water table could be accessed by a tunnel leading from the staircase. Skirmishes were fought between the warring camps of Saul and David on the edge of this ancient Canaanite pool (2 Sa 2:12–17).

From ancient times, ground water (rainfall that had seeped through the limestone rocks and collected underground) was drawn from deep wells—sometimes dug to a depth of 140 feet. However, once it was dug a well lasted for several generations. Besides family wells, there were community wells where villagers or city folk could draw water. There are several interesting Bible stories centered around these natural meeting places for people. Jacob met his future bride Rachel at one. The Samaritan woman had a life-changing conversation with Jesus at a well supposedly dug by the patriarch Jacob.

Cisterns: These were small reservoirs dug in the ground to collect and store rainwater. Dug to a depth of about 40 feet, they were bulb-shaped with a fairly narrow neck topped by a stone or wood cover. Water drained into the cistern from roofs, courtyards, streets, and—on occasion—open land. Water was drawn from the cistern using a bucket.

Cisterns were first built in the patriarchal period, and archaeologists have uncovered plaster-lined cisterns in Palestine with a capacity of 706 cubic feet. Many homes had their own cisterns, and they were especially popular in areas where there were no streams or rivers. There were probably communal cisterns as well.

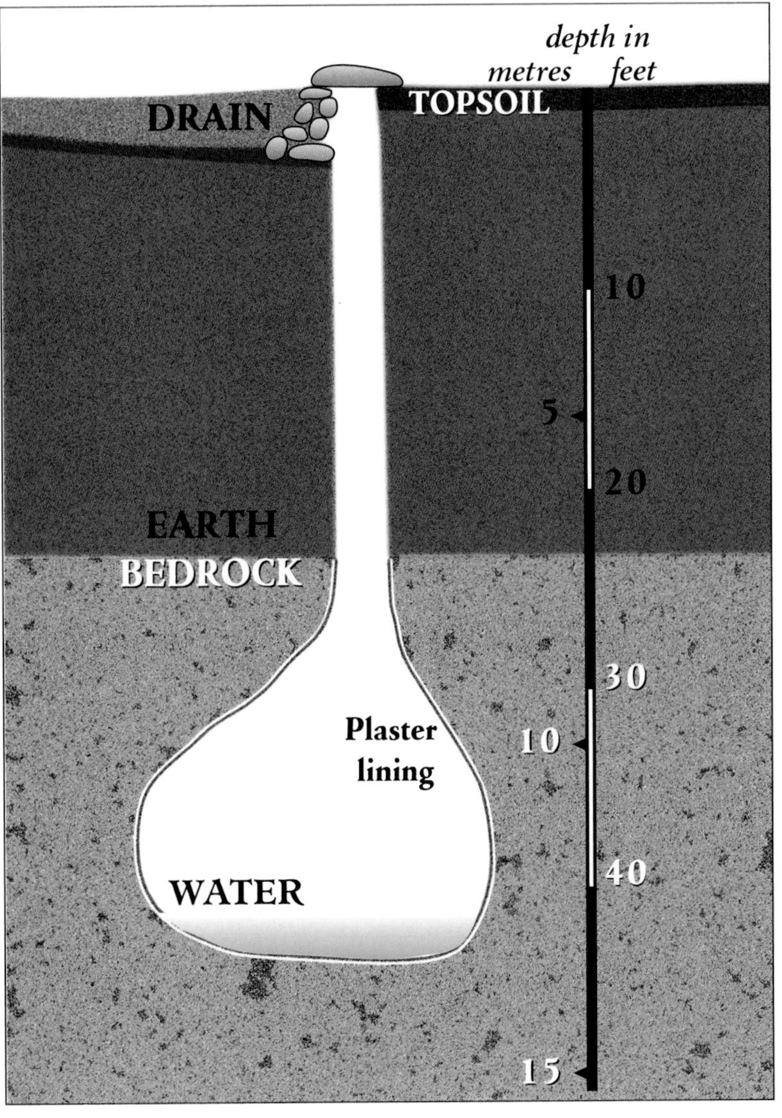

A cistern is a small reservoir for collecting and storing water. This example shows a typical cistern construction during biblical times.

Tunnels and channels: Certain settlements in Bible times were located in places with no water supply. Areas without rainwater or streams had to bring in water in from an outside source. To solve the problem, some remarkable underground channeling systems were developed. Tunnels and shafts were cut through the rocks beneath towns to bring in a good supply of water. During Hezekiah's reign, a tunnel was dug under the walls of Jerusalem to connect the city to a spring outside. The water was fed from the spring to a pool in the city. Over time, Jerusalem developed other systems, underground as well as above ground. Water brought in by tunnels or aqueducts emptied into open pools or large underground cisterns. Under the temple mount in Jerusalem, 37 cisterns have been found, and one huge cavern had a capacity of some two million gallons! The famous aqueduct at Caesarea and the cisterns of Masada are other excellent examples of the engineering ingenuity of people during Bible times. Even in dry or mountainous regions, the Israelites found creative ways to obtain and conserve water.

MINERALS

Copper was mined from early on, and iron came later. During Bible times, the land's other major resources were building stones, pitch, sand, and clays. A variety of chemical

"For the king had a fleet of ships of Tarshish at sea with the fleet of Hiram. Once every three years the fleet of ships of Tarshish used to come bringing gold, silver, ivory, apes, and peacocks." 1Ki 10:22

salts were obtained from the Dead Sea area, and today the Dead Sea itself yields potash, bromine, and magnesium. From biblical days on, many materials had to be imported. Israel conducted a busy import/export trade with its neighbors.

Fisheries

Although the Jews never really controlled the Mediterranean coast lands (and were not known to be seafarers), fishing was an important part of their lives. Fish was a natural food resource in Palestine. Most fishing was done on the Sea of Galilee (also known as the Lake of Gennesaret or the Sea of Tiberias). An inland freshwater lake (13 miles long and 8 miles wide), the Sea of Galilee supported the livelihood of many fishermen. It was from among this group that Jesus chose his first disciples:

As he walked by the Sea of Galilee, he saw two brothers, Simon, who is called Peter, and Andrew his brother, casting a net into the sea—for they were fishermen. And he said to them, "Follow me, and I will make you fish for people."

The waters of the Dead Sea are seven times as salty as the earth's oceans. Salt mounds, seen here, form naturally on the surface of the Dead Sea, located in the southern Jordan Valley.

Immediately they left their nets and followed him. (Mt 4:18–20)

Fish from the Sea of Galilee was sold fresh or it was dried and kept for eating in the winter. Much of the fish sold in Jerusalem was brought in by non-Jewish merchants from Tyre and other places. Unfortunately, Israel's other large body of water, the Dead Sea, has always been too salty to support life. The prophet Ezekiel had a vision of fisherman spreading out their nets to dry along the shores of the Dead Sea because the catch there was so great (Eze 47:10). This, of course, has yet to happen.

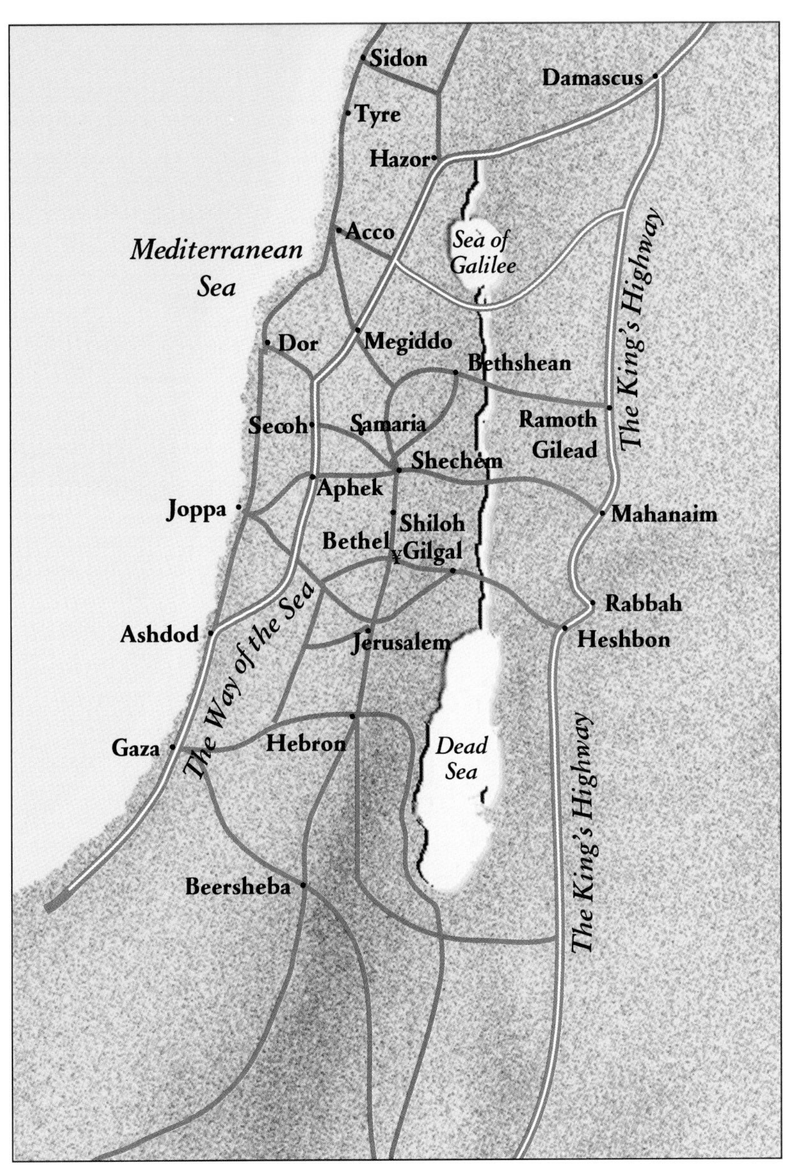

Primary roads and highways in the biblical world.

ROADS AND HIGHWAYS

Many journeys are recorded in the Bible. We read about Abraham moving from Ur to Canaan, the Israelites wandering through the desert, and the Queen of Sheba leaving Africa to visit King Solomon. We know that Jesus traveled around quite a bit, and Paul's journeys took him over land and sea.

Road and trade routes crisscrossed Palestine and extended north and south. There were few paved roads until the Romans came along and built a fine system connecting the provinces they controlled to Rome itself. Here is a list of some significant roads mentioned in the Bible:

The highway leading through Edom: This was blocked by the Edomites, forcing the Israelites to find another route (Nu 20:19).

The highway from Bethel to Shechem: Travelers from Bethel or Shechem went along this road to get to Shiloh to celebrate the yearly festival of the Lord (Jdg 21:19).

Opposite page: *In this colorful depiction by Danish artist Christian Dalsgaard (1824–1907), crowds wave to welcome Jesus to Jerusalem just before his crucifixion. Jesus rides in peacefully on a donkey, amid palm branches and words of blessing (Jn 12:12–14).*

The Jerusalem to Jericho road: The story of the good Samaritan took place along this road (Lk 10:30).

The Bethpage to Jerusalem road: Here Jesus mounted a young donkey and rode into Jerusalem on Palm Sunday (Mt 21:1–9).

The Jerusalem to Emmaus road: After his resurrection, Christ appeared to two of his followers as they were walking along this road (Lk 24:13).

The Jerusalem to Damascus road: Paul was converted to Christianity along this road (Ac 9:3).

A LOOK AT THE LAND—THEN AND NOW

During the time of Jesus, Jews considered Jerusalem to be the most important place in Palestine. The pulse of the country lay in Judea and Galilee, west of the Jordan, and on either side of Samaria. Jews avoided going through Samaria as much as possible, and would cross the Jordan twice just to avoid the Samaritans.

Most of the Jewish towns were in the hill country where cultivation was done on terraces and in small fields, and where livestock was raised. The northern end of this region looked down on the Plain of Esdraelon, a strategic place in the ancient world. The north-south route known as the *Via Maris* (the way of the sea) cut through the plain on the way from Egypt to Damascus and Mesopotamia. Because of its important location, the plain has been the scene of many battles from Bible times right up to the 20th century.

EARTHQUAKES

The Bible lands are situated on the edge of one of the main earthquake areas of the world. This belt extends from Spain eastward through the Mediterranean area and the Himalayan mountains. No wonder the Bible records several of these natural disasters! Some of them were part of the natural geological landscape, others were sent by God to communicate a particular message:

> "Now Mount Sinai was wrapped in smoke, because the Lord had descended on it in fire; the smoke went up like the smoke of a kiln, while the whole mountain shook violently."
> Ex 19:18

> "Now there was a great wind, so strong that it was splitting mountains and breaking rocks in pieces before the Lord, but the Lord was not in the wind; and after the wind an earthquake, but the Lord was not in the earthquake; and after the earthquake a fire, but the Lord was not in the fire; and after the fire a sound of sheer silence."
> 1Ki 19:11–12

> "And suddenly there was a great earthquake; for an angel of the Lord, descending from heaven, came and rolled back the stone and sat on it."
> Mt 28:2

> "About midnight Paul and Silas were praying and singing hymns to God, and the prisoners were listening to them. Suddenly there was an earthquake, so violent that the foundations of the prison were shaken; and immediately all the doors were opened and everyone's chains were unfastened."
> Ac 16:25–26

Not only did these scary tremors occur in ancient times, but earthquakes still happen in Palestine today.

The fertile Plain of Esdraelon is sandwiched between Galilee to the north and Samaria on the south. Although not a large area, it had strategic military and commercial value in Bible times, and many cities were located there, the most important being Megiddo. Today, Jews find it a prosperous farming region.

Beyond the Plain of Esdraelon, the upland ranges begin again, gradually rising to the mountains of Lebanon. These hilly ranges form the region of Galilee, a busy area with many trade routes. People from other cultures and places were constantly coming and going through this area, and it was marked by great diversity. This was also an area where people lived well off the fertile farmlands and the Galilee fisheries. It was in this region that Jesus spent his boyhood years.

However, it must be noted that over the centuries some natural features have changed in the Mediterranean. When Israel entered the Promised land, much of the higher elevations were wooded. Today, the forest landscape has almost gone. Trees were used for building and firewood, they were destroyed in times of war, and animals were allowed to destructively graze in forested areas. Consequently, woods were gradually replaced by a thorny scrub known as maquis, which is common throughout the Mediterranean lands.

During the last 50 years, some reforestation has taken place, and other landscape changes are in progress. Marshy areas have been drained and cultivated, groves of fruit trees have been planted in former woodlands, and some desert soils have been cultivated.

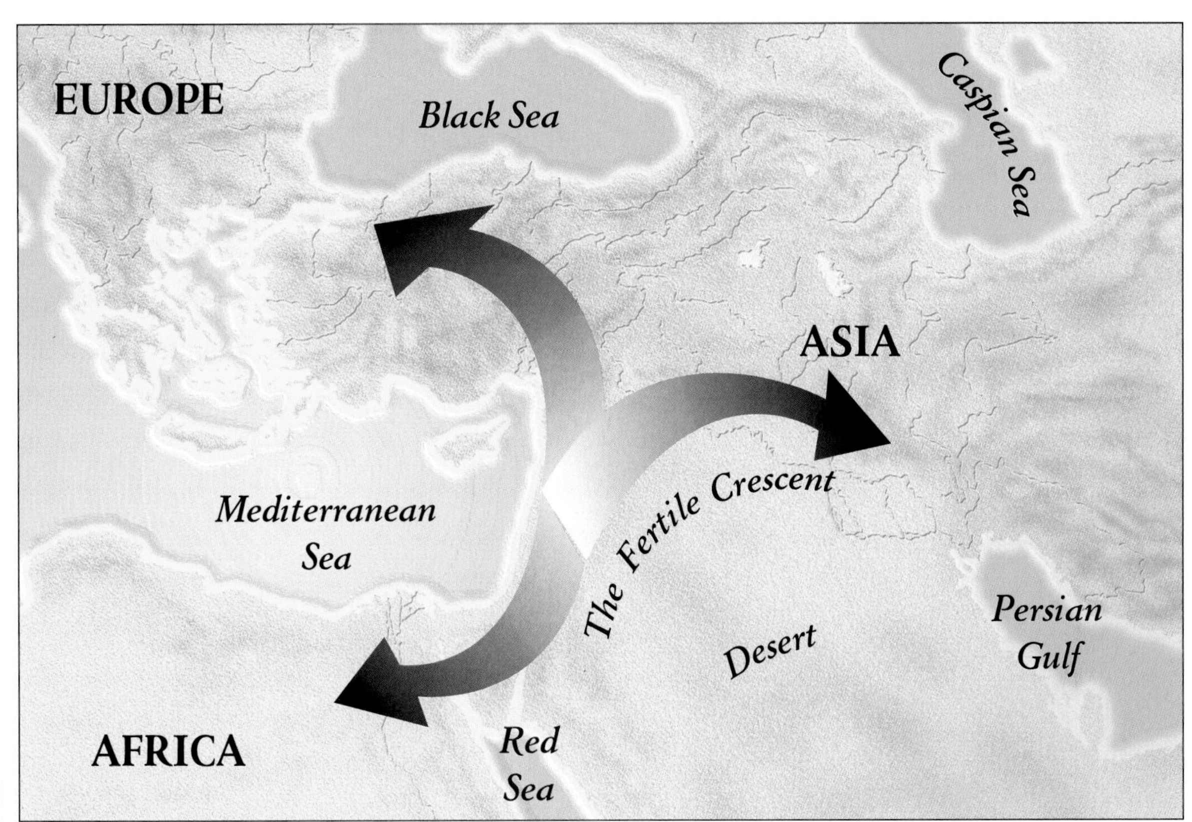

Palestine was a strategic link to Europe, Asia, and Africa.

This is the land of the Bible—a small place on the earth's surface with some attractive features and many natural problems. In spite of lush fertile areas, Palestine is primarily known as a barren, eroded, and hilly country with few natural resources. A narrow band squeezed between the desert and the sea. Temperatures can be oppressively hot or freezing cold, rainfall is often unpredictable (and in some places almost nonexistent), and to top it all off, Palestine is part of one of the world's main earthquake zones!

Yet in spite of all this, the land of Israel has been one of the most desirable countries in the world. It is the vital land bridge to three continents: Europe, Asia, and Africa. This busy corridor (which narrows to as little as 56 miles) has been fought for time and again—from the days of the ancients until now.

Bible Geography—20 Fascinating Facts

Salty and Deadly: The Dead Sea—the lowest point on the face of the earth—is the saltiest body of water in the world. The water is so dense you can't sink. This makes it the world's largest natural flotation device!

New Roads from Old: Until the Romans came along, roads and paths in biblical times were dirt tracks, which

Prominent in Bible times, the En-gedi oasis—fed by warm springs—is located on the west coast of the Dead Sea, in the territory of Judah, about 35 miles southeast of Jerusalem (near modern Ain Jidi). Here, David and his men took refuge while fleeing from Saul (1 Sa 23:29).

became impossibly muddy during rainy seasons. The pathways of these dirt roads would keep changing as caravans searched for smoother ground to cross.

Is it a mirage? Oases were wonderful places of relief set in the heart and heat of the desert regions. The Israelites stayed at the oasis of Kadesh-barnea in the northern Sinai desert. En-gedi, in the Judean wilderness near the Dead Sea, is known for its famous spring and waterfall.

Down to Jericho: Did the Good Samaritan really go down from Jerusalem to Jericho? Actually, he went east and down. Jericho is 3,300 feet lower than Jerusalem—an amazing drop for a journey of only 15 miles!

Jerusalem—An Out-of-the-Way Place: Jerusalem was difficult to get to. It was not located on either of the great trade routes (The Way of the Sea or The King's Highway). So even though tiny Israel was squeezed between powerful empires—and armies frequently marched through it on their missions of conquest—Jerusalem remained fairly secure as Israel's capital.

Hell on Earth: The Hinnon Valley in Jerusalem was a place where residents burned their rubbish. As a result, it gained a reputation as a place of fiery abominations and it even became symbolic of hell. Its Hebrew name—ge'hinnom—formed the basis for the New Testament word *gehenna,* which means "hell."

Egypt's Highway: The River Nile has always been the great highway of Egypt. It flows through the desert, with a fertile margin of cultivatable land on either bank.

Water from Below: The Jebusites who lived in Jerusalem before King David were responsible for an ingenious tunnel system that brought fresh water into their city from a hidden spring in the valley below. They tunneled straight down through the hill above the spring and tapped into an underground stream. They would lower buckets and fill them from this stream and not have to venture outside the city walls.

Mt. Hermon? It just might have been on the slopes of Mt. Hermon, in the far north of Palestine, that the disciples saw Jesus at his glorious transfiguration (Mt 17:1–8).

Antioch—Second Center of Christianity: It was in Antioch in Syria that the followers of Christ were first called Christians. This ancient city was founded in 300 B.C. by a general of Alexander the Great. It became the third city of the Roman Empire, after Rome and Alexandria. Antioch was famous for its boulevard and colonnade with trees and fountains, and its fine buildings. It was known as "Antioch the Beautiful." It was also called "Queen of the East" because its population included people from Persia, India, and China. Romans were also living there, as well as a large colony of Jews.

Mount Hermon, the highest mountain in Palestine, (9,332 feet above sea level), is the probable site of the transfiguration of Christ.

"The sun shall be turned to darkness, and the moon to blood, before the great and terrible day of the Lord comes."
Joel 2:31

Opposite page: *An interior view of the Church of the Holy Sepulchre, showing the altar at the 11th station of the Cross. This is the traditional site of Calvary, where Jesus was crucified.*

Where Did Jesus Die? Jesus died at a place called *Golgotha,* which is Aramaic for "skull." Its exact location is disputed. Many scholars believe that the present-day church of the Holy Sepulchre marks the true site of Golgotha.

Where Was Jesus Buried? The rock-cut Garden Tomb near Gordon's Calvary is thought by some to be the site of Jesus' burial, but it is possible the tomb is somewhere under the present-day church of the Holy Sepulchre.

Jericho—the World's Oldest City: A fine spring waters Jericho, which was first occupied in 9000 B.C. It was an oasis in the Jordan Valley and was called the "City of the Palms" in the Bible. The Israelites captured it under Joshua in the famous incident when its walls collapsed. It lay as a sparsely inhabited ruin for more than 1,000 years, until it was rebuilt by King Herod.

Where Was Tarshish? The Book of Jonah tells us that Jonah took a ship going to Tarshish rather than go to Nineveh, as God had commanded him. Tarshish was either part of the island of Sardinia (off the coast of Italy) or a region in far-off Spain. Jonah wanted to get as far away from Nineveh as possible!

A Bloody Moon: The Bible mentions eclipses several times as prophetic signs of God's judgment (Am 8:9; Joel 2:31).

Cavernous Caves: Caves were abundant in Palestine. Most caves were formed by the action of underground water. After the water table receded, the dry caves became useful as dwellings, hiding places, burial caves, and storage.

Water from Above: Palestine depended heavily on rain. Without rain, drought set in and famine was just around the corner. In contrast, Egypt and Mesopotamia had great river systems that provided water for their crops.

How Fast Can a Camel Go? People walking on foot could travel about 15 miles a day in Bible times. Donkey caravans could travel about 20 miles a day. Fully loaded camel caravans could cover 18 to 20 miles a day. But someone riding a fast camel could travel much farther—up to 70 miles a day!

Is it Red or Reeds? The Red Sea was also known as the Sea of Reeds. The Israelites crossed it coming out of Egypt during the Exodus.

Masada: One of the most spectacular sites in the Holy Land, the city of Masada sits on the flat top of a high rock bluff above the wilderness floor near the Dead Sea. The city began as a fortified Jewish community in the second century B.C. The Romans captured it in 6 A.D. Then, in 66 A.D., the Jews revolted and reclaimed it.

The Everyday World of the Bible

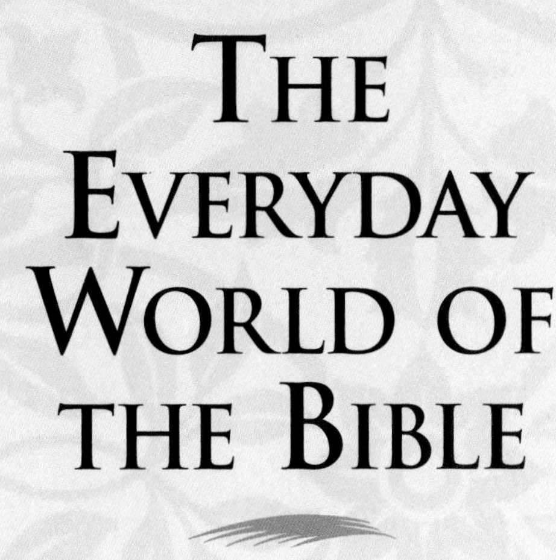

THE DAY-TO-DAY life for the Israelites and early Christians wasn't as dramatic as those breathtaking moments recorded in Scripture. What was this everyday world like? How did the average person live, work, and worship during the writing of the Bible? The answers to these questions will help us see that the Bible is populated with real people who had many of the same feelings and concerns that we have today.

PEOPLE AT HOME

In biblical times, the home was at the hub of people's lives. Birth, marriage, and death all took place there, and it was often the center of social activity, a workplace, and somewhere to eat and sleep as well. Several generations might live under the same roof.

Back then, there was variety in housing from place to place and period to period. Just as the Native American tepee is different from the 20th-century urban town house, so too was the bedouin tent in the time of the patriarchs different from the flat-roofed house in Capernaum during the time of Jesus.

TENT DWELLINGS

In this painting by Raphael, Moses receives the Ten Commandments from the Lord. In the valley below, the tent dwellings of the Israelite camp can be seen. The Israelites used the portable tent homes during their long journey from Egypt.

Tents were the most common dwellings in the ancient world. They were constructed by setting poles in the ground and stretching a covering of skin over them. The covering was fastened to stakes driven into the ground. Sometimes occupants used curtains to divide their tents into rooms, and they used mats or carpets to cover the ground. The sides of the tents could be folded back or even taken down to let fresh air circulate through during the heat of the day.

These dwellings, often made of goatskin, were the homes of the patriarchs. For hundreds of years, Abraham and his descendants lived in tents—in Canaan, in Egypt, and then in the desert. These tent dwellers moved around from place to place with their flocks and herds in search of fresh pasture and water. Their portable, practical homes were easily taken down, bundled up, and moved to a new site. When the Israelites conquered the Canaanites, they took over their towns and homes, and copied their style of building. Life became settled and more predictable in the land flowing with "milk and honey" (Ex 3:8).

THE COURTYARD HOUSE

The typical house in Palestine during the time of the patriarchs was built off the side of a courtyard. The simplest house had one small room and a circular, stone-lined pit inside the house for storing grain. Houses were built together and sometimes back-to-back. Entire terraces of these small homes (no bigger than an average bathroom or kitchen today) have been excavated. Surprisingly, these cramped quarters provided shelter for entire families. Larger homes have been discovered, however. One found at Megiddo, dating from 1600 B.C., had nine rooms with a door to each room—a luxury in those days.

This circular watchtower has many of the same characteristics as early stone or brick homes in Palestine. They were built on secure bedrock foundation. Roofs were generally low, often only six feet from the floor, and many houses had just a single room, or two at most.

BRICK HOMES

Most average homes in Palestine were made of stone, but down in the Jordan Valley homes were built of bricks because there was so much rich mud available there. At first oval mud bricks were made by hand, but once wooden molds were designed and made, the mud bricks became rectangular in shape. After the mud bricks were baked, they were white or pale red in color.

The roof of the house was made by placing wooden beams across the brick walls, covering the beams with brush, and finally mud or clay. Long timbers were too expensive for ordinary homes, so most rooms were fairly narrow.

THE FOUR-ROOMED HOUSE

When the Israelites moved back into Palestine after Joshua's victories, they began building four-roomed houses. This became the standard pattern of homes for centuries. The design was simple: You entered a courtyard from the street. On one side there were one or two rooms for storage; on the other side, a cattle barn. At the end was a large room for living and sleeping. The roof was flat, and strong enough for work, rest, or play by family members.

ROOFTOP LIVING

To get to the roof of a typical Israelite house, people climbed an outside staircase or even a wooden ladder propped against the wall. The roof was surrounded by a parapet, required by Jewish law to safeguard against falling to the ground below. A variety of activities took place at this topmost level. This was the place to do weaving and washing. In the hot sunny weather figs, dates, and flax were set out and dried. Prayer and meditation took place here:

> "About noon the next day, as they were on their journey and approaching the city, Peter went up on the roof to pray."
> Ac 10:9

It was also the ideal location from which to make public announcements:

> "What I say to you in the dark, tell in the light; and what you hear whispered, proclaim from the housetops."
> Mt 10:27

Festivals and celebrations were often set up on the roof. Many families celebrated the week-long Feast of Tabernacles on the roof of their home.

This building—called the "Cenacle"—marks the traditional site of the Lord's Supper. It is located just South of Jerusalem's walls. The Bible says that Jesus ate his last meal in "a large upper room" of a house (Mark 14:13).

NEW TESTAMENT HOMES

Besides the typical Israelite house, there were other types of dwellings in Jesus' day. When Jesus ate his last supper with his closest followers in a large upstairs room, it was likely in one of Jerusalem's wealthier homes.

To enter a home like this, you had to pass through a door that was usually kept locked. This door opened into a porch furnished with seats or benches. On the other side of the porch there was a short flight of stairs leading to the rooms and the open court. This courtyard area was the center of the Jewish home. It let in light and air to surrounding rooms. The floor was paved with tile or rock. Sometimes homeowners built the court around a fountain or well (2Sa 17:18). The courtyard was used for celebrations and other social gatherings:

> *When these days were completed, the king gave for all the people present in the citadel of Susa, both great and small, a banquet lasting for seven days, in the court of the garden of the king's palace.*
>
> Est 1:5

The rooms surrounding this area opened onto the court, and in later centuries, many of these rooms had balconies or galleries that faced this central area.

A stairway made from stone or wood led from the court to the upstairs rooms, and to the roof. The upper rooms were often quite large and nicely furnished. Paul preached his last sermon in this type of setting. Some of the crowd may have been next to the wall lying on cushions beside the window casement. It would have been easy for Eutychus, asleep in this position, to have fallen to the street below:

> *A young man named Eutychus, who was sitting in the window, began to sink off into a deep sleep while Paul talked still longer. Overcome by sleep, he fell to the ground three floors below and was picked up dead. But Paul went down, and bending over him took him in his arms, and said, "Do not be alarmed, for his life is in him."*
>
> Ac 20:9–10

The master's quarters were downstairs and faced the entrance. This was the most lavish area in the house. His reception area was smartly furnished with a raised platform, a square table, and a couch (used as a bed at night).

Some of these homes had one or two rooms built over the porch or gateway of the house. This structure was called the alliyah, and it was used as guest rooms, a place to rest or meditate, or for storage. Steps connected the alliyah to the street and to the central court of the house. Jesus likely referred to such an area when he spoke of praying privately (Mt 6:6).

In ancient houses, windows were small rectangular holes facing the street (or inside—facing the open court). Sometimes a porch was built along the front of the house, carefully enclosed with latticework. This porch window was only opened for festive events and other special occasions.

Doors in these houses were not hung on hinges. Wooden doors were fixed to heavy posts that turned on stone sockets. Often the main door of the house was equipped with a lock and key made of wood or metal. Some of these ancient keys were huge and were clearly seen when carried in public.

HOW HOUSES WERE BUILT

When the Israelites moved into Palestine, most people built their own houses or moved into the ones left there by the Canaanites. But as society expanded and became more complex, the need for public buildings and large dwellings grew. As workers became more skilled, they became specialists in stone building, bricklaying, and carpentry.

Many homes throughout biblical times were built out of large, rough stones—limestone, basalt, and sandstone. Smaller stones were used to fill the gaps between the larger stones, and the rough walls were covered with mud plaster. Larger homes often had a double thickness of stones, and the corners and doorways were made of squared stones.

The remains of ancient stables in Megiddo, Israel, built during the reign of King David, ninth century B.C. The sturdy, vertical stone pillars still remain standing.

Floors were usually hardened mud, and they were covered with straw mats. In wealthy homes, floors might be paved with stone slabs and covered with plush carpets. Building materials were readily available in Palestine. The wealthy could easily obtain stone, brick, and the best timber for their homes. They used hewn stone and marble, cedar paneling, and gold, silver, and ivory for ornamental work.

Many wealthy landowners had "winter homes" and "summer homes." The latter were built partly underground, paved with marble, and constructed to bring in cool currents of air. They were a delightful sanctuary during the hot and humid summer months.

HOMES OF THE POOR

In contrast with the fine homes of the wealthy, the poor often lived in one-room huts with mud walls. These walls were strengthened with reeds or stakes, but they were still not very secure and often became the breeding ground for snakes and vermin.

The family and animals occupied the same room, although family members sometimes slept on a platform above the animals. The windows were small holes high in the wall, and to keep intruders out, the doors of these homes were made very low. A person had to stoop to enter and leave the home.

Most houses in biblical times were sparsely furnished. They contained the bare necessities—utensils for cooking, food storage jars, and an area for sleeping. Even the well-to-do lived simply compared to the modern world. The furnishings and utensils shown here would have been familiar in biblical times.

FURNISHINGS

If someone from the time of Jesus were to visit you, he or she would be amazed at the number and variety of furnishings in your home. Even the best-furnished house in Palestine would have appeared empty to us today. Here is a typical inventory of household furnishings back then:

Mats and rugs: In the average home, straw mats were used as a floor covering or for seating. Poor people may well have had only a skin or mat on the floor to use for eating, sitting, and sleeping. The wealthy homeowner, on the other hand, would have had beautiful rugs, skins to recline on, and cushions of rich fabric.

Stools, tables, benches, and chairs: Long before the time of Jesus, the rich Shunammite woman furnished the prophet Elisha's room with a bed, a table, a stool, and a candlestick (2Ki 4:10–13). This would be more than would be available in an ordinary home. In wealthy homes, the owner would have a bench in his quarters. We know, too, that some people in Bible times owned and sat on finely designed chairs. Examples of these have been discovered in the tombs of the wealthy of Jericho.

In ancient times, a table was a circular piece of leather placed on the floor mat. In the New Testament period, a three-sided couch (known as a triclinium) was introduced by the Romans. It extended around three sides of a rectangular table, and it was used for reclining at meals. It was likely in this setting that Jesus and his disciples observed the Jewish Passover feast, the Last Supper.

This rendition of the Last Supper shows Jesus, surrounded by his followers, reclining at a triclinium, the traditional Roman table used for meals.

Beds: At night, family members would put down thick, coarse mattresses to sleep on, and cover themselves with quilts made from goat hair. Pillows may have been made from goatskin stuffed with feathers, wool, or some other soft material. In the morning, bedding would be rolled up and put away. Even from Old Testament times, wealthy families had bedsteads made of ivory, wood, or other expensive materials (Am 6:4), and they stored their bedding in expensive trunks.

Pots, pans, and storage bins: Most household utensils during biblical times were made of earthenware or terra-cotta. Later on, wealthy homes sometimes had kitchenware made of metal. There were flat-based bowls and "dipper juglets" in Abraham's day, and a "pilgrim flask" was used as a drinking vessel by soldiers and travelers. There were particular jars for storing flour and olive oil, and pots for carrying and storing water. There were cooking pots, and bowls and cups for serving food and drink.

When Jesus washed the disciples feet (Jn 13:5), he probably used a large container called a *krater,* dating back to the time of the kings. This type of container had two or four handles, and was usually hung on wall pegs.

Every house had stone or clay storage bins for animal fodder as well as food for the family. Fire for cooking was made on the earth floor or sometimes in an earthenware pot.

Lamps: Lamps were common in Bible times. Light was important because homes were very dark. Olive oil, pitch, naphtha (a flammable liquid), or wax were used and wicks were made of cotton or flax. Poorer Israelites made their

During biblical times, washing dusty feet was a common courtesy. When a guest arrived at a Palestine home, his or her feet might be washed by a servant or by the woman of the house in a foot bath like the one shown here. At the very least, the guest was provided with water for footwashing.

Archaeologists have uncovered thousands of lamps from antiquity. Because distinctive forms emerged as time passed, ancient lamps from biblical lands can be dated accurately. This oil lamp is from the Herodian period, 37 B.C.–135 A.D.

lamps of clay, while the well-to-do had lamps of bronze and other metals. Lamps were left burning all night for a sense of security and for safety—a thief would be less likely to break into a well-lit house. For the Jews, the lamp was a significant symbol of the life and dignity of the family.

COMFORT AT HOME

In our society, many of us are protected from summer's heat and winter's cold by the touch of a thermostat that controls a central cooling and heating system in our homes. The Israelites were not so fortunate. During the summer, the average Old Testament home was stuffy and alive with insects. When it was cold, the house was filled with smoke from the smoldering fire built in a hole in the earth floor. In the rainy seasons, the roof and walls of the house leaked. Clearly, home was not always a comfortable or comforting environment.

From Solomon's day, however, wealthy families began to emerge, and for them life was quite different. Their homes were built differently—they had more space and greater amenities. By the time between the Testaments, wealthy people were adding bathrooms to their home, with tubs set into the tiled floors. By New Testament times, rich people living in Palestine built their homes in the Roman style, with two rectangular courtyards each surrounded by rooms.

FOOD AND DRINK

Jesus encouraged his hearers not to worry about food, drink, and clothing. He knew that for ordinary people these were basic concerns. Cereal crops, fruit, and vegetables were staples in the Hebrew diet, but they were subject to drought and pests (such as locusts). Some mutton and goat's meat were eaten, and fish was an important food in New Testament times. Here is a list of some basic Bible time staples:

An olive press. To obtain oil from the valuable fruit, olives were spread on a round stone basin and crushed by a heavy, rotating stone wheel. The first oil skimmed from the crushed fruit was considered the finest oil.

	Food	**Reference**
Grains:	barley	Jn 6:9
	corn	Gen 41:35
	millet	Eze 4:9
	wheat	1Sa 6:13
Fruit:	almonds	Gen 43:11
	figs	Jer 24:1–3

	Food	Reference
	grapes	Dt 23:24
	melon	Nu 11:5
	olives	Dt 8:8
	pomegranates	Nu 13:23
	sycamore	Am 7:14
Vegetables:	beans	2Sa 17:28
	cucumbers	Nu 11:5
	garlic	Nu 11:5
	gourds	2Ki 4:39
	leeks	Nu 11:5
	lentils	Gen 25:34
	onions	Nu 11:5
Meat and Fish:	calf	Lk 15:23
	goat	Gen 27:9
	lamb	2Sa 12:4
	oxen	1Ki 19:21
	quail	Ex 16:13
	venison	Gen 27:7
	fish	Jn 6:11
Various Foods and Drinks:	cheese	2Sa 17:29
	curds	Isa 7:15
	eggs	Lk 11:12
	honey	Mt 3:4
	locusts	Mt 3:4
	milk	Gen 18:8
	wine	Jn 2

"Do not neglect to show hospitality to strangers, for by doing that some have entertained angels without knowing it." Heb 13:2

Meals: In the typical Israelite home, there was no breakfast. A snack might be eaten on the way to work, and the midday meal was usually bread, olives, and maybe fruit. In the evening, the family sat on the floor to eat dinner, which was usually a vegetable stew from a common pot eaten with bread. The Hebrews were a hospitable people and welcomed guests to their homes.

Even in their nomadic past, travelers would be invited to stay with the clan in their tents. Flat loaves of bread and milk were always part of the meal.

In wealthy homes, more food was available and in greater variety. At mealtimes, people reclined on couches around a table as they enjoyed appetizers and a number of main courses, followed by pastries and fruit for dessert.

Food laws: In the Old Testament, strict food laws were laid down for all Jews. They were generally as follows:

1. Animals that chew their cud and have divided hoofs could be eaten.

Unleavened bread, shown here, is made without yeast or leaven. The Israelites were commanded to eat only unleavened bread during the week following Passover to remind them of Israel's hasty departure from Egypt at the time of the Exodus.

2. Pork could not be eaten. It was considered unclean.

3. Only fish with fins and scales could be eaten.

4. Scavengers and many other birds were not eaten.

5. Blood had to be drained from a carcass before it was cooked.

6. Meat and milk dishes were not to be cooked or eaten together.

7. Meat that had been offered to idols could not be eaten.

"For I am the Lord your God; sanctify yourselves therefore, and be holy, for I am holy. You shall not defile yourselves with any swarming creature that moves on the earth." Lev 11:44

The gecko, crocodile, and lizard were all off-limits, but locusts, crickets, and grasshoppers were just fine for snacks or meals! Although the reasons for these strict diet laws are not fully clear, they were likely given to protect the health of the Israelites, and to set this group apart as the people of God.

Drinks: Drinking water was not readily available in the Palestine area. Local wells provided fairly safe water, which was collected in earthenware jars. However, water collected from the roof in the family cistern sometimes contained impurities that were not fit to drink. Even during Roman times, when water was brought to the towns by aqueduct or by pipeline, maintaining sanitary conditions was a concern.

Other liquids had to be found to quench thirst. Milk from the family goat was popular, and people drank fresh juice from newly picked grapes. Since grapes grew well in the Mediterranean climate, and had to be fermented so that it would keep, wine was naturally the most common drink.

TEN QUICK FOOD FACTS

- The Israelites did not have sugar. Honey from wild bees was the main sweetener.
- Fig cakes were especially practical for taking on a journey.
- Butter was hardly used because it would not keep; but cheese and yogurt were very popular.
- Salt was used for preserving food. Small fish were dried, salted, and eaten with bread.
- Many vegetables were eaten raw.
- It was not until the time of the Romans that a divided oven was invented, with the fire separate from the cooking area.
- Most people ate with their fingers (although a spoon was used for something like soup).
- Before the time of the apostles, a Jew could not eat at the home of a non-Jew because of Jewish food laws.
- Flat loaves of barley bread were probably the most common type of bread.
- Although wine was a common, everyday drink, intoxication was always condemned.

BIRTH

Children were considered a gift from God, and a big family was a sign of God's special blessing. A childless family was perceived as having displeased God in some way, and "barren" women were looked on with disfavor, even ridicule. Among children, boys were valued more. In this male-dominated culture, boys were needed to carry on the family name and continue the work of the land. Girls were necessary workers, but considered less important.

At birth, salt was rubbed into the baby's skin to make it firm, and the infant was wrapped in tight cloths to make the limbs grow straight. The name of the infant was carefully chosen to reflect something about the child's character. Babies were not weaned until they were two or three years old.

When a boy was eight days old, he was circumcised by his father or rabbi. The firstborn son was considered to belong to God in a special way and had to be bought back (redeemed) a month after circumcision by a payment to the priest (Ex 13:13).

After giving birth, in order to be considered "clean" again a mother had to sacrifice a pigeon and then a lamb. In New Testament times, money was deposited in the offering boxes of the temple to "redeem" a firstborn son—a tradition that began during the Exodus, when Israelite freedom cost the Egyptians the lives of their sons.

GROWING UP

For Israelite children, play, work and education were all closely tied to the home. Parents taught children their first lessons and prayers, and the entire family attended worship on the sabbath and festival days. Schooling for boys started when they were about six. Girls, however, were not formally educated. The rabbi of the local synagogue gave moral and religious instruction based on the Torah, and the boys learned largely by repetition. In later times, there were also Roman schools throughout the empire where pupils studied philosophy, mathematics, literature, rhetoric, astronomy, and architecture.

Work was an important part of the growing years. Children had to help in the fields, workshop, or kitchen as soon as they could manage the simplest task. Of course, there was opportunity to play as well. Children in biblical times enjoyed toys and games. Rattles, dolls, and dollhouses have all been uncovered by archaeologists—even board and dice games, ball games, and target games!

A Jewish boy reading from the holy Scriptures at his Bar Mitzvah service. From New Testament times, a boy's 13th birthday marked the time when he became a "son of the law."

At thirteen, during New Testament times, a boy became a man in a special ceremony called the Bar Mitzvah ("son of the law"). After his coming of age, the boy was regarded as a responsible member of Israel in home, community, and in the synagogue.

Twenty Famous Bible Couples

Names	Description	Reference
1. Adam and Eve	the first couple	Gen 3:20
2. Abraham and Sarah	father and mother of Israel (Isaac)	Gen 11:29
3. Jacob and Rachel	father of Israel's twelve tribes, parents of Joseph and Benjamin	Gen 29–30
4. Amram and Jochebed	parents of Aaron, Miriam, and Moses	Ex 6:20
5. Moses and Zipporah	lawgiver and his Midianite wife	Ex 2:21
6. Boaz and Ruth	great-grandparents of King David	Ru 4:13
7. Elkanah and Hannah	parents of Samuel	1Sa 1:1–2
8. Nabal and Abigail	surly farmer and his clever wife	1Sa 25:3
9. David and Bathsheba	parents of Solomon	2Sa 12:24
10. Ahab and Jezebel	evil rulers over Israel	1Ki 16:30–31
11. Ahasuerus and Esther	Persian king and his Jewish queen	Est 2:16
12. Haman and Zeresh	cruel Persian official and his wife	Est 5:14
13. Hosea and Gomer	faithful prophet and his promiscuous wife	Hos 1–3
14. Zechariah and Elizabeth	parents of John the Baptist	Lk 1:5
15. Joseph and Mary	legal father and actual mother of Jesus	Lk 1:27
16. Zebedee and Salome	parents of James and John	Mt 4:21
17. Herod Antipas	ruler of Galilee and	Mt 14:3

and Herodias	his sister-in-law	
18. Ananias and Sapphira	died after lying to the apostles	Ac 5:1
19. Aquila and Priscilla	godly couple who assisted Paul	Ac 18:2
20. Felix and Drusilla	Roman governor of Judea and his Jewish wife	Ac 24:24

MARRIAGE

People in Israel married at an early age; to be married at 13 was not uncommon. Marriages were arranged by parents. In Old Testament times, marriages were arranged within the same clan—and often to a first cousin.

A man was allowed to have more than one wife, and by the time of the judges and the kings, men could have as many wives as they could afford. This arrangement, motivated by economic and political reasons, often created domestic strife. In the Israelite community after the Exodus, most marriages were monogamous, and such a marriage was viewed as ideal.

Since the bride was considered a working asset, she had to be paid for. The fee (called the *mohar*) was paid to the girl's father. In return, the young woman's father gave the couple a dowry. At the binding ceremony of betrothal, gifts were exchanged between the couple. On the day of the wedding in the evening, the bridegroom and his party went in procession to the bride's home, where she was waiting, veiled and in her wedding dress. A blessing was given, then the bridegroom took the bride through the village to his own home. Friends went in torchlight procession to the new home. The marriage celebration and feast that followed sometimes lasted as long as a week.

Marriage of the Virgin, as painted by Raphael. In Hebrew custom, the groom escorted his bride to their new home accompanied by friends and relatives. There, a wedding celebration took place. It might last for a week.

DEATH AND BURIAL

A death in a household is always a tragedy, and in biblical times elaborate mourning rituals followed such an event. The body was prepared for a quick burial because of the hot

Archaeologists have discovered that burial sites, such as these, are very important for understanding the beliefs and cultures of ancient people. Many ancient cultures interred their dead in elaborate tomb chambers above or underground, others were buried in simple, unmarked caves or sites dug into stone cliffs. These Jerusalem tombs belonged to nobility in the time of Jesus.

climate. It was washed and clothed, then wrapped in special grave cloths, with a linen napkin bound around the head. The body was then put on a wooden stretcher (a bier) and carried to the place of burial. Family and friends—and even hired professional mourners—made a great public display of sorrow: Weeping, wailing, tearing clothing, wearing ashes, and fasting were all part of the seven-day mourning ceremonies.

Ordinary Israelites buried their dead in common graves or caves. Some caves were large enough for all the members of the family. Wealthy families could afford to have tombs specially hewn out of rock and sealed with a boulder. Graves were painted white to draw attention to them. They were not to be touched, as any contact with the dead made a person "unclean."

FAMILIES: THE STRUGGLE TO SURVIVE

The family was a unifying force throughout biblical history. But families were constantly threatened by social, economic, and religious pressures. Some of these challenges were unique to the family in biblical times.

Childlessness: If a couple could not conceive, they viewed their situation as a punishment from God. A childless husband sometimes married a second woman, or even conceived children with a slave (Gen 16:2–4). These practices resolved the issue of childlessness, but often created many other problems.

Polygamy: It was not unusual for Hebrew patriarchs and Israelite kings to have more than one wife (1Ki 11:3). Often, the husband favored one wife over another and domestic strife resulted, including the need to decide whose child to honor as the firstborn son. However, after the Exodus, Israelite marriages generally became monogamous (Mk 10:2–9).

Death of a husband: If the widowed wife was childless, she was expected to continue living with her husband's family, and to marry one of her husband's brothers or a near relative (Dt 25:5–10). If this was not an option, the widowed wife with children was free to marry outside the clan, or even return to her family of origin. An elderly widow might be cared for by one of her sons. If she had become wealthy, she could choose to live alone. The destitute widow in Old Testament times faced great hardships, whereas the childless widow of the New Testament could turn to the church for help and support (1Ti 5:16).

Israelite mourning rites called for weeping, wailing, and other loud expressions of grief. This was expected from family members, neighbors, and—if possible—professional mourners, who were hired to give vocal expression to grief when there was a death in the family.

Rebellious children: It was considered such a serious offense to dishonor one's parents that Moses ordered the punishment of death for any person that cursed or struck a father or mother (Ex 21:15). Although there is no record of this punishment actually being carried out, the Bible does describe many instances in which children disrespected their parents (Mt 15:4–9).

Divorce: In ancient Babylon, a husband could simply say to his wife, "Thou art not my wife" and his words were a legal divorce decree. However, in Hebrew culture, the Law of Moses was supposed to deter divorce, not encourage it, and therefore divorce could not be done privately. Although Hebrew society allowed a husband to divorce his wife, the wife was not permitted to divorce her husband for any reason, and many women simply fled from unhappy situations, without a bill of divorce (Jdg 19:2). If she was given a certificate of divorce, the former wife was free to remarry any man except a priest (Lev 21:7). If a husband suspected his wife of adultery, she was taken to the priest and ordered to drink bitter water. If she were innocent, she remained unaffected by the water. A guilty verdict ensued if she became ill, and in that case she was stoned to death (Nu 5:11–31).

Clothing in all Bible lands was very similar, and was worn primarily for modesty and comfort. Clothes for special occasions and for the rich were set apart by their color and embroidery, not variety in style. A popular item was a shirt-like garment made of wool or linen worn by men in cooler weather.

CLOTHING AND FASHION

In biblical times, the type of clothing worn was affected by climate and the availability of materials. Over the centuries, five basic items of clothing evolved:

The kethon: In Old Testament times, this was a simple, everyday tunic made of animal skin. Later on, this basic item was made out of linen and silk and worn by the wealthy.

The simlah: Shem and Japheth, Noah's sons, used this outer garment to cover their father's nakedness (Gen 9:23). The simlah was like a large sheet with a hood. It was first made of wool, but camel's hair was used later. A type of coat, the simlah was used for additional warmth, and the poor used it as daily wear and as a covering at night.

The beged: For special occasions, the Israelites wore the beged. They believed that this article of clothing gave honor to the wearer. After temple rituals priests wore the beged, and Rebekah dressed Jacob in this garment when he went before his father Isaac to receive his blessing (Gen 27).

The lebhosh: This was a garment used for general wear, but it eventually became an outer garment for everyone in Israelite culture. It was possible for the lebhosh to be made out of sackcloth (for mourning), while a decorative lebhosh could be worn as royal apparel.

The addereth: In Bible times, the wearer of an addereth (an outer cloak) was a person of importance. Today, this is a common garment in Palestine that everyone wears.

Even in the Garden of Eden, fabric and clothing were important. After Adam and Eve realized they were naked, they made loincloths of fig leaves to cover themselves. Then God made the pair coverings of skin before sending them out of the garden (Gen 3). Later, a variety of fabrics were used to make clothes:

These early leather sandals were the type commonly worn throughout Bible times. They were made of wood, leather, or fiber soles and were held in place by leather thongs. The sandals of the rich were more elaborate and included heel caps or sides that extended over the arch of the foot.

Linen: This was made from the flax plant and was one of the most important fabrics for the Israelites. It could be made coarse, thick, fine, or delicate. The Egyptians had a wide reputation for their fine linen.

Wool: Sheep's wool was the principal material for making clothes.

Silk: This was a fabric of great value because of its quality and the vivid colors available. Only the rich could afford silk.

Sackcloth: The dark color and coarse texture of the goat's hair material made it ideal as a ritual sign of mourning and repentance. Sackcloth material was also used to make grain sacks.

Cotton: Although it is possible, we are not certain whether the Israelites used cotton for making clothes. Both Syria and Palestine grow cotton today.

The common loom in Palestine in ancient times was similar to the one shown here. An upright loom was made by driving two poles into the ground, with a third pole, known as the weaver's beam, balanced across the top. Threads were hung from the beam and weighted with stones. In ancient Israel, wool and rough linen were commonly woven on family looms.

MAKING AND CARING FOR CLOTHES

Preparing fabrics and actually making clothes were considered women's work. There were a number of steps in making any garment:

Distaff spinning: Jewish women would attach wool or flax to a rod or stick called a distaff, and then use a spindle to twist the fibers into thread (Ex 35:25–26).

Weaving: After raw materials were spun into thread, the thread was used to make cloth. The warp (lengthwise thread) was attached to a wooden beam on the loom, and the weaver stood while working. Various types of woven fabrics were made this way, including woolen garments, linen, and the embroidered clothing of the priests (Ex 28:4, 39).

"A woman shall not wear a man's apparel, nor shall a man put on a woman's garment; for whoever does such things is abhorrent to the Lord your God." Dt 22:5

Tanning: In the Jewish community the tanner's trade was not considered respectable. This line of work involved drying animal skins to make garments. Lime, the juice of particular plants, and the leaves or bark of certain trees were used to tan the skins.

Embroidering: The Jews were noted for their fine needlework, but it was different from embroidery as we know it today. Cloth was woven with a variety of colors, and then a design was sewn onto it (Ex 26:11). In another method, embroidery was done by weaving gold thread or designs right into the fabric. This type of fine work was only done on garments worn by the priests.

Dyeing: From early on in Bible history, the Israelites were familiar with the art of dyeing. Many natural colors were used for clothing. Purple goods were highly valued (Ac 16:14), but that often referred to anything that had a red hue to it.

Clothes were cleaned by washing the garments, which often included stamping on them and beating them with a stick in a tub of water. Niter, soap, and chalk were used for cleaning (Jer 2:22). Garments were often cleaned by a fuller, who did business on the outskirts of town (where water was available, and where the offensive odor of the cleaning business would not bother townsfolk).

WHAT PEOPLE WORE

The Israelites were not influenced by the dress of surrounding countries, and fashions tended to remain the same from one generation to the next. Although some of the clothing for men and women looked quite similar, women were forbidden to wear anything that belonged to a man, and men were forbidden to wear a woman's garment.

The poor had little clothing—even using their outer garment as a covering at night. The rich, on the other hand, had an extensive and colorful collection of apparel. The following is a sampling of the Israelite wardrobe:

MEN'S CLOTHING

Inner garment: close-fitting and made of wool, linen, or cotton and worn by both sexes

Girdle: a belt or band used to secure the inner or outer garment

Outer garment: coat, robe, or mantle made of linen or goat's hair

Purse or scrip: both were used to carry necessities

Sandals: a sole of wood or leather fastened with straps of leather and worn by both sexes

Robes of honor: very thin, fine garments worn over colorful tunics

Mourning garments: made of goat's hair material and worn next to the skin in times of deep sorrow

Winter clothing: fur robes or skins; cattle skins were worn by the poor

Rings: worn as a seal or token of personal authority

Headdress: worn on special occasions

A middle eastern woman modestly covers her face with a veil, part of traditional women's clothing for centuries. Sometimes a veil was worn to disguise a woman's identity, and in Israelite society, a bride wore a veil at the time of her wedding.

WOMEN'S CLOTHING

Inner garment: described as a coat, robe, or tunic

Girdle: used to secure the the outer garment

Outer garment: longer than a man's; the front could be tucked over the girdle to make an apron

Veil: worn to show modesty and to indicate an unmarried status

Sandals: never worn indoors

Anklets: often made of gold, these made a tinkling sound when the woman walked

Mourning garments: ashes were placed on the head while wearing sackcloth

Winter clothing: fur robes or skins

Earrings: worn by Hebrew and Egyptian women

Cosmetics and perfume: henna was used as a cosmetic stain; frankincense, myrrh, aloes, and nard were sources of perfume

Headdress: used to some degree; hair ornaments may have been worn

AMULETS AND PHYLACTERIES

In ancient times, idolatrous people wore magical charms to protect themselves from evil spirits. These amulets—earrings worn by women, or pendants worn around the neck by men—had sacred words or the figure of a god engraved on them. Another kind of amulet had words written on a scroll that was rolled tightly and sewn up in linen.

To counter this pagan practice, Israelite men began wearing phylacteries. One type was worn on the forehead and was called a *frontlet*. It had four compartments, and in each compartment there was a piece of parchment that contained a passage from the Law. All four pieces of parchment were

The only mention of phylacteries in Scripture is found in Matthew 23:5, where Jesus admonishes the Pharisees for their broad phylacteries and long fringes—made conspicuous to show off their religion. This head phylactery, first century A.D., was discovered in one of the Qumran caves, near the Dead Sea.

wrapped in animal skin in a small bundle and then tied to the forehead.

A second type of phylactery was made of two rolls of parchment on which the words of the Law were written in special ink. The parchment was enclosed in leather and worn on the arm. Some men wore their phylacteries at evening and morning prayers, others wore them only in the morning. Phylacteries were not worn on the Sabbath or on other holy days.

The Pharisees were known to make their phylacteries larger than normal so that everyone would see them and marvel at such holy men!

Phylacteries, common in Judaism from early on, and worn by Orthodox Jews today, are small boxes containing specific verses from the books of Exodus and Deuteronomy. Religious Jews wear phylacteries strapped to the forehead and left hand during times of prayer.

THE VILLAGE

In early Old Testament times, village life centered around a farming settlement. The lifeblood of the community was animals and crops, and villages grew up near a stream or brook that would provide water year round.

When Abraham settled in Canaan, each family was given a plot of land. This was a gift from God, and each family was expected to utilize the land in the following ways: live on it, grow crops, maintain animals, and perhaps bury family members there. Each parcel of land was supposed to be kept within the family and not casually bought and sold.

Every 50 years marked a time of Jubilee, when land that had been mortgaged or sold was returned to the family. This was meant to help equalize social standing between rich landowners and poor laborers.

By the time of the kings, however, a wealthy class of rulers and officials began to emerge. They bought up a lot of land and oppressed the poor. Estates took the place of family farms. When people lost their land, they had to hire themselves out as farm laborers. Life in the village changed. Bigger and better homes were built for the wealthy and grouped together in a certain part of town. Within the same community, the very poor suffered tremendous hardship, thus the prophets cried out against economic and social injustice:

Alas for those who devise wickedness
and evil deeds on their beds!
When the morning dawns, they perform it,
because it is in their power.
They covet fields, and seize them;
houses, and take them away;
they oppress householder and house,
people and their inheritance.

Mic 2:1–2

FIFTY POPULAR BIBLE PLACES

Place	Description	Reference
1. Akeldama	known as Potter's Field and purchased with the money that bought the betrayal of Jesus	Ac 1:19
2. Alexandria	home of Apollos	Ac 18:24–26
3. Ararat	mountainous land in western Asia	Jer 51:27
4. Ashdod	one of five main Canaanite cities	Jos11:22
5. Athens	capital city of Greece	Ac 17:15–34
6. Babylon	capital city of the Babylonian Empire	Ne 7:6
7. Baca	a valley of Palestine where many balsam trees are found	Ps 84:6
8. Beautiful Gate	a part of the east gate of Jerusalem where Peter and John healed a lame man	Ac 3:2
9. Bethany	where Lazarus was raised from the dead	Jn 11
10. Bethel	located north of Jerusalem, this is an important biblical site	Gen 13:3
11. Bethlehem	birthplace of Jesus	Jn 7:42
12. Cana	a village of Galilee where Jesus performed his first recorded miracle	Jn 2:1

"He has cast the lot for them, his hand has portioned it out to them with the line; they shall possess it forever, from generation to generation they shall live in it."
Isa 34:17

13. Canaan	the name of Palestine, the land given to Abraham and his offspring	Gen 11:31
14. Capernaum	main area where Jesus ministered	Mt 4:13
15. Carmel	a town in the mountains of Judah	Jos 15:55
16. Cenchreae	a harbor east of Corinth	Ac 18:18
17. Chebar	the Jewish exiles, including Ezekiel, lived along its banks	Eze 1:3
18. Cities of Refuge	six cities of the Levites were set aside as sanctuaries for criminals: Bezer, Ramoth-Gilead, Golan, Kedesh, Shechem, and Kirjath-arba	Dt 4:41–43; Jos 20:7–9
19. Corinth	the church in this city received two letters from Paul the apostle	Ac 18:1
20. Damascus	city connected with Paul's conversion	Ac 9:1–18
21. Decapolis	group of ten cities forming a Roman district on the plain of Esdraelon and the upper Jordan Valley	Mt 4:25
22. Elim	a resting place for the Israelites after they crossed the Red Sea	Ex 15:27
23. Ephesus	visited by Paul during his second missionary journey	Ac 18:19
24. Galatia	a district of central Asia Minor	Ac 16:6
25. Gath	a Philistine city, home of Goliath	1Sa 17:4
26. Gomorrah	a depraved city that was destroyed	Gen 19
27. Haran	a Mesopotamian city	Gen 11:31
28. Hebron	a city of refuge	Jos 20:7
29. Helbon	a village of Syria near Damascus	Eze 27:18

Paul in Ephesus: "He entered the synagogue and for three months spoke out boldly, and argued persuasively about the kingdom of God"
Ac 19:8

30. Hermon	this mountain marks the northeast boundary of Palestine	Dt 3:8
31. Israel	the northern kingdom of the Jews in Israel	2Ch 35:18
32. Jericho	where Jesus met Zacchaeus	Lk 19:1–10
33. Jerusalem	capital of the southern kingdom of Judah, 30 miles from the Mediterranean Sea and 18 miles west of the Jordan River	2Sa 5:5
34. Judah	the southern kingdom of Israel	2Ch 13:8
35. Lydda	a town on the Plain of Sharon	Ac 9:32
36. Masada	where David hid from Saul	1Sa 24:22
37. Nain	a village in Galilee	Lk 7:11
38. Nazareth	where Jesus grew up	Lk 2:39–40
39. Nineveh	ancient capital of Assyria	Jnh 1

One of the oldest cities of the world, Hebron was an early camping site for Abraham. A place of great historical significance, the tombs of Abraham and Sarah, Isaac and Rebekah, and Jacob and Leah are enshrined here.

Built on top of a hill, Samaria was the capital of the northern kingdom of Israel. In New Testament times, Herod the Great rebuilt the city and renamed it Sebaste. Jesus showed his concern for the Samaritans, who were despised by the Jews, by traveling through their community and spending time with Samaritans.

40. Rome	the church in this city received a great theological epistle from Paul the apostle	Ro 1:7
41. Samaria	capital of the northern kingdom of Israel	1Ki 16:24
42. Sea of Galilee	also called Lake of Galilee, a large lake in northern Palestine	Jn 6:1
43. Salt Sea	also known as the Dead Sea or East Sea, it is the body of water at the southern end of the Jordan Valley	Nu 34:12
44. Smyrna	city in Asia	Rev 2:8–11
45. Sodom	a depraved city that was destroyed	Gen 19
46. Tarsus	birthplace of Paul	Ac 9:11
47. Thessalonica	Paul established a church here	Ac 17:1–9

48. Thyatira	home of Lydia	Ac 16:14
49. Tyre	city of Ezekiel's great prophecy	Eze 26
50. Ur	birthplace of Abraham	Gen 11:27

TOWNS AND CITIES

The difference between village and town life in Bible times lay in their fortification. Villages were settlements without walls. Towns were walled settlements that were built on top of a hill or mound and near a good water supply. Towns were usually built in fertile areas, or at a strategic junction of trade routes. Unprotected villages often surrounded fortified towns.

Old Testament towns were often very small (six to ten acres) with about 150–250 houses inside the walls, and about 1,000 residents. Walled towns began to develop when nomadic tribes or clans started to settle down. The chief of the clan became the "king" of his own territory. There was no central government, and kings of different towns often had conflicts.

Town life was extremely cramped. Houses were small, joined together, and streets were narrow. The main open space in town was the fortified gateway. Here, cattle and human traffic came and went, disputes were settled, and

In his expressionistic landscape of Jerusalem, modern painter Oskar Kokoschka depicts the "city of peace" in colorful tones. Jerusalem, a pivotal location in the religion and politics of the mid-east today, was the central and most important of Israel's ancient cities.

workers, merchants, town elders, and others all gathered for meetings, business, and trade.

From the time of King Solomon, towns grew into cities as they expanded in size and importance. Government became large and central. In Jerusalem, the capital, Solomon installed an administrative cabinet with diverse responsibilities. Besides being the government center, Jerusalem also became the religious capital. A magnificent temple was built there, and Solomon constructed palaces and a number of other large buildings at this site.

Although the word "aqueduct" is not actually found in the Bible, these conduits were built during the Greco-Roman era. Constructed to carry water into Caesarea, this aqueduct was in use when Philip and Peter preached the gospel there.

The great cities of New Testament times were different from early fortified towns. With the coming of the Greeks and Romans, towns and cities were planned carefully. In some locations, particularly Samaria and Caesarea, streets were made wider and paved, piped water was brought in from aqueducts, shops and public baths were built in central locations, and effective drainage for waste water and sewage was put in place. Life in the cities improved, especially for the wealthy.

Jerusalem in Jesus' day was a bustling, heavily populated city. It boasted a dazzling white limestone and gold temple built by the Herods, many other grand buildings, and streets crowded with people buying and selling. On market days, shops and stalls sold everything from sandals and cloth, to luxury goods offered by merchants. Besides seven different markets, there were many shops and restaurants to serve the needs of possibly a quarter of a million people living in the city—a far cry from the small farming settlement of earlier times.

WORKING LIFE

In Bible times, much of the history of the Israelites was lived out in an agricultural setting. Work tended to reflect this type of environment, the most important occupations being farming, shepherding, fishing, and village carpentry and crafts. Besides these, the Bible notes several other occupations:

Occupations	References
Baker	Gen 40:1
Barber	Eze 5:1
Brickmaker	Gen 11:3
Cook	1Sa 8:13
Coppersmith	2Ti 4:14
Cupbearer	Gen 40:2
Embalmer	Gen 50:3
Embroiderer	Ex 38:23
Engraver	Ex 28:11
Fuller	2Ki 18:17
Gardener	Jer 29:5
Gem-cutter	Ex 28:4
Jeweler	Ex 28:17–21
Mason	2Ki 12:12
Mariner	Eze 27:9
Military officer	Ac 10:1
Musician	2Sa 6:5
Painter	Jer 22:14
Perfumer	1Sa 8:13
Physician	Gen 50:2
Porter	2Sa 18:26
Potter	Isa 64:8
Refiner	Mal 3:3
Silversmith	Ac 19:24
Smith	1Sa 13:19
Spinner	Ex 35:25
Stonecutter	Ex 31:5
Tailor	Ex 39:1
Tanner	Ac 9:43
Tax collector	Mt 9:10
Tentmaker	Ac 18:3
Toolmaker	Gen 4:22
Weaver	Ex 28:32
Worker in metal	Ex 31:3–4

"The farmer waits for the precious crop from the earth, being patient with it until it receives the early and the late rains. You also must be patient. Strengthen your hearts, for the coming of the Lord is near."
Jas 5:7–8

FARMERS, SHEPHERDS, AND FISHERMEN

The work of farmers was mostly done by hand, even though they did use simple machinery—a wooden plough pulled by an ox, a wooden sickle to cut the stalks of grain, and a pronged fork to winnow the fresh corn. Besides growing and harvesting grain, other major crops included grapes, olives, and figs. Crops were planted after the autumn rains had softened the ground.

Shepherding was also important. The shepherd was usually in charge of a mixed flock of sheep and goats that he had to feed and protect. It was important to watch for wild animals, including lions and jackals, which inhabited the Jordan Valley area. The flock was important because wool and goat hair were used for clothing, goats were important for milk, and both animals were a significant source of meat.

Seven of Jesus' disciples were fishermen and several of his miracles were associated with fish and fishing—an important industry in Palestine. Here the Italian painter Raphael represents the miracle of the great catch of fish recorded in Luke 5:1–11.

The Israelites were poor sailors, so there was little fishing in Old Testament times. But by the time Jesus was in Galilee, there was a thriving fishing industry. The Lake of Galilee was full of fish. Using a cast net or a seine net, fishermen were able to pull in a good catch. Some fish were sold right away, others were salted. The work of fishing was often dangerous, because the lake could become stormy without warning because of sharp climatic changes.

THE WORK OF WOMEN

The woman in Bible times was ruled by her husband. She had low status, few rights, and did much of the hard work. Every day she had to bake bread and collect water from the local spring or well. Both jobs involved many steps of backbreaking effort, from grinding grain into coarse flour to carrying heavy water pots home on her head or shoulder. She might also have to make cheese or yogurt from milk. There might be spinning and weaving to do, and clothing to be made. During the harvest, women sometimes worked in the fields and helped crush the grapes and olives in the presses. The long workday ended with the preparation and eating of the evening meal when the whole family gathered together.

SICKNESS AND HEALTH

When Jesus came into the world, he was not attended by state-of-the-art maternity care. There was not even running hot water in which to wash the new baby. He arrived like many other Palestinian babies, in an area where humans shared quarters with animals.

Medical practice in biblical times was basic and, for the Hebrews, based on the health and hygiene laws given in the Pentateuch. Unlike surrounding tribes who mixed medical practice with superstition, magic, and sorcery, the Hebrews trusted God for good health and believed that sickness indicated spiritual disobedience or lack of faith (Job 4:8).

Along with their religious responsibilities, local priests were expected to fulfill medical duties. The Book of Leviticus (12, 13) describes both religious and medical purification rites, including cleansing after childbirth and for leprosy. Prophets also had a role in medical care. Elisha purified the water of Jericho, and helped in the cure of Naaman the Syrian and the son of the Shunammite woman (2Ki 4–5).

The medical principles of the Israelites were written in the law of Moses, and until Greek times, it was the job of the priest to diagnose and prescribe remedies for illness. By the time of Jesus, medicine was a respectable profession. This Roman medical box dates from the first century B.C.

Various ailments are mentioned in the Bible, including physical and mental disabilities. By New Testament times, doctors were at work, trained in medical schools that taught basic anatomy and medical care. Excavations have revealed collections of surgical instruments and evidence that certain surgical procedures and operations were performed back then. The role of the apothecary was probably more important than that of the doctor. He prepared the oils, ointments, and potions for the sick, the spices for embalming, the incense and oils for the temple, and cosmetics for everyday use.

Diseases and Disabilities Mentioned in the Bible

Blindness	Lev 21:18
Boils	Ex 9:9–10
Deafness	Mk 7:32–35
Dropsy	Lk 14:2
Dysentery	Ac 28:8
Eczema	Dt 28:27
Fever	Mt 8:14–15
Gangrene	2Ti 2:17
Hemorrhages	Mt 9:20
Leprosy	Nu 12
Paralysis	Mk 2:1–12
Sores	Lk 16:20
Tumors	1Sa 5:6
Ulcers	Dt 28:27

TEN QUICK "MEDICAL" CURES

- Myrtle, saffron, myrrh, and spikenard were used in personal hygiene.
- Olive oil and "balm of Gilead" were used for wounds and sores.
- Wine mixed with myrrh was used as a painkiller.
- It was believed that mandrake roots would help a women to conceive children.
- Broken arms or legs were bound up tightly.
- A hole was bored in the skull to relieve pressure.
- Skilled midwives helped mothers give birth.
- A poultice of figs was applied to boils.
- Honey was sometimes mixed with oil and applied to a wound.
- Frankincense and myrrh were used to help stop bleeding.

JUSTICE AND THE LAW

In Israel there was no real separation between civil and religious law. Priests, Levites, and elders worked toward the same goals and shared the administration of justice. In the Old Testament, the gate of the city or town was the place where grievances were aired, local quarrels settled, and cases tried. During New Testament times, the high court was the Sanhedrin, a body of 70 men who met in the temple. The authorities in Rome allowed them to pass any sentence under Jewish law except the death penalty.

Major biblical trade routes by land and sea.

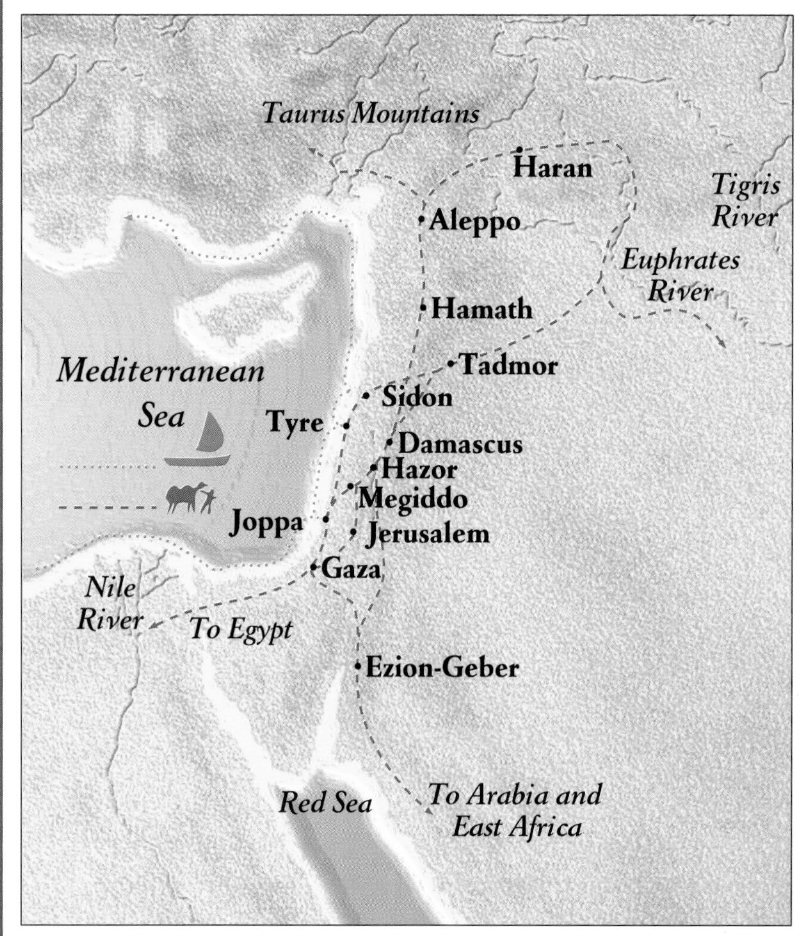

TRADE AND COMMERCE

Even from the time of Abraham, the buying and selling of land took place. It was a practice that was disapproved of, so there were laws to protect the property rights of families.

There were traditional customs connected with purchasing property. In the Book of Ruth, the seller took off his shoe and gave it to the buyer! When Jeremiah bought some land, there was a deed of contract and a copy was stored in a clay jar:

> *And I bought the field at Anathoth from my cousin Hanamel, and weighed out the money to him, seventeen shekels of silver. I signed the deed, sealed it, got witnesses, and weighed the money on scales. Then I took the sealed deed of purchase, containing the terms and conditions, and the open copy . . . and put them in an earthenware jar, in order that they may last for a long time. For thus says the Lord of hosts, the God of Israel: Houses and fields and vineyards shall again be bought in this land.*
>
> Jer 32:9–11, 14–15

Market places for local trade developed around the gates of towns and cities. Animals were sold there, as well as the merchandise of potters and smiths. Visiting foreign merchants also set up their stalls at the community gates.

Eventually, international trade developed as Israel expanded and experienced the growth of industries. As Israel conquered new territories, trade routes opened up; also, political leaders had an interest in buying luxury goods and creating wealth. All these factors contributed to a brisk import and export industry:

Exports	**Imports**
olive oil	tin, lead, silver, copper
honey	peacocks, apes
nuts	timber
aromatic gum	linen
myrrh	purple dyed cloth
wool	gems, gold, ivory
cloth	spices
woven garments	algum wood
wines	cotton, silk
	apples, cheese
	baskets
	slaves

Israel was positioned close to the Mediterranean Sea and between Asia Minor, Egypt, and Arabia. The Israelites took advantage of this location in their use of trade routes by land and sea. In Jerusalem's markets, however, goods were expensive and taxes were high. Jewish rabbis enforced strict business rules.

". . . O merchants of Sidon, . . . your revenue was the grain of Shihor, the harvest of the Nile; you were the merchant of the nations." Isa 23:2,3

In earlier times, trade was done by bartering, then gold and silver were introduced, and eventually money. Although not actually coins, a shekel or talent was a weight of gold or silver. Trading involved shekels and talents, which had to be weighed and measured. In New Testament times, however, there was a regular banking system, and money changers handled currencies of various countries.

This Athenian silver tetradrachma, about equal in value to the Jewish shekel (and equivalent to the American nickel), was worth about one day's wages for labor in New Testament times.

WEIGHTS, MEASURES, AND MONEY

Each time we read about weights, measures, and money in the Bible, we are confronted with terms and amounts that are foreign to our world of ounces, gallons, kilometers, dollars, and bankcards. It is also hard to compare purchasing power across the centuries. Measuring distances back then was quite different from the way we approach and understand it today. In comparing ancient measures with modern equivalents, it is important to note that this table is simply a rough approximation.

In early Bible times, before coins were used, people purchased either by exchanging goods or by paying an agreed weight of silver, gold, or bronze. The seventh century B.C. weights seen here are each inscribed with their value in shekels.

Term	**Biblical equivalent**	**Approximate modern equivalent**
Bath	ephah (dry measure)	38.5 pints
Beka	½ shekel	0.25 ounces
Bushel	8 quarts	15 pints
Cab	¼ seah	3.5 pints
Cor	Homer	48.5 gallons
Cubit		17.5 inches
Daric		$5
Denarius	a day's wage	one penny
Didrachma	½ Jewish shekel	32 cents
Drachma		16 cents
Farthing		¼ cent
Fathom		6 feet

Finger span		¾ inch
Furlong		202 yards
Gerah		1/40 ounce
Hin	1/6 bath	6 pints
Homer	10 baths	90 gallons
Koros		114 gallons
Log		0.5 pint
Measure		9 gallons
Mile (milion)		1,618 yards
Mina	50 shekels	1.6 pounds
Mite		1/8 cent
Omer	1/10 ephah	38.5 pints
Pace		1 yard
Palm		3 inches
Pot		1 pint
Pound (litra)		7.5 pounds
Quadrans		¼ cent
Quart		1.7 pints
Reed	6 cubits	8 feet, 9 inches
Saton		21 pints
Seah		13 pints
Shekel (royal)		0.5 ounce
Shekel (common)		0.4 ounce
Shekel (temple)	½ or ⅓ shekel	0.2 ounce
Span	½ cubit	9 inches
Talent (light)	3,000 shekels	66 pounds
Talent	125 libra	88 pounds

GETTING AROUND IN BIBLE TIMES

Journeys were commonplace in the Bible. Abraham moved from Ur to Canaan, the Israelites wandered around in the desert for several years, and the travels of Paul on land and sea are on record as well. These are just a few of many journeys we read about in the Scriptures. How did people move from one place to another? This is what travel and transport looked like back then:

On Foot: In Bible times most people walked from one place to the next.

Animals: The working animal of the Bible was the donkey. It was the chief means of transport for the average citizen all through biblical history. After about 1000 B.C., camels were used, especially in international trade. Horses were also used in New Testament times.

Caravans: To protect themselves against marauders, traders traveled together in a caravan—donkeys, camels,

"You shall not cheat in measuring length, weight, or quantity. You shall have honest balances, honest weights, an honest ephah, and an honest hin:... You shall keep all my statutes and all my ordinances, and observe them: I am the Lord."
Lev 19:35–37

As early as 3000 B.C., donkeys were domesticated and used in Mesopotamia to draw wheeled carts. When Mary, Joseph, and the baby Jesus left Bethlehem for Egypt, it is possible that they traveled by donkey.

goods, and men—along the main trade routes of the Mediterranean world.

Vehicles: In the Old Testament, horse-drawn chariots were used by armies and nobility. Carts drawn by donkeys were used on farms. In New Testament times, when roads were much better, a variety of chariots were popular. People who could afford it traveled in litters on the narrow city streets. Litters were couches with a framework that had curtains to conceal the traveler. The litter rested on poles which were carried by men or sometimes by horses.

Roads: The Romans built a system of excellent roads connecting the provinces to Rome. Some sections still remain in fine condition today. Even so, they did not go everywhere and many journeys had to be made on the old, unsurfaced roads, worn by many travelers over the centuries.

Inland waterways: Besides the Nile, the Tigris, and the Euphrates, no other rivers in Bible lands were used for travel and transport. Barges with sails were used on the Nile to bring corn to the seaport.

Travel by sea: The seafaring nations of the Old Testament were the Egyptians and the Phoenicians, who dominated travel in the east Mediterranean Sea. During this period, Israel had limited success in maritime trade. By the time of Jesus, Rome controlled the Mediterranean. The Gospels record several times when Jesus crossed the Sea of Galilee by boat, and in Acts Paul's Mediterranean journeys are well documented.

WARFARE, WEAPONS, AND WARRIORS

War was very much a part of the history of Israel—even though God's law protected life and spoke out against murder. From early on, every man was expected to be a soldier to help defend God's "holy people" from the pagan tribes that often attacked them, and to help establish the Israelites in the land promised to them. Although the Israelites were given clear rules of warfare, the biblical record of their history shows repeated violations of these principles. Thus, at times Israel's battles and skirmishes were seen as God's way of punishing them for wrongdoing and faithlessness. Idolatry, superstition, and greed often led the people to disregard God's rules, and by the time of the divided monarchy, the kings of Israel and Judah paid little attention to divine directives concerning warfare.

PRINCIPLES OF WARFARE AMONG THE ISRAELITES

Justice and righteousness: Before going into battle, the people of Israel made sacrifices to God and consulted him as the leader of their army. When they fought under his direction, the battles were considered "holy wars" and were fought to promote and protect divine morality (Jdg 4:14).

The protection of God: In a just war, God promised to protect his people (Dt 20:1–4). The enemies of Israel were considered God's enemies, and the Israelites were expected to trust God for victory.

INSTRUMENTS OF WAR

Item	Reference
Armor	1Sa 17:38
Ax	Jdg 9:48
Battering ram	Eze 4:2
Bow and arrow	Gen 27:3
Chariot	Ex 14:23
Girdle (belt)	2Sa 20:8
Greaves (leg protection)	1Sa 17:6
Helmet	1Sa 17:5
Horse	Ex 14:23
Military engine for throwing rocks and arrows	2Ch 26:14–15
Shield	1Sa 17:7
Sling	1Sa 17:4
Spear	Jdg 5:8
Staff of God	Ex 17:8–9
Stone	1Sa 14:49
Sword	Gen 27:40
Trumpet	Nu 10:9

These ancient fortress walls are located in Dan, a city in the northernmost section of Palestine. Originally known as Laish, it was renamed after it was captured by the Danites.

The presence of God: The ark of the covenant was a symbol of God's presence with the Israelites during battle, and it went before them in their conquest of the Promised Land.

Ritual cleanliness: Before engaging in any "holy war," God's people were instructed to be completely separate from anything that had to do with sin and pollution. In turn, the people made strong vows to the Lord, and made themselves ritually clean (Dt 23:9–14).

Victory was anticipated: The priests blew trumpets before battle commenced to honor God, to show that they expected victory, and to thank God for it (Nu 10:9–10).

Military conscription: In early Israelite history, the army was made up of all men who were 20 years or older (Nu 1:2–3). At other times, particular battles were fought by a limited number of men (Nu 31:3–6).

Exemptions from service: If a man had recently built a home that had not yet been dedicated, he was excused from war. Anyone who had not yet harvested his vineyard was not expected to serve (Dt 20:5–6). Too, newlyweds were exempt for a year (Dt 24:5), and those fearful of serving were excused in case their presence demoralized the troops (Dt 20:8). For religious and family reasons, Levites were not expected to serve, but some of them voluntarily joined the armed forces (Nu 1:48–49).

Peace terms: Before attack, a peace agreement was offered to the enemy, which included subjection of the enemy to forced labor, making them vassals of Israel (Dt 20:10–15). In return for Israel's protection and mercy, the vassal pledged total obedience.

Conquest: Nations outside Palestine that rejected Israel's offer of peace and subjection received death for every man. Women, children, livestock, and everything else became Israel's property (Dt 20:12–14).

Protection of natural resources: The Law of Moses forbade the destruction of fruit trees in pursuit of war (Dt 20:19–20).

Paying the troops: Provisions were made for compensating the armed forces, including allowing them to take booty as their pay (1Sa 30:16). A portion had to be set aside for the Lord's temple (Nu 31:28–30) and for maintenance of government (2Sa 12:30).

WAR DURING BIBLE TIMES

The everyday life of the Israelite family was ordinary and routine, jolted only here and there by the attack and invasion of warriors. Here is a look at what war was like during Bible times:

- The tribes of Israel rallied together to resist and defeat desert tribes who constantly raided Israel.
- When Saul was appointed king, he chose 3,000 men as the first permanent army of Israel.
- King David was a military genius. Under him, the Israelites learned new methods of warfare, and he was the first king to have a bodyguard of great warriors.
- For a long time the army was made up entirely of foot-soldiers.
- The kings built fortresses to protect the land.
- Soldiers usually went to war in spring, when food was available.
- War was rarely declared; the element of surprise was important.
- The ram's horn was blown to gather troops.
- Before battle started, the priest offered a sacrifice to God.
- When Israel was plundered by desert tribes, the invaders rode in on camels, destroyed crops, and took cattle and captives.
- An attack on a city often took place just before dawn.
- From the city walls, defenders of a city hurled down burning arrows, boiling oil, and stones in an attempt to keep the attackers at bay.

"When you go to war against your enemies, and see horses and chariots, an army larger than your own, you shall not be afraid of them; for the Lord your God is with you. . . "
Dt 20:1

***"But to what will I compare this generation? It is like children sitting in the marketplaces and calling to one another,…"* Mt 11:16**

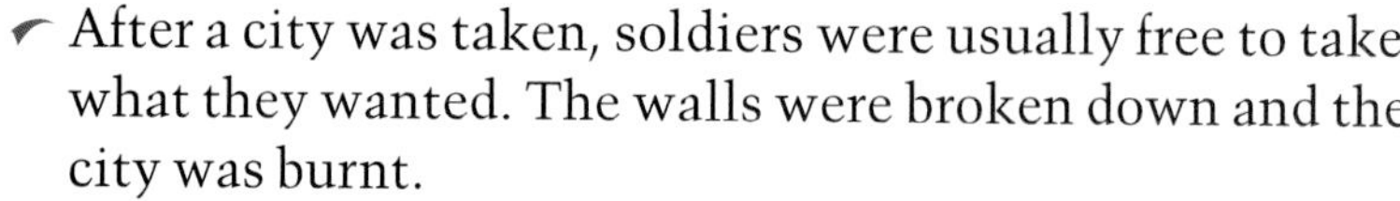

- After a city was taken, soldiers were usually free to take what they wanted. The walls were broken down and the city was burnt.
- The New Testament was not written against a background of war. The Mediterranean world was at peace under Roman government.
- At times, Jews rebelled under Roman authority; these rebellions were quickly crushed.
- Companies of Roman soldiers were stationed within the provinces (for example, Caesarea) to keep the peace.

GAMES, SPORTS, MUSIC, AND DANCING

Although the people in Bible times had to work hard to live, they did have time for social activities. For a start, God had ordered one day in seven—the sabbath—to be set aside from ordinary work. It was a time to rest, relax, and worship him. The wealthy had slaves and servants to do the hard labor so that there was more time for them to choose to do as they pleased. The religious festivals provided opportunity for holidays and fun festivities for everyone.

Just as they do today, most board games in Bible times required throwing dice. Gambling was also a common part of playing games, and from the Gospel accounts, we learn that dice were thrown when the Roman soldiers gambled for Jesus' robe.

Children then played as children do today. Of course, there was no knowledge of baseball and the like, but dolls and board games were common. Children played outside, in the market, and at weddings—even funerals. Children also played ball and target games, and marbles were popular in Egypt.

Casting lots—dice games—were popular with adults, although the religious leaders strongly disapproved of gambling. Shooting with bows and arrows was also a pastime, and children practiced with slings and stones. Wrestling was a favorite Bible sport, and in Babylon they wrestled while holding on to the opponent's belt.

For the Greeks, public entertainment became very popular. People even made a living at it. The Sadducees enjoyed this kind of recreation while the Pharisees believed it to be wrong. King Herod built a stadium for gladiators, and an amphitheater for chariot racing in Jerusalem. Greek games and athletics were also performed in the stadium. In his writings, Paul the apostle uses the strict training of an athlete as an example of living the Christian life effectively:

> *Do you not know that in a race the runners all compete, but only one receives the prize? Run in such a*

way that you may win it. Athletes exercise self-control in all things; they do it to receive a perishable wreath, but we an imperishable one. So I do not run aimlessly, nor do I box as though beating the air; but I punish my body and enslave it, so that after proclaiming to others I myself should not be disqualified.

1Co 9:24–27

Music and dancing were also an important part of the social—and especially the religious—life of the Israelites.

Everyday Life in the Bible—50 Quick Facts

1. Children were encouraged to ask questions and find out about their history and religion.

2. Children were taught to respect their mother even though she had low status in the society.

3. Time was not rushed in the homes of the Jews.

4. In Bible times, the day started at sunrise.

5. The skeletal remains of loved ones were sometimes removed from graves and stored in stone chests called ossuaries.

6. When putting on shoes, the right sandal was always put on or taken off before the left.

7. The Israelites of the Old Testament normally grew their hair long.

Several burial sites have been excavated by archaeologists providing accurate pictures of burial practices during biblical times. Many ancient tombs typically held several generations of a family. The bones of deceased family members were placed in stone boxes (ossuaries), and then stored in long, narrow chambers within the family tomb.

8. In the Old Testament, the days of the month were marked by putting a peg into a bone plate that had three rows of ten holes.

9. As a sign of mourning, men shaved off their beards.

10. The Egyptians were skilled at making beautiful jewelry.

11. For a wedding banquet, oxen and fat calves were killed and cooked.

12. Even though Israelite society was patriarchal, family life was not always oppressive to women.

13. Pastoral life changed very little over the centuries.

14. The four biggest problems for farmers were lack of water, locusts, wild animals, and invading armies.

15. Measurements of distances in the Old Testament were based on a day's journey or even a bowshot.

16. There were twelve months in the calendar, with five days added at the end of the year.

17. In later Bible times, the day started at dusk. A whole day became an evening and a morning.

18. Merchants had two sets of weights: one when they were buying, the other when they were selling. Sometimes they used the weights dishonestly and cheated their customers.

19. In Old Testament times slavery was accepted in Israel.

20. In New Testament times there were both Jewish and non-Jewish slaves in Palestine.

Scales—or balances—were used in Bible times to weigh money, grain, and other merchandise. The Mosaic law warned the Israelites to use honest scales and weights (Lev 19:36), yet the prophet Amos accused God's people of cheating with dishonest balances (Am 8:5).

21. It was common for Israelite farmers to live in a village or fortified town near the farm they owned.

22. In New Testament times the tunic and cloak were the basic dress.

23. Canaanite and Philistine pottery was far more artistic and decorative than Israel's pottery.

24. In the warm climate of the Mediterranean, pork was not eaten because it was considered "unclean" according to the law.

25. The Greek tunic was often sleeveless.

26. Only Roman citizens could wear the Roman toga.

27. In Egyptian schools for adults, many subjects were taught and discipline was strict—no wine, women, or music.

28. It is not known when schools for Hebrew children first began.

29. The Levites taught the Law of God, but the prophets complained that they often did a bad job.

30. By the time of Jesus, Greek education had become world-renowned.

31. The Jews disapproved of Greek athletes because they practiced and competed in the nude!

32. Cavalry and chariots for war were introduced in Israel under Solomon.

33. The soldier's shield was made of a wicker or wooden frame covered with leather, which needed oiling regularly.

34. Since the streets were not clean in most towns, the Romans made pavements and stepping-stones so pedestrians could avoid dirt and mud.

35. When the clans of Israel settled in permanent homes, the normal family unit became smaller—father, mother, and children.

36. Israelite children kept pets, such as birds.

37. Soldiers did not wear sandals. They wore high-topped leather shoes that laced up to the knee.

38. When he was a boy, Jesus probably went to a synagogue school, where he learned the Torah.

39. Grain—the lifeblood of the Mediterranean world—was stored in silos and barns in the ancient world.

40. Leaven (to make the bread rise) was used to make round, flat loaves. The unleavened bread of Bible times was much like today's pita bread.

41. When the Israelites were in the desert wilderness they ate manna and quail, which they found bland and uninteresting compared to the spicy food they ate while in Egypt.

42. If someone fell into debt in Israel, he could sell some property—or even himself into service—to repay the debt.

43. Stoning was a form of execution for certain crimes.

44. Embalming was a uniquely Egyptian invention.

45. The Hebrews used large, standing stone slabs to commemorate important events or covenants. Jacob used a stone for a pillow at Bethel, and then set it up as a memorial of his encounter with God and poured oil on it.

46. An important part of Jewish family life was the blessing of the children by their parents. Today, many Jewish children are blessed at the sabbath meal.

47. The Israelites were taught to make tassels for the corners of their outer garments. They would tie a blue thread to each tassel to help remember God's commandments.

48. The Romans constructed amazing aqueduct systems for cities throughout their empire. Jerusalem's aqueducts brought water into the city from as far away as 25 miles.

49. Execution by crucifixion was usually reserved for the lower classes in Greek and Roman societies. It was a slow, excruciatingly painful, and humiliating death.

50. Washing and bathing were done in all biblical periods for religious and health reasons. The Bethesda Pool in the northeast corner of Jerusalem was an especially popular bathing spot. This pool was believed to possess healing properties.

"So Joseph stored up grain in such abundance—like the sand of the sea—that he stopped measuring it; it was beyond measure."
Gen 41:49

Religion and Worship in the Bible

ROM THE WRITING of the Ten Commandments to the teachings of Jesus, the Bible reveals how God helps to guide humanity with his holy hand. In return, his people strive to show their love and thanksgiving to the Lord. The Israelites built great temples and offered sacrifices to prove their faithfulness. Early Christians humbly prayed together in homes to express their personal commitment to God. Worship—whether by song, poetry, feast, or prayer—is at the heart of the Bible. This chapter examines some of the religious traditions and practices of Jews and Christians.

ISRAEL AT WORSHIP IN THE OLD TESTAMENT

The Israelites loved and worshiped God. They were thankful to him for his goodness to them, and they stood in awe of his great power. At times they were disobedient, turning away from him, his laws, and his leading. Yet they always came back to him in repentance, with renewed hearts ready to worship. Indeed, religion was at the core of the nation's life, and the Israelites responded to the living God in many ways and at many places throughout their history. How did this journey begin?

The biblical practice of making animal sacrifices to God may be traced back to a tradition established after the Fall. This scene depicts the acceptable sacrifice of Abel, the fat portions of the firstlings of his flock, and Cain's unacceptable offering—fruits of the soil (Gen 4:3–7).

FIRST GLIMPSES OF GOD

The first clear act of worship is recorded in Genesis. The children of Adam and Eve brought two types of offerings to God. Cain brought the fruit of the ground and Abel brought an animal offering. God responded to their actions, accepting Abel's offering and rejecting Cain's. This distinct interaction between God and these two established a pattern in worship—that is, God is vitally involved with his followers.

Israel's religion really began when Abraham was called by God to leave his nomadic life, move to a new land, and become the founder of a great people. Abraham obeyed God, and the seed of the nation Israel was born. In his dialog with God, Abraham learned that God honored and wanted animal sacrifices and the worship of his fledgling people.

As God had promised, the new nation continued to grow from Abraham's progeny: Jacob (Abraham's grandson and Isaac's son) and his 12 sons formed the clans of Israel. They were a nation on the move, and wherever they settled they built altars (and sometimes stone monuments) and offered sacrifices to God:

> *Jacob set up a pillar in the place where he had spoken with him, a pillar of stone; and he poured out a drink offering on it, and poured oil on it. So Jacob called the place where God had spoken with him Bethel.*
>
> (Gen 35:14–15)

Certain trees and wells were marked as sacred because they were tangible reminders of God at work in their lives at particular times (Jos 24:26; Gen 16:14).

Worship during this time was often spontaneous. God acted and spoke when he chose, calling a few of his people to worship him at any given time. Altars were outdoors, exposed to the weather, affecting the time of the ceremonies.

The Ten Commandments

1. . . . you shall have no other gods before me.
2. You shall not make for yourself an idol, . . .
3. You shall not make wrongful use of the name of the Lord your God, . . .
4. Remember the Sabbath day, and keep it holy.
5. Honor your father and your mother, so that your days may be long in the land that the Lord your God is giving you.
6. You shall not murder.
7. You shall not commit adultery.
8. You shall not steal.
9. You shall not bear false witness against your neighbor.
10. You shall not covet your neighbor's house; you shall not covet your neighbor's wife . . . or anything that belongs to your neighbor.

The Collection of Law

The Ten Commandments were God's covenant with his people Israel. However, in Israel's law books, Exodus to Deuteronomy, there are three major collection of laws. The first follows the Ten Commandments in Exodus (21–23) and deals with moral, civil, and religious laws. In Leviticus (17–26), the second collection, known as "holiness" laws, focus on worship rituals. The third collection in Deuteronomy (12–25) underscores the detailed commands given in Exodus and Leviticus, and spells out the duties of the king. Given in the form of a sermon by Moses, the third set includes encouragement to the people to keep the Law.

The purpose of the Law was to direct the nation in how to live in relationship with God and others. It was not intended to be an impossible list of do's and don'ts, but was there to provide guidance as its name in Hebrew "torah" (meaning "instruction") suggests.

The Law reflects God's holy, just, and good character. He wanted his chosen people to imitate and reflect his character. Indeed, on several occasions God told Israel to be holy in the same way that he was holy (Lev 11:45; 19:2; 20:26).

Worship During the Time of Moses

Worship changed during the time of Moses and extended far into Jewish history. It began when Moses led God's people out from Egypt. His reason for leaving that country was so that the Israelites could worship God together. Group worship was a new concept for God's people.

In dramatic, surreal style, Russian artist Marc Chagall (1887–1985) portrays Moses receiving the tablets of the Law from above while the people watch in awe. According to biblical history, the Ten Commandments were given to Israel by God at Mount Sinai in 1450 B.C.

When Moses climbed to the top of Mt. Sinai, he received from God much more than the Ten Commandments. Moses received a plan for an enclosed worship center. This place of worship was distinctly different from the altars put together under the open sky. The tabernacle became the place where the Israelites worshiped God on their journey from Egypt to Canaan. Each time the Israelites camped, the newly ordained priests—Aaron, his sons, and men from the clan of Levi—set up the tabernacle for worship. This center of Israel's religious life was a constant reminder that God was always with them. The "tent of meeting," as the tabernacle came to be called, was the dwelling place of God, and the place where he met with his people.

THE TABERNACLE—A MOBILE WORSHIP CENTER

The tabernacle was a large tent supported by a frame of acacia wood. The walls of the tabernacle were made of goat-hair coverings. The roof was made of rams' skins, dyed red.

The inside was draped with colorful violet, purple, and scarlet tapestries that were sewn together into two sets of five curtains. It was divided into two rooms. The smaller, inner room was called the "holy of holies;" it could only be entered by the high priest once a year. An embroidered linen curtain separated this sacred place from the larger room, called the "holy place." The entrance to this room was covered by another linen curtain.

The ark of the covenant stood in the holy of holies. It was a rectangular box made of acacia wood and overlaid with gold. The covenant box contained the two stone tablets of the Ten Commandments, a golden pot of manna, and Aaron's rod. On top of the box was the "mercy seat," a slab of gold with a cherub at each end.

In the holy place, there was an incense altar in front of the curtain. It was made of acacia wood, overlaid with gold, and decorated with horns. The seven-branched lampstand—the only source of light in the tabernacle—was also in this room, along with a table for the Bread of Presence.

The tabernacle was erected in a courtyard, which itself was enclosed by a screen of linen curtains. There was an

The tabernacle, the portable worship center of the Israelites, was first erected in the middle of camp at Mount Sinai by those of the Exodus generation. Eventually it was set up at Shiloh, and later moved to Nob and then Gibeon. Solomon transported the tabernacle and its furnishings to the new Temple, and that is the last mention of these sacred relics (1Ki 8:4).

entrance on one side with an embroidered linen curtain drawn across it. Within the tabernacle courtyard was an altar made of acacia wood and lined in copper. A huge bronze basin called the "laver" was used by the priests for washing their hands and feet each time they were about to enter the tabernacle or offer a sacrifice.

When the Israelites pitched camp the tabernacle was erected at the center, with the priests' tents around it, and beyond that the many tents of the 12 tribes. In the Bible we learn that it was set up at Shiloh soon after the Israelites entered Canaan, then it was moved to Nob, and on to Gibeon. Solomon brought it to his temple, but beyond that we have no knowledge of its whereabouts.

So they brought up the ark of the Lord, the tent of meeting, and all the holy vessels that were in the tent; the priests and the Levites brought them up. King Solomon and all the congregation of Israel, who had assembled before him, were with him before the ark, sacrificing so many sheep and oxen that they could not be counted or numbered. Then the priests brought the ark of the covenant of the Lord to its place, in the inner sanctuary of the house, in the most holy place, underneath the wings of the cherubim.

1Ki 8:4–6

The Age of the Kings

During this period, the Israelites developed a deep sense of regal splendor. They liked the idea of having kings rule over them, but they understood that these earthly rulers were a pale reflection of their heavenly king—the Lord God whom they worshiped. It was in this age that God made a new promise to his people that the dynasty of King David would never end. In this assurance lay the hope of a coming Messiah.

When King Solomon built the temple in Jerusalem, worship and religion finally took place in a permanent home.

From this point on, Jerusalem became the center of worship (although there were unapproved temples and false altars set up in other places). Solomon's temple was patterned after the tabernacle in its layout. It was a place known for its beauty. The cedar paneling, which lined the stone building, was covered with gold. Although not a large structure by today's standard, the temple was likely the largest building the Israelites had constructed up to that time. A detailed account of how the temple was built and furnished is given in 1Kings 5–7.

Solomon's temple, shown here, was not known for its size but for its beauty. Constructed according to Phoenician design, it took seven years to build, and 30,000 laborers from Israel to do the stonework and carpentry alone.

After the temple was completed, King Solomon held a grand dedication service. All the religious leaders and the people of Israel were there. Numerous animals were sacrificed, the ark of the Lord was placed in the inner sanctuary, and the cloud of God's glory filled the temple. It was a wonderful moment in Israel's religious history, and King Solomon himself led the worship, his hands spread out to heaven:

> *"Blessed be the Lord, who has given rest to his people Israel according to all that he promised; not one word has failed of all his good promise, which he spoke through his servant Moses."*
>
> 1Ki 8:56

THE PROPHETS

The prophets' job was to keep Israel true to the faith God had given his people. They spoke out fearlessly about false religion, empty rituals, and wrong behavior. This group was called to touch the conscience of Israel when the nation strayed from the Lord: they warned of God's punishing hand, encouraged repentance, and offered God's hope for a bright future.

These messengers of God were appointed by him for a particular task and place, and they were given a specific message. In their ministry they saw visions; they preached sermons; they used parables, drama, and poetry to get God's message across—often to a hostile audience.

From the time of Samuel, the prophets came and went at crisis points in Israel's history. Their tasks were many and

WHO'S WHO AMONG THE PROPHETS

The words and actions of some of the prophets were second-hand accounts recorded in the Scriptures by others. Some prophets, however, wrote their own stories. This partial list of biblical prophets includes both writers and non-writers with a brief description of their ministry.

Prophet	Description	Reference
Amos	spoke out against social injustice and unrighteousness	*Am 5:24*
Anna	a prayer warrior who foretold the coming of Jesus, the Messiah	*Lk 2:36–38*
Deborah	predicted the victory of Barak over the Canaanites	*Jdg 4:4–9*
Elijah	opposed Baal worship in the time of Ahab and Jezebel	*1Ki 17–2Ki 2*
Elisha	Elijah's successor who performed many miracles and predicted the salvation of Samaria	*2Ki 2–13*
Enoch	prophesied before the Flood about God's judgment of sin	*Jude 1:14–15*
Ezekiel	foretold in dramatic action the siege of Jerusalem	*Eze 4–5*
Gad	told David about the kind of judgment that would fall upon him for his sin in numbering the people	*2Sa 24*
Hosea	declared God's great, forgiving love for unfaithful Israel	*Hos 11:8–9*
Huldah	predicted the prosperous reign of King Josiah	*2Ch 34*
Isaiah	spoke out against outward worship that was not rooted in right, holy living	*Isa 6:5–9*
Jeremiah	predicted captivity and disaster, but also the promise of restoration for Jerusalem	*Jer 13–17;30–33*
Joel	offered the hope that if Israel repented there would be a coming day of God's blessing	*Joel 2:28, 32*
Jonah	a rebellious prophet, God gave Jonah a second chance and showed mercy to the people of Nineveh	*Jnh 3*
Nathan	condemned King David for his adultery with Bathsheba	*2Sa 12*
Zechariah	prophesied about the promise of blessing for Jerusalem and the coming Day of the Lord	*Zec 8, 14*

varied. It was through Samuel that God appointed Saul—and later David—as Israel's leaders. Through Elijah, God successfully challenged Israel's rampant worship of the Canaanite gods Baal and Asherah, and the work of their pagan prophets in the land of Israel. Through Elijah and his successor Elisha, many miracles of healing were performed.

The Exile was a crisis point in Israel's history, and many prophets spoke out before, during, and after this period. The wayward Israelites had broken faith with God countless times, and after several warnings and calls to repentance delivered by the prophets, God allowed his beloved Israel to be taken captive.

LESSONS LEARNED DURING THE EXILE

On the willows there we hung up our harps . . . How could we sing the Lord's song in a foreign land? Ps 137:2, 4

Captivity in Babylon was hard for the Israelites. Their city and temple were destroyed, and they were taken thousands of miles away from Jerusalem to a new land. It's no wonder they sat down by the rivers of Babylon and wept when they remembered home. Even then, God's people used this time of hardship wisely. They rediscovered who they were as the people of God, and they renewed their relationship with him. Many Israelites saw this period as a time of purification and discipline for the nation.

After 70 years, small groups of Israelites returned home from captivity to rebuild the temple in Jerusalem. Those that returned (probably less than 75,000) were determined to follow the Law in serving God. They returned to strict observance of the Sabbath, to the ritual of circumcision, and to following the Jewish food laws.

PRIESTS WHO MADE A DIFFERENCE

Melchizedek	a great king-priest who offered bread and wine to the war-weary Abraham	*Gen 14*
Aaron	head of the priesthood and in charge of national worship	*Ex 28*
Eli	the temple priest at Shiloh who raised Samuel	*1Sa 1–4*
Zadok	loyal high priest in David's court who also anointed Solomon king	*2Sa 15*
Jehoiada	high priest who saved Joash from the murderous Queen Athaliah	*2Ki 11–12*
Azariah	high priest who stopped King Uzziah when the arrogant ruler tried to take over the duties of a priest	*2Ch 26*
Hilkiah	high priest who cleared the temple of all traces of Baal worship during the reign of Josiah	*2Ki 22–23*
Jeshua	Judah's first high priest following the Exile	Ezr 2
Ezra	outstanding priest, teacher, and scribe during the rebuilding of Jerusalem's walls	*Ezr 7*
Eliashib	high priest during the days of Nehemiah who rebuilt the Sheep Gate in Jerusalem	*Ne 3; 13*

THE WORK OF PRIESTS

The priests were considered the most "holy" group within Israel. They were the ones in charge of the tabernacle and temple, and only they could offer sacrifices. Priests were originally appointed from the family of Aaron (the brother of Moses), and the priesthood continued through his descendants. Within this group, the "high priest" was the only individual allowed to enter the holiest place once a year, on the Day of Atonement. Subordinate to the priests were the Levites, the tribe set apart for religious duties. They had to be supported by the other clans, who gave a tenth of all their harvests and livestock for the work of God.

Most of the work of priests and Levites centered around tabernacle and temple sacrifices and worship. A group from the Levites formed the temple choirs and may have composed some of the Psalms we have in our Bible. The priests and Levites were also responsible for deciding when to go out to battle in the name of God. But perhaps the most important task of these religious leaders was to teach the people the Law of God. Unfortunately, the prophets often had to scold these messengers of God for failing to teach true knowledge of God.

WHAT THE PRIESTS WORE

The high priest wore elaborate and splendid robes of gold, blue, purple, and scarlet. He wore an ephod (similar to a waistcoat) with shoulder straps. Each shoulder strap had an onyx stone engraved with the names of six of the tribes of Israel; these were carried before the Lord whenever the high priest entered the tabernacle or temple.

Attached to the ephod shoulder straps by rings and gold chains was a breastplate made of linen in gold, blue, purple, and scarlet. It had four rows of stones, each stone representing one of the 12 tribes. The breastplate was a double square into which the "Urim" and "Thummim" could be placed. These were sacred stones that the priest used to determine God's will for the people. If the Thummim was picked from the pouch in response to a question, the answer from God was "yes"; if the Urim was selected, the answer was "no."

Under the ephod, the high priest also wore a blue or velvet robe with gold bells attached to the skirts. This made a wonderful sound as he moved about the house of

Aaron's priestly vestments, described in Exodus 28, included a breastplate with four rows of precious stones, 12 stones in all, each representing one of the sons of Israel. The Bible lists the names of the stones but does not identify the order of the names to be inscribed on them. Attempting to identify a certain stone with a particular tribe would be guesswork.

God specified the design of the high priest's garments in Exodus 28. These robes were almost royal in character. They were gold, blue, purple, and scarlet and made of the finest linen. The priest also wore an ephod (somewhat like a kilt) that had bells on its skirts, a breastpiece, and a turban with an engraved insignia.

the Lord. He also had a coat and turban made of fine linen. Affixed to the turban was a plate of pure gold on which was engraved "Holy to the Lord."

Compared to the garb of the high priests, the clothing of the other priests seemed almost ordinary. The main distinctive item was the sash each priest wore, which was decorated according to his rank.

SACRIFICES AND THEIR PURPOSE

The practice of sacrificing offerings to the Lord was an ancient and basic part of Jewish religion and worship. The Book of Leviticus spells out the details and purpose of the sacrifices. Here are five basic facts:

1. A sacrifice was always made to God alone; he deserved the best that could be offered.
2. Sacrificing was a way given by God for humans to make peace with him.
3. Sacrifices were for everyone.
4. Sacrifices could not take away sin. They were an act of obedience and a mark of repentance. Direct pardon could only come from God.
5. Often, the death of an animal was seen as a substitution for the person who brought the sacrifice. Wrongdoing that deserved death could not be atoned for by sacrifice, but after repenting of sin and obtaining God's forgiveness, the sacrifice was offered as a sign of sorrow for sin.

"Then Noah built an altar to the Lord, and took of every clean animal and of every clean bird, and offered burnt offerings on the altar" (Gen 8:20).

TYPES OF SACRIFICES

Burnt offering: A whole animal—except for the skin, which went to the priests—in perfect condition was sacrificed. The blood of the animal was sprinkled on the altar to dedicate the sacrifice to God.

Grain offering: This offering of flour, grain, or baked cakes along with oil and frankincense was a goodwill offering to God. Part of it was burnt on the altar, the rest was a contribution to the priests.

Offering of well-being: This offering was similar to a burnt offering, except here only the fat (the best portion as far as the Israelites were concerned) was burnt on the altar. The meat was shared by the family offering the sacrifice. Since God shared in the sacrifice too, it was considered a friendship meal with him.

Offering for sin: When someone sinned against another person or against God, this sin defiled the holy place of the tabernacle or temple, which then had to be cleansed. The blood of the animal was sprinkled about to symbolize that the contamination had been removed by the death that had taken place. Some of the meat was given to the priest. When he ate the meat without incident, the worshiper took this as a sign that God had accepted his act of repentance.

FESTIVALS

Religious festivals played a significant part of Jewish life and were connected to the seasons and the farmer's year. Most of the festivals and holy days existed from Israel's earliest history (the celebration of Purim and Hanukkah began to be observed much later). After the seventh century B.C. these festivals were held only in Jerusalem. Crowds of pilgrims would descend on the city for these annual events of thanksgiving and reflection. There would be rejoicing, feasting, music, sacrifices, and occasions to honor God for all his blessings.

Passover or Unleavened Bread: One of the most important Jewish festivals, it served as a reminder of the time God rescued the Israelites from Egypt, and spared the lives of firstborn Jewish children. Celebrated in the Jewish month of Nisan (March/April), celebrations began in the evening when each family sacrificed a lamb and ate unleavened bread at the Passover meal. This remains one of the most important Jewish festivals today (Ex 12).

Firstfruits: Celebrated during Nisan, this ceremony was held on the last day of the Festival of Unleavened Bread. The first sheaf of the barley harvest was given to God (Lev 23:9–14).

Weeks: This festival took place seven weeks (or fifty days) after Passover

THE CALENDAR AND FESTIVALS

Calendar		**Farmer's Almanac**	**Festivals**
Month 1	Nisan	Barley harvest	Passover or Unleavened bread, Firstfruits
Month 2	Lyyar	General harvest	
Month 3	Sivan	Vine tending	Weeks, Pentecost
Month 4	Tammuz	First ripe grapes	
Month 5	Ab	Summer fruit	
Month 6	Elul	Olive harvest	
Month 7	Tishri	Ploughing	New Year, Trumpets, Day of Atonement, Tabernacles or Booths
Month 8	Heshvan	Grain planting	
Month 9	Kislev		Dedication or Lights
Month 10	Tebeth	Spring growth	
Month 11	Shebat	Winter figs	
Month 12	Adar	Pulling flax	Purim

> ***It shall be to you a sabbath of complete rest, and you shall deny yourselves; on the ninth day of the month at evening, from evening to evening you shall keep your sabbath.***
> *Lev 23:32*

and it marked the end of the grain harvest. It was celebrated during the month of Sivan (May/June). Later on it became known as Pentecost (from the Greek word "fiftieth"). People celebrated God's gifts at harvest, and the priest offered animal sacrifices and two loaves of bread made from new flour (Lev 23:15–21).

Trumpets: On the first day of Tishri (September/October), the seventh month of the Jewish year, the trumpets sounded for a special celebration. It marked the beginning of the most solemn month of the year, and was a day of rest, worship, and offerings. After the Exile, it became a religious festival (known as Rosh Hashanah) to mark the New Year (Nu 29:1–2).

Day of Atonement (Yom Kippur): Also commemorated during the month of Tishri, this marked a national day of mourning for Israel. The nation confessed their sin and asked for God's forgiveness. The priests offered a sacrifice for their own sin, and a second sacrifice for the sin of the people. This was the only time of year when the high priest (dressed in white linen) entered the inner sanctuary, the most holy place of the tabernacle or temple. There he sprinkled blood from the sacrifice. Then, after laying his hand on a live goat (a "scapegoat"), the high priest let it go free in the desert as a sign that the sin of the people had been taken away (Lev 16).

Tabernacles or Booths: This week-long festival, held during the busy month of Tishri, was a popular and joyful celebration marking the end of the fruit crop harvest. Water was poured out and prayers offered for the coming season. Part of the festivities included camping out in gardens and on rooftops in tents or huts made from tree branches as a reminder of the time when Israel lived in tents in the desert (Lev 23:39–43).

Dedication or Lights: Celebrated today as Hanukkah during the month of December (Kislev), this festival called to remembrance the cleansing and rededication of the temple by Judas Maccabaeus in 164 B.C. after it had been desecrated by Antiochus IV Epiphanes, the Syrian ruler. During the festival, lamps were placed in houses and synagogues each evening (1Mac 4:52–59).

Purim: This festival—celebrated during Adar (February/March)—traced its roots to the time when Esther and her cousin, Mordecai, saved the Jews from massacre during the reign of the Persian King Xerxes (Ahasuerus). The name of the celebration refers to the lots cast by Haman, the king's hateful chief minister, to decide the day of the bloodbath (Est 9).

Besides annual festivals, Israel regularly had other celebrations, the most important being the Sabbath. This was

commemorated every seventh day and was set apart for rest, remembering God's goodness, and serving him (Isa 58:13–14).

The appearance of the new moon marked the beginning of each month, and at this time trumpets were sounded and sacrifices were made. This helped the Israelites remember that God had created an ordered world. On this monthly public holiday there were special meals and religious instruction (Nu 10:10).

Every seventh year was designated as a time of rest for cultivated land. Thus fields lay fallow seven years after they were sown. Anything that grew in the seventh year could be harvested by the poor. This was a reminder to Israel that the land ultimately belonged to God, not to them (Lev 25:1–7).

The year of Jubilee occurred every 50 years. The Law intended this to be a time when land and property were returned to original owners, slaves would go free, debts would be canceled, and the land allowed to lie fallow. The law of Jubilee was a wonderful idea but difficult to enforce. It finally came to be looked on as a time that only God himself could bring about. It was a time promised by the prophet Isaiah and declared by Jesus to have arrived (Isa 61:1–2; Lk 4:16–21).

The Jewish celebration on the 14th and 15th days of the month before Passover is known as the Feast of Esther (Purim). It marks the deliverance of the Hebrews through the efforts of Mordecai and Esther from the plot of Haman to exterminate God's holy people (Es 9). An important holiday, it continues to be celebrated among Jews today.

Fasts

Part of Israel's religion included fasting. Praying and fasting were often done together as a sign of repentance. Fasting meant having nothing to eat or drink. Other rituals connected with fasting included tearing clothing, wearing sackcloth and ashes, and remaining unwashed.

However, only one day annually was set apart for a national fast in the Old Testament laws. This was the Day of Atonement. During the Exile, special fasts were held to mourn the destruction of the temple. After this period in Israel's history, other fasts were held to remember the siege of Jerusalem and the final capture of the city.

Thus says the Lord of hosts: The fast of the fourth month, and the fast of the fifth, and the fast of the seventh, and the fast of the tenth, shall be seasons of joy and gladness, and cheerful festivals for the house of Judah: therefore love truth and peace.

Zec 8:19

Music and Worship

Music was an important part of everyday life among the Israelites and surrounding cultures. Social functions were not complete without music, and it played an important role in festivals, weddings, funerals, and even war. Although Hebrew music tended to be rhythmic rather than melodic, music-making developed to serve the specific needs of the people. For example, the shofar was an ideal instrument for sounding signals or alarms; lighthearted social occasions called for the lilting tones of the pipe; and some psalms were best put to set tunes.

Even though God directed the development of Israel's religious and social life, music, like other aspects of its culture, was influenced by surrounding societies. King Solomon married an

Music was always an important part of Israel's everyday life. In this painting by Dutch artist Jan DeBray, the musician David plays the lyre for King Saul to help soothe the monarch's troubled heart and mind (1Sa 16).

Egyptian woman whose dowry included 1,000 musical instruments! (It is likely she brought her own musicians to the new culture to play these instruments in the traditional Egyptian manner.)

Those who ministered in the temple took care, however, to avoid using music and instruments associated with pagan worship. The prophet Amos judged those "who sing idle songs to the sound of the harp" (Am 6:5). There were definite ideas about music suitable for worship.

Music served as an accompaniment to many religious rituals prescribed by the Lord. There were singers and musicians who took part in temple worship. Only certain instruments were allowed in the temple orchestra, and the singers were males from Levite families.

The Psalms—religious songs—were written to be sung, and many of them carry notes regarding tunes and musical directions. The term "selah," included in many Psalms, probably marked some kind of musical interlude. Some Psalms were jubilant songs that encouraged worship with the backing of a full orchestra; other Psalms were written for processions to sing to cel-

MUSICAL INSTRUMENTS OF THE DAY

Instrument	Description
Percussion Instruments	
Bells	Tiny, pure gold bells were fastened to the hem of the high priest's robe. They made a sound when they touched each other.
Cymbals	Made of copper, they were the only percussion instrument in temple orchestras.
Rattler-sistrum	A handle was attached to a small U-shaped frame, and small objects were strung on bars stretched across the frame to make noise.
Timbrel	Similar to a tambourine, it was carried and beaten by the hand.
Gong	Made of metal, it was used for weddings and other celebrations.
Stringed Instruments	
Harp	Lavishly made, it was used in the temple orchestra. (Some Bibles use viol, psaltery, or dulcimer to refer to the harp.)
Lute	This three-stringed triangular instrument was usually played by women.
Lyre	A small version of this harplike instrument (kinnor) produced a pleasing sound, and was used in secular and sacred settings. Skilled artisans made lyres of silver or ivory and decorated them extravagantly.
Trigon	Probably borrowed from the Babylonians, this was not a common instrument in Israel.
Wind Instruments	
Clarinet	A primitive version of today's clarinet, this instrument was popular at banquets, weddings, and funerals.
Flute	A big pipe with a mouthpiece, the biblical flute produced a sound rather like an oboe. Because of its sharp, penetrating sound, this instrument was often used in processions.
Pipe	Used in the temple for religious celebrations and social events. (Some Bibles use the terms organ and flute to refer to the pipe.)
Shophar, Shofar	This instrument, best known as a "ram's horn," was used to give signals and announce special events. (Some Bibles use trumpet, horn, and cornet.)
Trumpet	Bones, shell, or metals were used to make trumpets. These instruments were often used in pairs, and their high, shrill sounds announced battles and ambush, and called people to assemble for various secular and religious events. Similar to the shophar, trumpets were used by the priests.

ebrate a victory or pilgrimage; still others were probably sung as pilgrims wended their way up to Jerusalem for religious festivals and worship (Ps 120–134).

Your solemn processions are seen, O God,
the processions of my God, my King, into the
sanctuary—the singers in front, the musicians last,
between them girls playing tambourines:
"Bless God in the great congregation,
the Lord, O you who are of Israel's fountain!"
Ps 68:24–26

In the Scriptures, the use of cymbals is restricted to religious rites. These clanging, percussive instruments were a permanent part of the temple orchestra, instituted in David's time. The cymbals shown here are from Anatolia, Turkey, about 2100 B.C., and the limestone fragment depicts a participant in the dedication of a temple in ancient Ur.

Beyond temple worship, music was a part of other religious functions, and instruments not allowed in the temple were used at these events, particularly feast days. Music often led the festivities, and music, dancing, and singing were part of the celebration. Women singers and musicians were allowed to take part in these events.

RELIGION BETWEEN THE TESTAMENTS—TEN QUICK FACTS

- Under Persian rule, the temple at Jerusalem was maintained on a lavish scale (Ezr 1; 6:1–12).
- During the age of the Greeks, Jewish religion (Judaism) was strongly influenced by Greek culture (Hellenism).
- Two parties arose among Jews with regard to Greek religion: those who embraced the foreign ways (Hellenists), and conservative Jews (Hasidim), who strongly believed that hellenism and Judaism were mutually exclusive.
- With the support of some leading Jewish families, Antiochus IV Epiphanes transformed Jerusalem into a Greek city. He forbade the practice of Jewish religion and desecrated the temple.
- Judas Maccabaeus built a new altar to replace the one defiled by Antiochus, and the temple was rededicated in 164 B.C. (1Mac 1–4).
- From 165–63 B.C. Judea was an independent state ruled by the Hasmonean priest-kings.
- By the time of Jesus, the Roman conquest had long taken place and Judea was a Roman province.
- At this time, Jewish religious belief turned toward the future. Many hoped for the coming of the warrior Messiah who would rid the Jews of hated foreign rule.
- This was an era when Jews studied and debated ideas about the resurrection, angels, demons, and other apocalyptic themes.

The Law was studied and extended as never before, and a variety of religious groups came into being.

JEWISH RELIGION IN THE NEW TESTAMENT

The world to which Jesus came was in the hands of the Romans, and although they encouraged Greek culture, they allowed the Jews to practice their own religion. During this time, the temple in Jerusalem was still at the heart of Israel's worship. Pilgrims trekked there for the great annual festivals, sacrifices were offered there, and it was the center of religious instruction.

Jews agreed on the authority of the Torah (the Law) and the importance of temple sacrifices, yet a number of groups within the nation had different ideas on the way these beliefs should be worked out in everyday life.

The Hasidim: These were faithful followers of the Law who resisted the influence of Greek ideas and culture into the Jewish way of life. Many of them joined the sects of the Essenes and the Pharisees.

In this colorful representation by Peter Paul Rubens (1577–1640), Jesus has dinner in the Pharisee's house. A sinful woman, forgiven by Jesus, anoints his feet with ointment because of her deep gratitude (Lk 7).

The Pharisees: The Pharisee sect grew out of the Hasidim of an earlier time. As well as the Torah, the Pharisees accepted the oral law that had grown up around it, and tried hard to live up to a multitude of burdensome rules. They expected others to do the same, and were contemptuous of "sinners" who did not abide by their strict codes. The Pharisees (meaning "separated ones") wanted above all else to avoid "uncleanness" so they devoted themselves to keeping each minute detail of every ritual and moral commandment. Besides this preoccupation with the letter of the law, the Pharisees also believed in apocalyptic teaching, angels, and the resurrection.

The Sadducees: Most Sadducees were members of influential priestly families. They had political standing and believed in working along with the ruling power. They accepted only the first five books of the Bible as their Scripture, and would not accept the oral law that was embraced by the Pharisees, or any beliefs that were not taught in the Torah. They did not believe in angels, demons, the resurrection, or apocalyptic predictions of the last days. They did, however, emphasize the sacrifices at the temple and the role of the priests.

For in every city, for generations past, Moses has had those who proclaim him, for he has been read aloud every sabbath in the synagogues. Ac 15:21

The Essenes: This small sect had emerged in the second century B.C. to protest Greek influence on Jewish religion. The Essenes were even stricter than the Pharisees about keeping the Law. Disillusioned with Jewish society and—in their view—the nation's loose interpretation of the Law, they formed their own monastic communities. There they studied the Torah and made careful copies of it as they waited for the coming of the Messiah. The Jewish settlement at Qumran (near the Dead Sea) was probably an Essene commune.

The Zealots: These nationalists (similar in spirit to the Maccabean revolutionaries) firmly believed that only God was their authority. They refused to pay taxes to the Romans and prepared themselves for the war that would usher in God's kingdom. They led several guerilla revolts against the Roman authorities. Unfortunately, one of their revolts ended with the Roman destruction of Jerusalem in 70 A.D.

The Scribes: Originally, scribes wrote down the words of others. Then they became copyists and explainers of the Law. By the time of Jesus, they had become official interpreters of the Law and decided how it should be applied to everyday life. The scribes were an influential group of people, many of whom belonged to the Sanhedrin (the supreme Jewish court).

The synagogue, a place of worship and prayer for Jewish believers, came into being during the Babylonian captivity. It flourished in Palestine and scattered Jewish communities thereafter. Pictured here is the modern Great Jerusalem Synagogue, Israel.

JEWISH WORSHIP IN THE SYNAGOGUE

The synagogue probably came into being during the Exile when the Jews were without the temple and living far away from Jerusalem. By the time of Jesus, the local synagogue was an important place for prayers and Scripture readings on the Sabbath. The synagogue itself was a plain, practical building that served as the local school, the center for local government, as well as a place for worship.

Inside each synagogue was a chest in which the scrolls of the Law were kept. During services, the religious leaders sat in front of the chest facing the people. The men sat in one section, the women in another. The synagogue was regularly attended by Jesus, and it was a popular place during the ministry of the apostle Paul.

Jewish Religion and Everyday Life

The practice of Jewish religion in New Testament times was not very different from the past. Festivals, sacrifices, and fasting were basic components, as were tithing, food laws, and rituals concerning uncleanness. In the home, Jews were expected to pray 18 benedictions each morning, afternoon, and evening; and the father of the household said a blessing before every meal. However, not all Jews observed these rituals and laws.

After the Exile, some Jews settled in different parts of the Persian Empire. In New Testament times, there were probably more Jews living in Alexandria than Jerusalem. These Jews who moved away from Palestine were known as the Jews of the Dispersion (or Diaspora). Synagogue worship kept their faith alive, but their language was Greek and they used the Septuagint (the Greek translation of the Old Testament) as their Scriptures. They were less strict than their counterparts in Palestine, influenced as they were by the local culture.

Herod's Temple

When the Jews returned to Jerusalem to rebuild Solomon's temple, which had been destroyed earlier, they completed the work in 515 B.C. Although it was in use for 500 years, little is known about this second temple (Zerubbabel's). We do know that it was desecrated by the Syrians, then restored and rededicated under Maccabean rule three years later (an event still remembered at the Jewish festival of Hanukkah).

In 20 B.C. King Herod the Great started to build yet another temple in Jerusalem. He wanted to impress the Roman world and win the hearts of the Jews. Ten years later the main construction was complete, but work continued for many years following.

This model gives us a good idea of what Herod the Great's magnificent temple looked like in the time of Jesus. Early church historian Josephus has provided detailed information on Herod's expansion and beautification of Jerusalem's second temple—no doubt one of the wonders of the ancient world. The temple was destroyed by the Romans in 70 A.D.

Early visitors at the manger were a group of shepherds who had been tending their flocks on the Bethlehem hills. Angels announced to them the birth of the Messiah, and the shepherds hurried to the place where the kingly infant was born.

This third temple, although built on the same plan as Solomon's, was the most extravagant ever seen. It was a dazzling, gigantic structure, with special areas for Jews and non-Jews, a court designated for women, and the Court of Israel for Jewish men. Herod's temple was destroyed by the Romans at the time of the Jewish rebellion in 70 A.D. and its priceless treasures were taken back to Rome.

THE LIFE AND MESSAGE OF JESUS

Jesus made an impact on the Jewish world from the moment he was born (about 5 B.C.). Angels announced the event, a bright star or comet appeared to mark the occasion, and shepherds came to honor him. When Jesus was presented in the temple soon after birth, Simeon, devoutly religious, and Anna, a prophet, were expecting him. They blessed the baby and praised God for the coming of the promised Messiah.

Some time later, wise men from the East hurried to Judah to worship the young king of the Jews. The ailing King Herod was threatened by news of the boy's arrival, and decreed that all Jewish male toddlers were to be killed. Joseph and Mary, the parents of Jesus, safely whisked him away out of Herod's reach.

After Herod died, the family of Jesus moved to Nazareth, where Jesus grew up. At twelve years of age, Jesus amazed the teachers of the law at the temple. Clearly, he had an understanding of the content and meaning of the Scriptures far beyond his young years. Even then, Jesus knew that he was unique and that God had called him to do special business.

When he was 30, Jesus began his ministry. This

THE BEATITUDES

Jesus pronounced blessings ("beatitudes") on the hungry, poor, and just. Those whose lives depend on God are happy and blessed, and the kingdom of God belongs to them.

"Blessed are the poor in spirit, for theirs is the kingdom of heaven."
"Blessed are those who mourn, for they will be comforted."
"Blessed are the meek, for they will inherit the earth."
"Blessed are those who hunger and thirst for righteousness, for they will be filled."
"Blessed are the merciful, for they will receive mercy."
"Blessed are the pure in heart, for they will see God."
"Blessed are the peacemakers, for they will be called children of God."
"Blessed are those who are persecuted for righteousness' sake, for theirs is the kingdom of heaven."
Mt 5:3–10

period was marked by unique events, just as his birth had been. Jesus was baptized by John the Baptist in the River Jordan, and God opened up the heavens, sent the Holy Spirit down on Jesus like a dove, and blessed his "Son, the Beloved" (Mt 3). Then Jesus spent forty days of fasting in the wilderness. There he was tempted by the devil, but resisted—appealing to the truth of the Scriptures to withstand the attack. The devil left in defeat, and angels came to take care of Jesus. From this point on, the ministry of Jesus began in earnest.

The Parables of Jesus

Much of Jesus' teaching was given in the form of stories known as parables. These were vignettes about everyday life—each tied to a spiritual truth or principle.

	Matthew	Mark	Luke
Lamp under the bushel basket	5:14–15	4:21–22	8:16
Houses on rock and sand	7:24–27		6:47–49
Unshrunk cloth on an old cloak	9:16	2:21	5:36
New wine in old wineskins	9:17	2:22	5:37–38
Sower, seeds, and soils	13:3–8	4:3–8	8:5–8
Tiny mustard seed	13:31–32	4:30–32	13:18–19
Weeds	13:24–30		
Yeast (leaven)	13:33		13:20–21
Treasure hidden in a field	13:44		
One pearl of great value	13:45–46		
Net thrown into the sea	13:47–48		
One sheep that went astray	18:12–13		15:4–6
King and his slaves	18:23–24		
Landowner and his laborers	20:1–16		
Man and his two sons	21:28–31		
Landowner and his tenants	21:33–41	12:1–9	20:9–16
Wedding banquet and guests	22:2–14		
Sign of the fig tree	24:32–33	13:28–29	21:29–30
Ten bridesmaids	25:1–13		
Talents (or Pounds)	25:14–30		19:12–27
Sheep and Goats	25:31–46		
Seed and harvest		4:26–29	
Creditor and debtors			7:41–43
Good Samaritan			10:30–37
Friend in need			11:5–8
Rich Fool			12:16–21
Watchful servants			12:35–40
Faithful slave			12:42–48
Fig tree without fruit			13:6–9
Places of honor at the banquet			14:7–14
Great dinner and the reluctant guests			14:16–24
Estimating the cost			14:28–33
Lost coin			15:8–10
Prodigal son			15:11–32
Dishonest manager			16:1–8
Rich man and Lazarus			16:19–31
Master and slave			17:7–10
Widow and the unjust judge			18:2–5
Pharisee and tax collector			18:10–14

The Teachings of Jesus

- The core of the message of Jesus was that the "kingdom of God" (the rule of God in people's lives) had arrived (Lk 17:21). This message was for everyone for the asking, even the poor and the beggars on the street.
- Jesus told people to repent (turn away from their sins) and believe in the good news that he came to bring (Mk 1:15).
- Jesus taught that he was the way to God. In order to have eternal life, people were to put their trust in him, the Son of God. Jesus even declared that "The Father and I are one." (Jn 10:30).

- Jesus brought joy to religious life (Mt 6:16–18).
- According to the Gospels, Jesus performed more than 30 miracles, including bringing the dead back to life.
- Jesus selected 12 disciples to learn from him, and to carry on his ministry after him (Mt 10).
- Jesus taught his hearers to approach God personally, as a child approaches his or her earthly Father. This was a revolutionary idea to many people.
- Jesus taught his followers how to pray (Lk 11:1–4).
- Jesus treated women and children with unique dignity and respect.
- Jesus regularly attended the local synagogue and went to the festivals in Jerusalem.
- Jesus did not bring a new system of laws; he came to fulfill the Law, establish a new covenant, and bring the hope of salvation (Mt 5:17).
- New believers were expected to follow Christ's example: meet with other converts, pray, study the Scriptures, and speak to others about him.
- The Lord's Supper was instituted by Jesus so that his followers would remember his death when they shared bread and wine together (Lk 22:14–20).

When Jesus began his ministry, one of his first tasks was to select a group of 12 men who would become his close followers, helpers, and friends. In this representation by 19th-century Danish artist Christian Dalsgaard, Jesus calls his first disciples.

CHRISTIAN WORSHIP IN NEW TESTAMENT TIMES

The new Christians—as the followers of Christ came to be called in the Book of Acts (11:26)—drew much from their Jewish background for their forms of worship. They also created new practices. They met in the temple for fellowship and worship, but they also met in the homes of believers for the same purpose.

It soon became clear to the early Christians that temple sacrifices were no longer necessary; the death of Jesus was the final and complete sacrifice for sin. Christians began to break away from temple worship, especially when they came into conflict with practicing Jews. However, for decades many Jewish Christians continued to attend the synagogue, and the apostle Paul often preached and worshiped there—until he was forced out!

Other elements of New Testament worship were unique to the first Christians; some were new interpretations of old rituals. The following are the most significant practices:

- The Jewish Passover ritual is reflected in the Lord's Supper practiced by Christians. At first this "breaking of bread" was part of an actual meal that took place in homes. Eventually it moved from homes to a special building and was no longer part of a meal.
- The synagogue service, with its prayer, Bible reading, and sermon became the model for early Christian services.
- The Christian rite of baptizing new converts came from a Jewish practice that developed during the time between the Testaments. Non-Jews who became converts to Judaism were baptized in water as a sign of cleansing. John the Baptist baptized many people as a sign of their repentance and inward cleansing by God. Christian baptism was regarded as a symbolic death, burial, and resurrection reflecting the work of Christ on behalf of the believer.

The Law required washing with water for ritual purification. During the time of Jesus, the Jews used bathing pools for this purpose. However, John's baptism went beyond these requirements. His baptism was a public act of repentance and commitment to God. John baptizes Jesus in this 15th-century painting by Andrea del Verrocchio.

- Prayer was an important part of the life of the early church. Many of these prayers were spontaneous, but they reflected the language and spirit of the Old Testament.
- The New Testament church had a set of beliefs not only expressed in writings, but also in their spoken words and songs of worship. Some of their early creeds and statements of faith were short and simple. For example, "Jesus is Lord," and "one Lord, one faith, one baptism." One early statement of faith is a creed in the form of a hymn (1Ti 3:16), and an even more detailed confession of faith is expressed by Paul in his letter to the Philippians (2:6–11).

- New terms and words were introduced into the language of New Testament religion:

Marana tha: These two Aramaic words meaning "Our Lord, come!" were addressed to Jesus, calling him "Lord," the Jewish term reserved for God alone (1Co 16:22).

Abba: An intimate term of endearment, this Aramaic word implies "dear father" or "dad." Jesus encouraged his disciples to use this term when addressing God, their heavenly father (Mk 14:36).

Amen: This Hebrew word was used in temple and synagogue services at the end of prayers. It underscored the certainty of the words that were said whether it was a blessing, a request, or an expression of praise (Ro 9:5; 15:33; Gal 1:5; 6:18).

THE YOUNG CHURCH

Just before the ascension of Jesus, he gave his disciples some last instructions about the work before them, and he promised to send the Holy Spirit in his place to be their helper. The Book of Acts recounts the story of how the good news spread from Jerusalem to the surrounding lands and on to the capital of the Roman Empire mainly through the work of Peter and a new convert, the apostle Paul. This period was highlighted by unique events and remarkable teaching:

- Jerusalem was packed with pilgrims for the festival of Pentecost. The dramatic coming of the Holy Spirit was experienced and witnessed by many at this time.
- As the new Christian church grew and flourished, they were persecuted for their teaching and beliefs by the religious authorities, particularly the Sadducees.
- Empowered by God, the apostles performed many miracles.
- The apostles were called "heralds" because they proclaimed God's message for all to hear.
- The gospel spread to Africa through an Ethiopian official who became a convert after Philip explained the good news about Jesus.
- Cultural and religious prejudice between Jews and Gentiles was a fixed and deep gulf up to this point. Through a pointed and explicit vision from God, Peter was given a clear call to take the gospel to non-Jews, eat in their homes, and extend the fellowship of the church to them. This was a

The ascension, depicted by 19th-century Danish artist, Andreas Hunnaeus. In Christian theology, Jesus' ascension to heaven 40 days after his resurrection represents his exaltation, the sending of the Holy Spirit, and the promise of his bodily return to earth in the future.

revolutionary step, and it transformed religion and worship in the history of the church.

- Paul's contribution to the Christian church was outstanding. He was the primary apostle to non-Jews, and traveled hundreds of miles, always breaking new ground with his preaching and teaching. He was imprisoned, beaten, and poorly treated because of his faith. But he always clung joyfully to his hope in Christ, encouraging others even when he was in dire circumstances:

> *I want you to know, beloved, that what has happened to me has actually helped to spread the gospel, so that it has become known throughout the whole imperial guard and to everyone else that my imprisonment is for Christ; and most of the brothers and sisters, having been made confident in the Lord by my imprisonment, dare to speak the word with greater boldness and without fear.*
>
> Php 1:12–14

"But you will receive power when the Holy Spirit has come upon you; and you will be my witnesses in Jerusalem, in all Judea and Samaria, and to the ends of the earth."
Ac 1:8

Paul's letters to the early church provided the theological framework for the Christian faith for all believers—Jews and every other ethnic group.

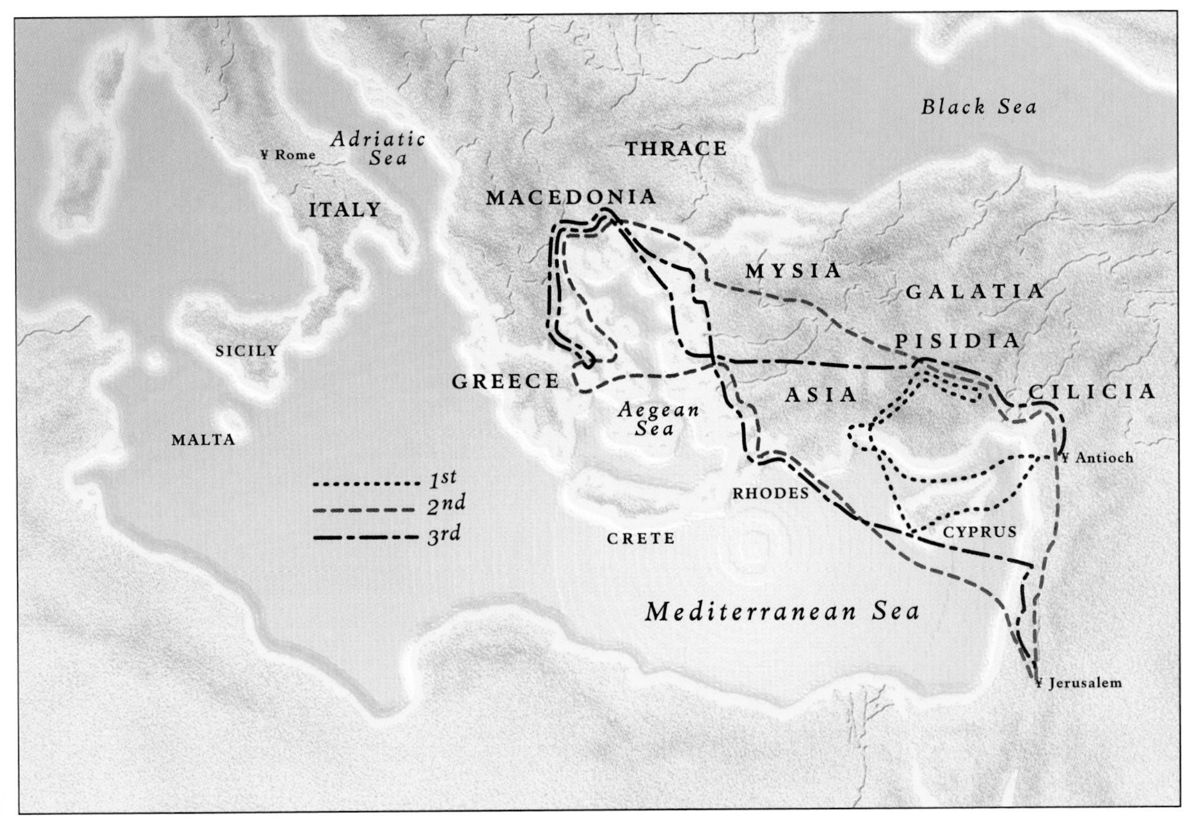

Paul's missionary journeys. He preached the gospel in key places throughout the Empire.

The Religious Beliefs of Other Groups in Bible Times

From the earliest days, Israel's religious faith was unique compared to the beliefs practiced by surrounding nations. Yahweh, the God of the Hebrews, revealed himself to his people, and he was to be the only God they served. In ancient times in the Near East, monotheism was an uncomfortable concept, and time and again Israel was attracted to the familiar paganism of the groups around them.

The religion of Egypt: The Egyptians worshiped many gods at local shrines and in their great temples. They believed in life after death, and every care was taken to prepare for this new life by putting provisions in the tomb where the carefully embalmed body of the dead person was laid. The Pharaoh, Egypt's king, was the intermediary between the gods and the people. Priests played an important role in the religious life, and magic was a significant part of faith and practice.

Baal, Astarte, and the religion of the Canaanites: According to Canaanite belief, the god Baal controlled the forces of nature, and his wife, Astarte, ruled over love and war. El, the chief of gods, was a shadowy figure at the time of the Israelite conquest of Canaan. There were several other deities with varying levels of power and popularity. The Canaanite gods were notoriously brutal and capricious. They interfered in human affairs only to delight themselves, with no thought of the consequences. In fact, the gods were considered no more or less than reflections of those that worshiped them. The Canaanites had rich temples for their gods, with priests, choirs, and temple servants. There were altars for sacrifices and altars for incense, and there were pillars in the temples thought to be the homes of gods or spirits.

Even though the Canaanites and Hebrews shared several words for sacrifices, priests, and common expressions for other religious issues, the two systems of belief were extremely dissimilar. Worship of the Canaanite gods was not demanding, without rules of conduct, and without any apparent joy and happiness. On the other hand, the Israelites had strict laws and rituals, and one true God who demanded total loyalty. Hebrew worship expressed joy and delight in the one whom they served.

Assyrian and Babylonian religion: Like other groups in the ancient world, the people of Babylon and Assyria worshiped the great powers of the universe and also had favorite

Although the Canaanites were great traders, fine artisans, and the first to develop an alphabet, their religion was pagan and debased. This image of Baal, worshiped by the Canaanites, was the weather god, who was also associated with fertility and war.

local gods. These deities were in control of everything but they were unpredictable. Anu was the chief god, and Enlil, his son, ruled over the earth's surface. Ishtar, the wife of Anu, was far more prominent in religious life than her husband. Marduk (Bel) was the patron god of Babylon, and eventually he became the king of all the gods. The national god of Assyria was Ashur, and he came to be identified with Enlil as Assyria increased in power.

The Ammonites traced their ancestry to a son of Abraham's nephew Lot. At first their relations with neighboring Israel was amicable. Later on, the Ammonites betrayed Israel and from that point there was deep enmity between the two nations. This statue of an Ammonite king dates from the time when Ammon joined with Moab and Edam to attack Judah (ninth century B.C.).

Babylonian religion was a mix of demons and evil spirits, divination and omens, and the ghosts of the underworld. Worship centered around the local temple or shrine, and animals and goods were offered as presents to the gods. A priest performed the rites on behalf of the worshiper. In spite of the fact that this religion included many myths about creation, the history of the world, and the role of the gods, Babylonian religion offered minimal information about the future. It was a set of beliefs that offered little hope.

Persian religion: These beliefs were based on the life of herders, and the gods reflected nature and the world of ideas and speech. Worship rituals included the sacrifice of animals and imbibing intoxicating drinks. The prophet Zoroaster encouraged everyone to worship Ahura-mazda as the supreme deity. Zoroaster's ideas influenced the Persian kings and many other people—even influencing Jewish thought.

Jupiter (depicted here along with Thetis, a sea-goddess) was chief of the Roman gods. His Greek name was Zeus, and from his home on Mount Olympus in Greece, he ruled over the other gods and was worshiped throughout the Greek and Roman world.

The religion of the Greeks and Romans: The supreme god of Greece was Zeus. He ruled all the other gods, who lived on the mountain Olympus. When the Romans conquered the Greeks, they took over their gods, giving them Roman names. Zeus became the Roman god Jupiter; His wife Hera became the Roman Juno.

Although the ordinary person worshiped many gods, it had little effect on daily life. In the final analysis, belief and

Contrary to biblical theology, the humanist Marsilio Ficino believed that the soul could find union with God through the contemplation of beauty. This mystical approach to spirituality is reflected in this delicate work by Sandro Botticelli (1444–1510), the Florentine painter. The Birth of Venus portrays the ethereal goddess surrounded by Zephyrs.

behavior were not really important to the Greek or Roman. What was important was good citizenship and loyalty to the state. By the time of Julius Caesar, educated Romans often had little use for the gods. Some, like the Greeks, turned to philosophy or new religions to find deeper meaning in life. Those who wanted a more personal faith turned to the "mystery" religions or foreign cults. One of these, Mithraism, proved to be a serious rival to Christianity.

In their vast empire, the Romans were tolerant of other religions so long as they did not prove to be a threat to the state. Judaism was allowed, and—at first—Christianity was tolerated. As time passed, however, Christians were required to compromise their faith, and they were persecuted when they resisted.

The apostle Paul was constantly challenging the early church to remain true to the gospel they had been taught. The Roman world was filled with so many eclectic religious beliefs and philosophies that it was not difficult to confuse the truth. In fact, at Lystra Paul and Barnabas were mistaken for Hermes and Zeus:

> *When the apostles Barnabas and Paul heard of it, they tore their clothes and rushed out into the crowd, shouting, "Friends, why are you doing this? We are mortals just like you, and we bring you good news, that you should turn from these worthless things to the living God, who made the heaven and the earth and the sea and all that is in them. . . . Even with these words, they scarcely restrained the crowds from offering sacrifice to them.*
>
> Ac 14:14–15, 18

In Ephesus a great temple was built in honor of Artemis, an eastern fertility god with a Greek name.

In spite of the various religions and philosophies of the day, Judaism survived, and the spread of Christianity continued throughout the world.

RELIGION AND WORSHIP—TEN QUICK FACTS

While Moses was on Mount Sinai receiving the Ten Commandments, Aaron fashioned an idol of gold to appease the Israelites, who then worshiped the icon—a golden calf. This depiction is from the Psalter of Ingeburg of Denmark, a 13th century manuscript.

- The temple at Ur (whose ruins are more than 4,000 years old) tells us that religion was important in ancient times.
- Covenants were popular in Moses' day. However, God's covenant was in a class by itself—he promised Israel unequaled benefits and blessings!
- Moses was so angered by the Israelites for worshiping a golden calf (fashioned by Aaron for the people), he ground the idol to powder, mixed it with water, and made the Israelites drink it!
- Shechem and Shiloh were important worship sites for the tribes of Israel. Shrines in these places housed the ark of the covenant at various times during the period of the judges.
- The Philistines—who gave their name Palestine to the whole country of Canaan—worshiped the Canaanite deities of Dagon, Ashtoreth, and Beelzebub.
- The Stoic philosophy in Paul's day emphasized the importance of reason, harmony with nature, and virtue over pleasure.
- Founded by Epicurus, the Epicurean philosophy stressed pleasure as its chief aim.
- The early Christians expected Jesus to return at any time. For them, his second coming would complete the Day of the Lord, prophesied by the prophets, and begun with the first coming of Jesus.
- Gnosticism was a mixture of astrology, reincarnation, and Greek philosophy. Gnostics believed in a spiritual world, which was good, and the material world, which was evil. Gnostic beliefs affected the early church, and Paul spoke out against them in his letters to the Corinthian and Colossian churches.
- In idolatrous Athens, Paul found an altar with the inscription "To an unknown god" (Ac 17:23). Using this as a starting point, the apostle preached a stirring message about the one true God.

TRADE AND INDUSTRY IN THE BIBLE

IN OLD TESTAMENT times, the Israelites were primarily shepherds, wandering around with their flock. But as they settled in towns and cities, new trades and small industries began to emerge. From necessities like clothing and masonry to the luxuries provided by jewelers, trade in biblical times had much in common with our modern world. During ancient times there were important legal documents, personal bills of sale, and even pottery fragments that recorded business transactions. In fact, many of the tools in the carpenter's workshop of the ancient world were almost identical to those found in the modern tool box. This chapter studies the development of industry throughout biblical history.

A chariot could be imported from Egypt for six hundred shekels of silver, and a horse for one hundred fifty; so through the king's traders they were exported to all the kings of the Hittites and the kings of Aram. 1Ki 10:29

THE BEGINNINGS OF TRADE

Merchants and traders of the ancient world took their camel caravans and donkeys to the far corners of the near East to peddle their wares. There were not always roads between cities, so merchants often had to transport their merchandise by sea, or trek across the desert to get from one destination to another.

Sometimes they spent more than a year in countries other than their own. Trading was done in person, and along with their goods, traders exchanged news and ideas with those they encountered. This opened the way for new discoveries about the world—and for this reason, trade strongly influenced society in biblical times.

Buying and selling was hazardous work. Robbery was so common along trading routes that traders were always in need of protection. Nations allied with one another provided military protection for traders as they shuttled back and forth in peacetime. During war, trading became extremely difficult. Roads were filled with armies, goods soared in price, and some kings banned trade with certain nations altogether.

Ancient trade routes developed as the desire for raw materials expanded among groups and nations. Archaeologists have discovered evidence of a network of trade routes across Bible lands—from the Persian Gulf to Asia Minor, Syria, Canaan, and Egypt—that existed before 3000 B.C.

EARLY TRADE: 25 FASCINATING FACTS

1. Egypt was rich in gold and silver and controlled the ancient market in precious metals.
2. Wood, turquoise, and copper were not available in Egypt and had to be imported.
3. Linens and papyrus were two of Egypt's great contributions to civilization.
4. Canaan was a favorite trading place as it lay exactly on the major trade routes.
5. Honey, olive oil, grain, wine, and spices were Canaan's staple trading commodities.
6. The ancient world needed tar and oil, which Canaan produced in large quantities.
7. Local trade followed the principle of supply and demand: what was needed most cost the most.
8. In biblical times, merchants conducted most of their business at the city gate.

The Phoenicians occupied a strip of land some 185 miles along the eastern Mediterranean coast located in what is now Lebanon. They were an industrious and highly adventurous people, known as fearless sea traders. Tyre was their main port and commercial center.

9. Both women and men transacted business deals.
10. In King David's time, neighboring nations gave up large sums of money and various goods to keep peace with Israel.
11. Both Tyre and Phoenicia traded with Israel.
12. King Solomon continued the practice of accepting payments from weaker nations to keep peace, just as his father David had. Solomon was sovereign over all the kingdoms from the Euphrates to the land of the Philistines, even to the border of Egypt; they brought tribute and served Solomon all the days of his life (1Ki 4:21).
13. Some income for Israel's treasury came from merchants who wanted special favors, and paid to get them.
14. Solomon was a well-known international dealer. The king "made silver as common in Jerusalem as stones, and he made cedars as numerous as the sycamores of the Shephelah." (1Ki 10:27)
15. When Israel was divided into two kingdoms, the wealth of the nation decreased.
16. During the period of the divided monarchy, Phoenicia became the dominant commercial force in Palestine.

One of the godly kings of Judah, Jehoshaphat continued the reforms of his father Asa. He commissioned the priests to teach God's law throughout all the towns of Judah. God rewarded his efforts by blessing Judah with peace and prosperity.

17. The Phoenicians developed sea routes to Egypt, Cyprus, Crete, Sicily, Carthage, Italy, and Spain. They traded with Africa, Arabia, and India from the Red Sea.

18. After the Phoenicians, the Arameans became the great traders.

19. The Edomites became a strong trading power, and made good use of their key location on the trade routes between Egypt and the Arabian Desert.

20. On the verge of a massive trade endeavor, the fleet of ships built by Jehoshaphat and Ahaziah were wrecked before they sailed on their first voyage.

21. Under King Uzziah, Judah's business interests improved, and he brought the port of Ezion-geber under Judah's control.

22. When Babylon defeated Judah, the southern kingdom's friends laughed at the misfortune of their former ally.

23. After the Exile, the Israelites were cautious in strengthening trading ties with other nations.

24. Before New Testament times, Judah's big trading days were over.

25. During the time of Jesus, Jews were farmers and shepherds, and many traded with Greeks and Romans.

Israelites were people of the land, and their economy and life depended on what could be grown or raised. All of life's necessities—food, clothing, shelter—came from the land. Men worked the land, but Israelite women helped when they were needed in the fields.

ITEMS OF TRADE

The prophet Ezekiel noted many objects that were traded in ancient times in Bible lands. He listed raw materials, manufactured goods, animals, clothing, metals, and precious stones. Besides identifying traded goods, Ezekiel listed where they came from:

> *Tarshish did business with you out of the abundance of your great wealth; silver, iron, tin, and lead they exchanged for your wares. Javan, Tubal, and Meshech*

traded with you;. . . The Rhodians traded with you; many coastlands were your own special markets; they brought you in payment ivory tusks and ebony. Edom did business with you because of your abundant goods; they exchanged for your wares turquoise, purple, embroidered work, fine linen, coral, and rubies. Judah and the land of Israel traded with you; they exchanged for your merchandise wheat from Minneth, millet, honey, oil, and balm.

Eze 27:12–13, 15–17

Some of the primary goods in trade included:

Gold: Pharaoh's government owned all of Egypt's abundant gold. The desert was rich in gold ore, and the Egyptians used every available method to mine the precious metal. Israel's land was without gold, and what was given to them by the Egyptians was used to decorate the ark of the covenant and the tabernacle. When Israel gained military power, other nations paid tribute in gold and silver (1Ki 9:14). Even then, the Israelites did not use the valuable resource for money, but for decorations in their royal and religious settings and for jewelry (Nu 31:50).

Silver: In early times, people used silver for money. In those days, there was a set value for a given amount of silver, and it became an important factor in trading. Silver came from northern Syria and parts of Egypt. It was used to pay tribute and as a gift to the temple in Jerusalem (1Ch 29:3–4).

These Canaanite weapons, dating from the 15th century B.C., were discovered in Kadum, Samaria. The type of weaponry seen here—daggers and an ax-head—would have been used in hand-to-hand combat.

Copper: Canaan, rich in copper and bronze, learned the art of smelting as early as 3500 B.C. Solomon used large amounts of copper in building the temple at Jerusalem, and it is believed that it was imported from the Arabah desert. Copper, a hard metal, was easier to find than gold or silver, and it had many more uses than the pricier metals. Armies used copper for weapons and coats of armor. Religious objects, kitchen utensils, and many musical instruments were also made from the useful substance. King David accepted bronze (an alloy of copper and tin) as part of the tribute required from Hadadezer of Aram (1Ch 18:8).

Tin: Although the Phoenicians sold tin, it is not certain where it came from. People in biblical times combined it with copper to make bronze, a stronger, tougher metal.

Iron: Ironworks began in earnest in Asia Minor around 1400 B.C. In Israel's early history, they depended on the Philistines for their iron farming tools instead of developing their own iron industry. In King David's time, great quantities of iron were stored for building the temple, and David got as much iron as necessary for weaponry and other military needs. However, as far as we know, the Israelites never practiced iron smelting, and depended on imports from Syria, Cyprus, and Asia Minor. Iron was in popular demand in the ancient world, and merchants throughout the near East traded with it.

Ivory: Hard to get and highly desirable, most of the ivory used in the near East came from Asiatic elephants. Finely carved ivory was used in palaces and in the homes of the rich. Solomon's merchant ships brought ivory for his throne (1Ki 10:18–22), and ivory was sought after to make decorative household objects. Amos the prophet spoke of the rich Samaritan houses of ivory that would be destroyed because they had been created on the backs of the poor (Am 3:15). Later, when the Assyrians captured Samaria in 722 B.C., they looted the royal palaces and took the ivory to Sargon II.

Ivory was highly valued in the ancient world and was part of almost every ancient culture of the middle East. Obtained from the elephant, hippopotamus, and some other animals, ivory was used in expensive furnishings, decorative items, and jewelry. This ivory box found in Megiddo dates from the 13th–12th century B.C.

Glass: Archaeologists have discovered an Egyptian glass factory that was in operation about 1400 B.C. It produced small glass bottles that were exported to several locations, including Palestine. Glass was rare, and therefore considered a precious form of wealth (Job 28:17). The Mesopotamians, Phoenicians, and Egyptians also manufactured and exported various types of glass objects.

Wood: In early times, the near East had fine forests in several areas. Over the years, the trees were steadily cut down to make homes and furniture, farm implements, and idols for worship. The wood was used for fuel (Dt 4:28). Solomon imported

An ancient Egyptian wooden sculpture of a cat. Although the Bible does not mention cats (and they were almost unknown in Mesopotamia), we do know that they were worshiped in ancient Egypt.

cedar lumber from Lebanon, and also ordered a variety of timber for building the palace (2 Ch 2:16). Bashan was known for its fine oak forests, and the Israelites made oars and furniture from oak. Today, many of these previously forested areas lie rocky and bare, leaving much of Israel a barren landscape.

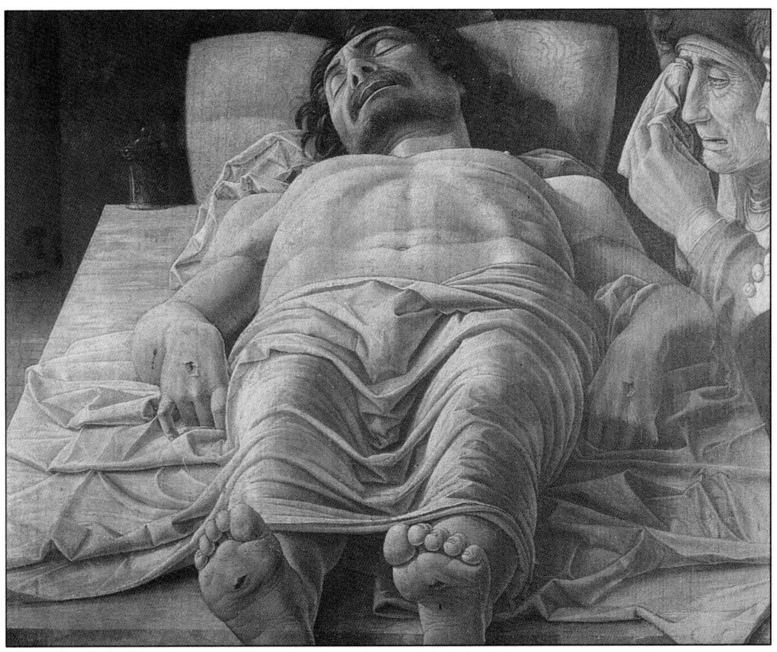

Flax was grown in the Jordan Valley and in Galilee. It was processed and then woven into cloth. As early as Solomon's time, guilds of textile workers produced linen from the fibers of the flax plant. Fine bleached linen would have been used to make the shroud for the body of Jesus.

Bitumen: In the Bible, the word pitch refers to bitumen, a thick type of oil found in pits by the Dead Sea. It was a useful commodity, and Noah used it to make the ark waterproof (Gen 6:14).

Flax: Fine linen was made from the Egyptian flax plants that grew along the Nile. The Egyptians were skilled at making a soft, comfortable cloth worn by royalty, and also used for wrapping the embalmed bodies of the dead. The Israelites also grew flax near Jericho and in the Galilee area. And although the cloth they produced was not as fine as that of the Egyptians, linen was used among the Israelites, even to wrap the body of Jesus for burial (Lk 23:53).

Cotton: The humid climate of upper Egypt was excellent for raising a good crop of cotton. It was spun into cloth by Egyptian weavers, and the mummies of Egypt were wrapped in this material. The cotton plant was brought to Palestine shortly after the Captivity.

Wool: From very early on, the people of the near East raised sheep and goats, so they usually wore clothing made of wool. Weavers and dyers of biblical times became expert artisans at weaving, dyeing, and making cloth. Many towns developed famous cloth-making industries. For example, a famous dyeing industry at Tell Beit Mirsim was uncovered by archaeologists.

THE GROWTH OF INDUSTRY IN THE BIBLE

Today's big factories, modern way of manufacturing, and fast-paced international trade are far removed from the cottage industries, local workshops, and limited ways of transporting goods found in ancient times. Yet even back then, people pooled their energies and resources to create rustic manufacturing "plants." Jeremiah the prophet suggests that in the sixth century B.C., potters and bakers had their own work areas of the city (Jer 19:1–2; 37:21). Nehemiah refers to a place where artisans worked together (Ne 11:35), and the Old Testament speaks of a guild of linen workers and a group of royal potters (1Ch 4:21–23). How did these ancient artisans actually manufacture their wares?

THE CLOTHING TRADE

Most clothes in biblical times were made from wool because it was more readily available than linen or cotton. After the sheep was sheared, the wool was washed, bleached, and beaten by the "fuller" using a purifying soap. The natural oils were also removed from the fibers before the wool could be dyed, spun, and woven. The Fuller's Field, set up to process wool on the east side of Jerusalem, was noted for its foul smells, and was established away from the residential part of the city and close to running water.

After harvest, flax was dried in the sun, then soaked in water for several days to loosen the fibers. After this, the fibers were separated, beaten with a wooden mallet, and finally combed. Although linen was usually kept white, sometimes fine clothes and curtains in Bible times were dyed purple or scarlet. Dyeing was an ancient art, and the valuable and popular color of the day (purple) was extracted from the murex shellfish native to the Phoenician coast.

BARTERING—AN ANCIENT PRACTICE

In biblical times, bartering was a common business practice; that is, one item or service was exchanged for another. A carpenter would help a fisherman build his house in exchange for fresh and salted fish; a shepherd might trade wool for a farmer's grain.

There are several interesting examples of bartering mentioned in the Bible. In the Book of Genesis, livestock was traded for grain when famine was rampant and money ran out (Gen 47:13–16). In prosperous and peaceful times, people traded on the basis of need and available materials and services. King Solomon traded wheat and fine oil for cedar and cypress timber in order to build the temple (1Ki 5:1–11). Jacob bartered his services to Laban in order to have Laban's daughter as his wife (Gen 29:15–30). In another instance, the Bible tells us that the tribe of Levi traded their services as priests for some of the food and meat brought to the temple for sacrifice (Nu 18:25–32). A curious barter was the prophet Hosea's exchange of silver, barley, and wine in order to pay for a wife (Hos 3:2).

A contemporary stained-glass depiction of Hosea and Gomer by Joep Nicolas. In the prophet Hosea's message, his adulterous wife Gomer was a symbol of Israel's unfaithfulness to God.

Bartering is still practiced in bible lands today. A part of each modern city is designated as the place where merchants, farmers, potters and the like can meet to exchange goods and services.

A spindle was used to spin the wool or linen into yarn. Wooden-framed looms were used to weave the yarn into cloth. Most clothes would be sewn by hand from two or three pieces of woven cloth; however, some robes were seamless.

THE POTTERIES

The potter's work was significant in Israelite society, and the art of making pottery was a specialized trade by the time of Saul and David in the Old Testament. Potters lived in settlements in the lower part of Jerusalem, and in the neighborhood of Hebron and other locations where clay was in abundant supply. Because of the constant demand for their wares, the potter's work was a dawn-till-dusk operation, with little time off from the steady routine of making and selling. Often, several potters worked together, and in one potter's shop uncovered by archaeologists, there was space for preparing the clay, an area for storing both clay and fuel for the kiln; there was also a drying area, and a storage area for pots that needed further treatment. A stone mortar, pottery templates, and objects for cutting clay were among the tools found in the ancient workshop.

A contemporary artist creates a tapestry on an upright loom. One of the oldest of the ancient crafts, woven cloth was a highly prized trade item as early as 2500 B.C. It is still popular as an art form today.

The potter fashioned bowls, jars, and other utensils from clay as it rotated on a wheel. Once a vessel was shaped and had dried, it was dipped in a solution to seal the pores. Although decoration was rare in the days of the kings, sometimes designs were applied at this stage by painting, scratching, or rubbing the surface. Then the piece of pottery was baked with a batch of others in an oven or kiln. Firing took several days because the temperature of the kiln was raised and lowered slowly to keep bowls and jars from cracking and breaking.

Pottery-making and pottery itself were integral parts of ancient life. They became important symbols used in the Bible to illustrate God's power and influence.

Commercial Documents

During biblical times, a great deal of business was conducted without a written bill of sale. Even so, although they did not have the equivalent of a cash receipt back then, large transactions were documented in specific ways. Jeremiah's purchase of land was transacted with money, a sealed deed of purchase, an open copy, and all before several witnesses:

> Take these deeds, both this sealed deed of purchase and this open deed, and put them in an earthenware jar, in order that they may last for a long time.
> Jer 32:14

When Abraham bought a family burial place, the verbal transaction took place at the city gate in front of many witnesses, and the biblical record notes that he paid 400 shekels of silver for the land:

> So the field of Ephron in Machpelah, which was to the east of Mamre, the field with the cave that was in it and all the trees that were in the field, throughout its whole area, passed to Abraham as a possession in the presence of the Hittites, in the presence of all who went in at the gate of his city.
> Gen 23:17–18

The equivalent of today's scrap paper would be broken bits of pottery (known as ostraca) used in the world of the Bible. Business transactions, dates, and names of people were often listed on them. Potsherds uncovered from the eighth century B.C. list a variety of commodities delivered to the palace in Samaria. In Egypt in the fifth century B.C., legal paperwork controlled most business arrangements: contracts were drawn up for supplying commodities, statements of building rights, securing loans, and settlements of claims. Excavations have uncovered many personal seals throughout the land of Palestine. These were affixed to documents, packages, and handles of food jars to authenticate ownership; this was yet another form of commercial documentation.

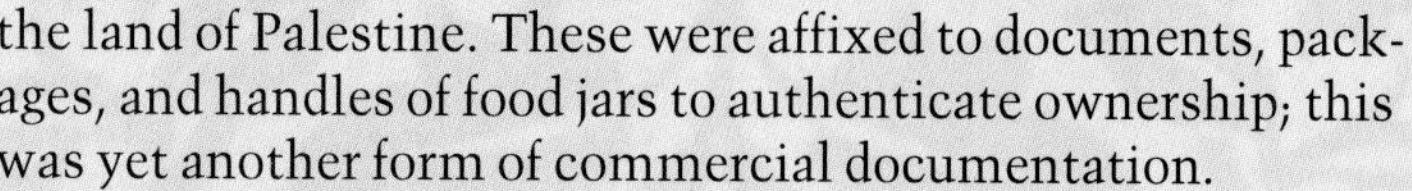

Legal and business proceedings often took place at the city gate, a very public and busy spot, where people could be called on to witness the signing of documents, or attest to word-of-mouth business deals and the exchange of money.

Metalworking

In the ancient world, metal was hard to obtain and the melting process difficult to control. Metal workers were prized artisans, and metal tools were expensive. It was not until around 1000 B.C. that the business of metalworking was mastered.

Decades before Israel appeared in Palestine, the Canaanites forged bronze or copper implements and weapons. During the patriarchal period, molds for molten metal were crafted out of limestone blocks, and their discovery indicates that the Israelites had knowledge of the processes of metalworking. Several biblical passages also suggest this (2Ki 24:14; Jer 6:29–30; Eze 27:12).

Without any extensive metal deposits, Israel had to import metal and ores. Commercial ships from Tarshish brought silver, iron, tin, and lead and exchanged them for Israel's wares. Copper was likely imported from Cyprus because the ore deposits in the Wadi Arabah were insufficient for Israel's needs.

Iron became common in Israel after Philistine's power over them was broken by Saul and David. In later periods, skilled metalworkers banded together in guilds and made a variety of tools and weapons, including axes, sickles, ox-goads, knives, spearheads, javelins, and swords. The metal industry flourished and found a ready market. Although the apostles did not refer to the business of metals, it presumably continued to thrive in New Testament times.

THE BUILDING TRADES

In biblical times, important buildings and the houses of the rich were built using ashlar masonry (that is, carefully cut blocks of limestone fitted together without mortar) and stone masons were needed to do this kind of work. The best example of ashlar masonry can be found at the Wailing Wall in Jerusalem (known today as the "Western Wall"). Some of the building blocks in the wall are so large, it must have taken a large group of builders back then to place them in position.

Ancient quarries have been found near Jerusalem, in Megiddo, Samaria, Hazor, and several other places. Most building projects would have utilized local limestone quarried throughout the hill country by groups of stonecutters.

Another important worker in the building business was the brickmaker, who worked with two kinds of bricks in Bible times. There were baked clay bricks, which became popular in Palestine in New Testament times. There were also sun-baked mud bricks (mixed with sand and chopped straw) widely used in Egypt, which were probably made by the Israelite slaves before their liberation from Egypt.

Mud or clay bricks were common building materials in ancient Egypt (but were rarely used in Palestine). Mud was mixed with water, and sometimes straw was added to make the bricks stronger. The mixture was pressed into wooden frames, and the oblong bricks were left to dry in the sun.

Early mud bricks were fashioned by hand and were oval in shape. Eventually a wooden mold was made to frame the bricks, which then gave them a more standardized shape. Once the bricks had set, the molds were removed and the bricks were left to dry in the sun. These bricks were used in Egypt for most structures. Important buildings, however, were constructed in stone. In Palestine, the upper part of a building was often constructed from unbaked or partially baked brick.

But by New Testament times, bricks baked in kilns had become common, popularized by the Romans, although they had long been in use throughout Mesopotamia.

Woodworking

From patriarchal times, Canaan had a tradition of fine woodwork. Carpenters not only made excellent furniture, they made carts and wagons, and worked in the home-building trade. Israel had some wood—cypress and cedar, olive groves, and sycamore trees grew in the foothills. There also may have been limited supplies of acacia, oak, and ash in that area. For large projects—such as the construction of the temple—long timbers were needed, so wood was imported from Lebanon and other places.

The Bible not only describes how the carpenter selected wood, but it also provides details concerning actual carpentry, from measuring to the use of tools. Archaeologists have unearthed many woodworking implements used in Bible times, from saws and hammers to various chisels and awls. By New Testament times, Joseph and Jesus, two well-known carpenters, would also have had wood planes and spoke shaves in their collection of tools.

A carpenter at work uses a string lathe to cut wood. Among other things, woodworkers in biblical times made roof beams, fishing boats, farm tools, and furnishings for the home—such as chairs, tables, and bed frames. Jesus' peers probably found it incredible that the carpenter who had made plows for their plot of land was also the Messiah.

Boat Building

Many New Testament stories focus on boats, fishing, lakes, and seas. Jesus sometimes taught from a boat or traveled in one, many of his disciples were fishermen, and the apostle Paul went on several journeys by ship. However, there is no evidence that the people of Israel were great ship builders at any time in their history, and they may have even feared the sea—holding the ancient Semitic view of personifying the mysterious deep water as a power of evil that wrestled against God. When Solomon used a fleet of ships to conduct trade in the Red Sea area, he had Phoenicians build the boats and serve as sailors, since they were veteran seafarers.

The ships were carefully constructed of fine imported wood, the sails and flags were made of embroidered linen, and the deck awnings of dyed cloth. Experienced shipwrights caulked the seams with flax and bitumen. The oarsmen hailed from coastal areas. This was a fine fleet indeed:

They made all your planks of fir trees from Senir;
they took a cedar from Lebanon to make a mast for you.
From oaks of Bashan they made your oars;

they made your deck of pines from the coasts of Cyprus,
inlaid with ivory.
Of fine embroidered linen from Egypt was your sail,
serving as your ensign;
blue and purple from the coasts of Elishah
was your awning.
The inhabitants of Sidon and Arvad were your rowers;
skilled men of Zemer were within you,
they were your pilots.
The elders of Gebal and its artisans were within you,
caulking your seams;
all the ships of the sea with their mariners were within you.

Eze 27:5–9

Commercial ships had a rounded hull, raised prow and stern, and they were used for trade along the coast. Another type—the long ships—were much larger, and had two banks of oars from the sides, and two steering oars from the stern. There was a central mast and a high upper deck, and it is believed that this type of vessel may have been the ships of Tarshish frequently mentioned in the Old Testament.

Jewelry Making

Although most industries were centered around the necessities of life, the Israelites and other Bible groups enjoyed trinkets and ornaments and other indulgences. Thus, the luxury industries developed, dealing in gold, silver, ivory, and precious stones. The Old Testament mentions several precious stones including rubies, sapphires, topaz, emeralds, jasper, and amethyst.

Egyptian jewelers at work, from the Tomb of Nebamun, Amenophis III (1411–1375 B.C.). Archaeologists have made important finds in Egypt and Mesopotamia of spectacular gold jewelry set with precious stones.

Back then, as now, precious stones were set in gold and silver, and some examples have been discovered hidden under floors and in graves. There were wealthy goldsmiths in the prophet Nehemiah's day. And in New Testament times, there is mention of a guild of silversmiths in Ephesus who made silver images for worshipers at the temple of Diana.

Gold and silver were refined on charcoal braziers by the smiths. Melted in a small crucible, which stood on hot char-

> ***"I adorned you with ornaments: I put bracelets on your arms, a chain on your neck, a ring on your nose, earrings in your ears, and a beautiful crown upon your head."***
> ***Eze 16:11–12***

coal, molten gold or silver was sometimes poured into a mold to form a fine ornament. Silver was often difficult to purify because it was found in the same ore as lead. Even the psalmist refers to the lengthy process of purifying silver—seven times in the refiner's furnace of clay (Ps 12:6).

Jewelers had particular tools for polishing, engraving, and preparing the stones and the settings. It is clear from some Jewish writings from the first century A.D. that the jeweler's techniques remained much the same from early to late Bible times.

Just like today, many people could not afford expensive jewelry and had to make do with substitute ornaments from baked clay, bone, limestone, wood, and leather. Beads were often made from inexpensive stones, bone, or clay, and they were likely fashioned at home, instead of by a professional jeweler.

TRADE, INDUSTRY, AND CRAFTS— 20 BIBLE FACTS

1. Abraham came from a trading port, Ur of the Chaldees, located on the Euphrates in today's south Iraq.
2. The embalming practices of the Egyptians required vast imports of spices and incense.
3. Tyrians brought fish and merchandise into Jerusalem and distressed the prophet Nehemiah by trading and selling on the Sabbath.
4. In New Testament times, much of the trade and commerce were controlled by the Romans.
5. In some cities there were whole streets occupied by one trade (Street of Sandalmakers or Street of Weavers, for example) and certain workshops would employ several workers.
6. Some towns were given over to an entire industry. At the town of Debir, baskets full of loom weights and equipment for dyeing were uncovered by archaeologists.
7. Pottery, spinning, weaving, and metal work were among the earliest trades in Bible times.
8. The earliest kind of metalworker in Bible times was likely the tinker who traveled from place to place to do his work. A painting on an Egyptian tomb shows a group of tinkers with their goatskin bellows.
9. The Phoenicians were the most expert dyers in ancient Bible times; the Israelites themselves probably only made

vegetable dyes, using almond leaves for yellow and the madder plant for red.

10. The carpenter's craft covered all kinds of work. Besides making doors, furniture, and farm equipment, the carpenter was at the same time joiner, cabinetmaker, cartwright, wood sculptor, and shipwright.
11. Many of the tools in the carpenter's workshop of the ancient world would be almost identical to those found in the modern tool box.
12. The finest stone masons came from Phoenicia. The Great Gate at Megiddo is an outstanding example of the stone workers' skill. The stones were laid so carefully—and without mortar—that not even the thinnest knife could be inserted between the blocks.
13. The work of the tanner involved treating the hides of dead animals to make leather for shoes, tents, shields, and flooring. This occupation was scorned by the Jews because the tanner would deal with animals listed as "unclean."
14. In their line of work, which involved scouring wool and bleaching cloth, fullers usually worked outside towns and near running water. The fuller used large vats of water and beat or pressed the materials with his feet!
15. Many "factories" and workshops were deep recesses cut into the walls of a town or city.
16. Jewish rabbis had strict rules for business deals, and market inspectors saw to it that they were carried out.
17. The temple was likely the most important factor in Jerusalem's commerce. A brisk trade in goods required for worship at the temple, especially animals for sacrifice, went on in the area.
18. Jesus threw out buyers and sellers who were trading and doing various business deals in the temple court.
19. In earliest times, trade was done by bartering. Coins were not used until the seventh century B.C.
20. By New Testament times, trade between countries required a regular system for banking and the services of money changers.

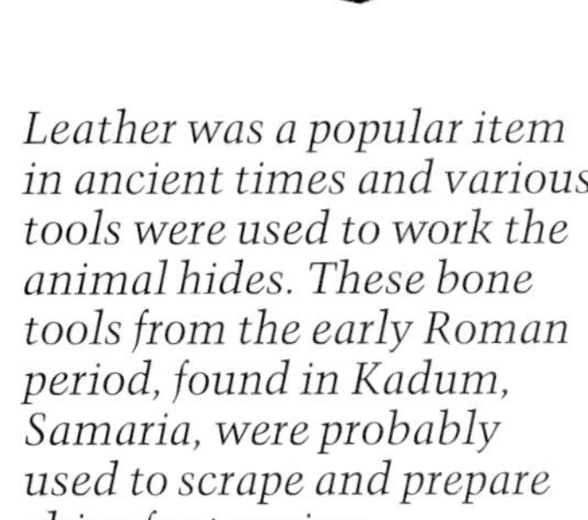

Leather was a popular item in ancient times and various tools were used to work the animal hides. These bone tools from the early Roman period, found in Kadum, Samaria, were probably used to scrape and prepare skins for tanning.

The People of the Bible

MANY BIBLE personalities are familiar to us. We are well acquainted with Adam and Eve and their transgressions in Eden. The saga of Moses—from the hiding place in the bulrushes to the view of the Promised Land—is well known to us. But how many of us are as familiar with Elymas, Onesiphorus, or Epaphroditus? And what about Jesus? The Bible portrays him as a sinless human being, the Son of God, a great teacher, and a law-abiding Jew. But did you know he also broke many Sabbath rules, chased people out of the temple, and overturned tables! This chapter should reveal more about some of the characters you thought you knew—as well as introduce some of the ones you didn't!

People You Should Know

These quick sketches of some major Bible characters indicate the main highlights of their lives, and also include little-known facts that bring them to life before our view.

***Aaron* (15th century *B.C.*)**—Aaron (oldest son of Amran and Jochebed) was Moses' brother, a Levite, and the high priest of Israel. He helped Moses free the Israelites and lead them out of Egypt. Aaron was Moses' public speaker, and he used his rod to perform many miracles, even to strike the waters of Egypt and turn them to blood. In the wilderness, he helped Moses defeat the Amalekites. When his authority was questioned, Aaron's rod budded, blossomed, and bore ripe almonds—a sign that he was God's choice as high priest.

To demonstrate the power of God to Pharaoh and his court, Aaron's staff became a snake and consumed the snakes of the wise men and sorcerers in a contest orchestrated by the Lord himself. This scene, depicted by 19th-century artist James Tissot, is recorded in Exodus 7:8–13.

At times, Aaron disobeyed God. He allowed the Israelites to build an idol in Moses' absence, and another time he sided with Miriam against Moses. On both occasions, Moses begged God to show Aaron mercy, and God did so. Aaron died when he was 123, just before the Israelites entered the Promised Land. (Ex 4:14)

***Abraham* (22nd century *B.C.*)**—Abraham (Abram) and his family were called by God to leave Haran and go to a new land. Abraham obeyed. He moved his family and flocks from place to place, even going to Egypt for food, until God directed him to the new land, Canaan. God promised to make Abraham the founder of the Hebrew nation, and Hagar, his wife's slave-girl, bore him a son. This, however, was not the promised child.

When Abraham and his wife Sarah (Sarai) were old, she gave birth to Isaac—the firstborn of the Hebrew nation. Some years later, God tested Abraham's faith when he told him to offer Isaac as a sacrifice. Again, Abraham obeyed. Just as he was about to lay the knife on his child, God's angel stopped him. Isaac's life was spared and God renewed his promises to

Abraham—one of the Bible's most outstanding example of faith. (Gen 11:26)

Daniel (6th century B.C.)—The fine son of a wealthy Jewish family, Daniel was taken captive to pagan Babylon when he was young. While Daniel and three Jewish friends were in training as King Nebuchadnezzar's courtiers, they honored God and grew strong on a basic diet allowed by Jewish law.

Filled with godly wisdom, Daniel was able to interpret Nebuchadnezzar's strange dreams. Years later, when Belshazzar was king, the elderly Daniel deciphered an ominous message that appeared on the palace walls. That same night the king was killed and the Persians captured Babylon.

Daniel's fame grew and he became an important official. Others were jealous of his position and plotted against him. Daniel was thrown in among lions, but God preserved his life. Daniel went on to record a number of dreams, visions, and prophecies concerning the future. (Da 1:6)

David (970 B.C.)—David, youngest son of Jesse of Bethlehem, was a shepherd boy when Samuel the prophet came and secretly anointed him as Israel's next king. Time passed and David was sent to take food to his brothers in the army. While there, he took up the challenge to fight big Goliath, the champion soldier of the Philistines. After he killed the giant, King Saul became jealous of the young shepherd, whose music often soothed the temperamental king.

After Saul's death, David became king in Judah. His popular reign was marked by many achievements. He made Jerusalem his capital, brought the ark of the covenant there, and made preparations to build the temple.

David's great life was not without tragic personal failings: He committed adultery, plotted murder, experienced the death of a child, and had trouble with his sons. Yet David always turned to the Lord for forgiveness and renewal. He was a great king, a fearless soldier, and a creative writer and musician. Many psalms are attributed to David, the man whom the Bible describes as close to the heart of God. (Ru 4:17)

Deborah (12th century B.C.)—One of Israel's greatest judges, Deborah was the only woman on record to hold this position of leadership. She was highly regarded for her moral authority and wisdom. When the Israelites were being oppressed by the Canaanites (led by Jabin), Deborah was given instructions from God. She told Barak of Naphtali to gather an army on Mount Tabor to face the enemy. Barak would only agree to go if Deborah went with the army. She complied, providing essential leadership and inspiration. As the Canaanites advanced, a violent rainstorm flooded the

"David became greater and greater . . . David then perceived that the Lord had established him king over Israel, and that he had exalted his kingdom for the sake of his people Israel." 2Sa 5:10,12

ISRAEL'S KINGS AND RULERS

The United Kingdom

Saul	Israel's first king (1Sa 9–10)
David	Israel's second and best-loved king (2Sa 1–24)
Solomon	David's son, known for his wisdom and riches (1Ki 1–11)

Some scholars believe that these large chambers, carved out of the bedrock of Ophel Hill in Jerusalem, are the tombs where many of Israel's kings were laid to rest.

The Northern Kingdom (Israel)

Jeroboam I	left Israel with a legacy of idolatry (1Ki 11:26–14:20)
Nadab	son of Jeroboam I, continued idol worship (1Ki 15:25–28)
Baasha	ruled for 24 years, and was cursed for his sin by the prophet Jehu (1Ki 15:27–16:7)
Elah	son of Baasha, killed while drunk (1Ki 16:6–14)
Zimri	committed suicide after ruling for a week (1Ki 16:9–20)

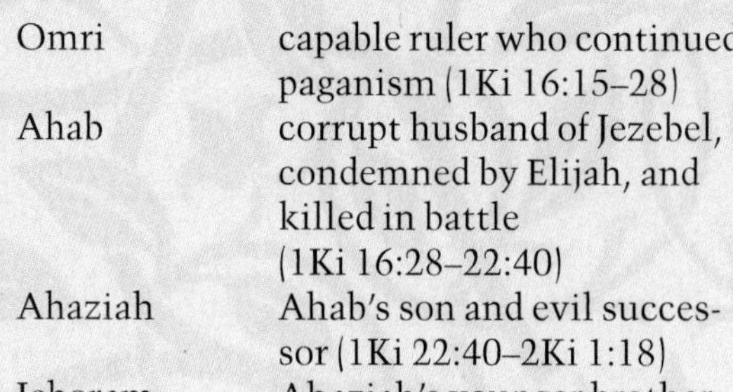

Omri	capable ruler who continued paganism (1Ki 16:15–28)
Ahab	corrupt husband of Jezebel, condemned by Elijah, and killed in battle (1Ki 16:28–22:40)
Ahaziah	Ahab's son and evil successor (1Ki 22:40–2Ki 1:18)
Jehoram	Ahaziah's younger brother and successor, he ended Baal worship but did not fully reform (2Ki 3:1–9:25)

Jehu, the 10th king of Israel, was the son of Jehoshaphat. A military commander, Jehu was anointed head of state by both Elijah and Elisha. The king put an end to the evil house of Ahab, and banned Baal worship in Israel. Jehu reigned in Samaria for 28 years.

Jehu	famous for his chariot riding and ending Ahab's pagan dynasty (2Ki 9:1–10:36)
Jehoahaz	Jehu's son, his army was almost destroyed by the king of Aram (2Ki 13:1–19)
Jehoash	son of Jehoahaz, he was king of Israel for 16 years (2Ki 13:10–14:6)
Jeroboam II	reigned during the time of Jonah the prophet (2Ki 14:23–29)
Zechariah	son of Jeroboam II; reigned for six months and then was assassinated by Shallum (2Ki 14:23–15:2)
Shallum	reigned for a month and then was killed by Mena hem (2Ki 15:14–22)

Menahem	an exacting, cruel king, he reigned for 10 years (2Ki 15:14–22)
Pekahiah	Menahem's son, he ruled for two years, then was killed by his army captain, Pekah (2Ki 15:22–26)
Pekah	ruled for 21 years and maintained idol worship in Israel (2Ki 15:27–31)
Hoshea	last king of Israel after the monarchy split; he was defeated by King Shalmaneser V of Assyria; Samaria, the capital of Israel, was captured and the people taken captive to Assyria (2Ki 17)

The Southern Kingdom (Judah)

Rehoboam	Solomon's son, whose stubborn arrogance sparked a civil war with the northern tribe of Israel (1Ki 11:43–12:24)
Abijam	defeated Jeroboam I in battle (1Ki 14:31–15:8)
Asa	son of Abijam, Judah's first godly king (1Ki 15:8–14)
Jehoshaphat	Asa's son, another godly king (1Ki 22:41–50)
Jehoram	married Athaliah, the evil daughter of Ahab and Jezebel (2Ki 8:16–24)
Ahaziah	son of Jehoram and Athaliah (2Ki 8:24–9:29)
Athaliah	seized the throne after Ahaziah's death and had all the royal offspring murdered except Joash, who was hidden from his brutal grandmother (2Ki 11:1–20)
Joash	Ahaziah's son and ruler after Athaliah was executed (2Ki 11:1–12:21)
Amaziah	son of Joash (2Ki 14:1–20)
Azariah (Uzziah)	son of Amaziah; powerful king who fortified Jerusalem; he allowed idolatry and was struck with leprosy (2Ki 15:1–7)
Jotham	Azariah's son who fortified Jerusalem (2Ki 15:32–38)
Ahaz	Jotham's pagan son who reigned for 16 years (2Ki 16:1–20)

Among Hezekiah's accomplishments was this underground tunnel, which allowed fresh water from the Gihon spring outside Jerusalem's walls to flow into the city.

Hezekiah	king of Judah after his father, Ahaz; Hezekiah put an end to idol worship; God saved Judah from Assyria, and added 15 years to Hezekiah's life (2Ki 18–20)
Manasseh	son of Hezekiah (2Ki 21:1–18)
Amon	Manasseh's son, killed by his own servants (2Ki 21:19–26)
Josiah	leader of national reform (2Ki 22:1–23:30)
Jehoahaz	Josiah's son, deposed after 90 days (2Ki 23:31–33)
Jehoiakim	Josiah's son who persecuted Jeremiah (2Ki 23:34–24:5; Jer 36)
Jehoiachin	Jehoiakim's son who provoked God's anger (2Ki 24:6–16)
Zedekiah	uncle of Jehoiachin, blinded and taken into exile in Babylon (2Ki 24:17–25:30)

area, bogging down their horses and chariots in mud. The Israelites were able to overpower them. Sisera, the Canaanite general, fled and was later killed. (Jdg 4–5.)

Elijah (9th century B.C.)—Elijah the prophet lived and worked in Israel during King Ahab's reign. He was sent by God to judge the king and his pagan wife Jezebel for worshiping Baal and killing God's prophets. God sent a drought, and Elijah had to go into hiding for his own safety. God provided him with food from the mouth of ravens, and later from the hands of a widow—whose dead son was brought back to life by Elijah's prayer of faith.

In the third year of the drought, Elijah confronted Ahab and they agreed to a showdown at Mt. Carmel between the prophets of Baal and Elijah's God. Baal and his cohorts failed miserably, Elijah and the God of Israel won the contest, the priests of Baal were killed, and the drought ended that day. God protected Elijah in further dealings with the rebellious Jezebel and Ahab, and the prophet continued to warn and confront them about their wanton sins.

Before his work was finished, Elijah prepared Elisha to continue his work, and the prophet witnessed the death of the dreadful Ahab. After this, God took Elijah to heaven in a chariot of fire, and his prophet's mantle fell on Elisha's shoulders. (1Ki 17:1)

"Elijah was a human being like us, and he prayed fervently that it might not rain, and for three years and six months it did not rain on the earth. Then he prayed again, and the heaven gave rain and the earth yielded its harvest." Jas 5:17–18

Esther (5th century B.C.)—After King Ahasuerus (Xerxes) divorced his wife Vashti, he chose the lovely young Jewish woman Hadassah (Esther) to be his wife. When she moved into the palace, her cousin Mordecai, who had been her guardian, advised her to keep her Jewish identity hidden from the Persian royal court.

When Haman, the imperious and cruel chief minister, schemed to wipe out all the Jews in the area because of his hatred toward Mordecai, Esther stepped in. She approached the king, gained his pleasure and interest, then courageously revealed Haman's plan to exterminate her people. Outraged by Haman's conspiracy, the king ordered his death and appointed Mordecai chief minister in Haman's place. On the day Haman had appointed for the annihilation of the Jews, Esther's people turned on their enemies and wiped them out. This amazing turn of events is remembered at the Feast of Purim, an important festival in the Jewish calendar. (Est 2:7)

Eve—Described as the "mother of all living," Eve was created by God to provide companionship to Adam in the garden of Eden. She was tempted by the clever serpent into tasting the fruit from the tree of knowledge of good and evil—the one thing that God had instructed them to avoid.

WOMEN OF POWER

In biblical times, the status of women was restricted and perceived as much less important than the place of men. A woman was defined by her relationship to men: She was a father's daughter, a husband's wife or widow, a king's queen, or—for that matter—his concubine. Caught in a cultural bind, a woman had few rights or opportunities and seldom a career. Most women were mothers and homemakers. Yet throughout biblical history, there were exceptional women who defied their restrictive societal mold. These were women of extraordinary individuality and courage who were compelled to act and speak out. Some of these women were known for their godly ways and good deeds; others were notoriously evil; but all were women of power.

Jael: Pretending to offer Sisera protection and hospitality, Jael drove a peg into the army captain's temple, killing him while he slept in her tent (Jdg 4:17–22; 5:24–27).

Bathsheba: In spite of her ignoble entry into David's life, Bathsheba maneuvered herself into a position of political power in the royal court during David's latter years. She convinced David to make Solomon the next king of Israel, and after David's death she exerted power and influence over her son, King Solomon (2Sa 11–12; 1Ki 1–2).

Jezebel: A strong-willed and evil queen, Jezebel succeeded in forcing Baal worship on her husband Ahab, the royal household, and on Israel. She massacred God's prophets, arranged the execution of Naboth, and sent the prophet Elijah into hiding (1Ki 16:31; 18:4, 13, 19; 19:1–2; 21).

Huldah: A wise prophet who gave advice to Hilkiah the priest (and a deputation sent by King Josiah) on the ancient scroll of God's Law discovered in the temple (2Ki 22:14–20).

Judith: The apocryphal tale of Judith is one of resourcefulness and courage. When Israel was under siege by the Assyrians and the situation seemed hopeless, Judith encouraged the townspeople to trust God for a victory. Disarming the unsuspecting Assyrian general by her kind friendship, Judith overpowered Holofernes, cutting off his head. His troops fled, and Israel won an easy victory (Book of Judith).

In the apocryphal work the Book of Judith, the story is told of the delivery of Israel from its enemy Holofernes. Judith entices him to her tent. When he falls asleep, she cuts off his head. This depiction of Judith, her maidservant, and the severed head of Holofernes is by Italian artist Artemisia Gentileschi (c.1593–1653).

Herodias: When John the Baptist spoke out against the adulterous marriage of Herodias to King Herod (Antipas), she had John arrested and put in prison. Not satisfied with that, she asked for his head and had John the Baptist executed (Mk 6:17–29).

Priscilla: When Priscilla chose to marry Aquila, the Jewish former slave, she undoubtedly shocked her wealthy Roman family, and certainly those in her social setting. Priscilla and Aquila were clearly leaders in the early church, they were partners with Paul in tent-making, and they both had a part in the discipleship of the eloquent Apollos (Ac 18:24–26).

Phoebe: Probably an officer in her own church at Cenchreae, Phoebe was known for assisting the apostle Paul during his visits to Corinth and Cenchreae, for helping many other people, and for her community service. She was a valued member of the early church (Ro 16:1–2).

She persuaded Adam to join her in disobeying God, bringing sin into the world. Her curse was to experience suffering in childbirth and to have her mutual partnership with Adam give way to a relationship of conflict and inequity. God sent them out of the garden forever. Eve later bore Adam many children, including Cain, Abel, and Seth. (Gen 1:26–31)

"God made the wild animals of every kind, and the cattle of every kind, and everything that creeps upon the ground of every kind. And God saw that it was good." (Gen 1:25)

God—The biblical narrative is the story of God and his dealings with humanity. From Genesis to Revelation, God is pictured as the beginning and end of history—its Creator, Sustainer, and Redeemer. The Bible does not contain a formal definition of God, nor do any of its writers argue for his existence, which is presumed throughout Scripture. Yet even though we cannot fully capture the essence and character of God because he is limitless, we can be certain of many things about him from the biblical record—his word and his revelation to us. Here are a number of important facts about the Lord:

- God is self-existent (Ex 3:13–14).
- God is self-sufficient (Ps 50:10–12).
- God is omniscient—he knows everything (Isa 40:13–14).
- God is infinite spirit—he is without the limitations of his creatures (Jn 4:24).
- God is eternal—in relation to space, he is everywhere; in relation to the universe, he is both within it and outside it (Ps 139).
- God is immutable—he cannot change (Heb 1:10–12).
- God is sovereign and all-powerful (Isa 46:9–11).
- There is only one God, and he reveals himself in three forms—Father, Son, and Holy Spirit (Gen 1:26; Mt 28:19; 2Co 13:14).
- God is holy and pure—he cannot tolerate sin (1Pe 1:15).
- God is true, righteous, and just (Heb 6:18; Ps 119:137).
- God is faithful and loving (Ps 89:1–2).
- God is kind, good, and compassionate (Ps 107:8).
- God is the Creator and Judge of the universe (Isa 40).

From beginning to end, God's story is one of profound love for humanity. We see him as a compas-

NAMES OF GOD

God is known in Scripture by many titles or descriptions. The following list identifies some of the more popular Hebrew names, and provides more insight into the nature of God.

Name	Meaning	Reference
Elohim	God—a plural term implying the power and richness of the God of Israel	Ps 19:1
Yahweh	the Lord, or Jehovah (appears some 6,800 times in the Bible)	Gen 2:4
Jehovah Jireh	the Lord provides	Gen 22:14
El Shaddai	God almighty	Ps 91:1
Lord of hosts	Savior and protector of Israel, a title used frequently by the prophets	Isa 6:1–3

sionate creator concerned about Adam's loneliness and as a shaper of history who called Abraham to faith. God revealed himself as a loving father when he led and disciplined his wayward people. He was a moral authority, thundering from Mt. Sinai, and a delighted father enjoying the baptism of his son, Jesus.

God's pure love and holy righteousness motivated him to send his son to deal with the problem of sin. The coming of the long-expected Messiah gave humanity the chance to come home to God. It was in the humanity of Jesus that God revealed himself most clearly. The Bible declares that God was the power behind the death, resurrection, and ascension of Jesus; and it was God who orchestrated the phenomenal spread of Christianity. However, God's leading and directing history did not end there.

He promises his people a hope and a future beyond the grave. It is he who will usher in the end of the age, and establish a new heaven and earth (Rev 21). By putting together what is yet to be with what has already been, the Bible makes it clear that all of history lies within the purpose and power of God.

Holy Spirit—Christian tradition has often relegated the Holy Spirit to a shadowy behind-the-scenes role in religious life. But this is by far an inaccurate picture. The Holy Spirit— who has always been present—is an equal partner in the Godhead. He was involved in the birth of Creation, active throughout the making of the Bible story, and he will be involved at the end of history, doing the work of God in particular ways.

The Bible best describes the Spirit as "wind, breath" (Hebrew, *ruah*; Greek, *pneuma*). This portrays his invisible power and ability to move freely everywhere. The Spirit of the Lord rushed on Samson, then left just as quickly (Jdg 14:19; 16:20). At the baptism of Jesus, the Holy Spirit descended on him like a dove, assuring him of God's love and delight in him (Mt 3:16–17). In the Pentecost narrative, the Spirit came in the form of rushing wind and divided tongues of fire, spreading power and unity over a crowd of waiting pilgrims (Ac 2).

This masterpiece by 16th-century painter El Greco reflects the passion and power of Pentecost and the coming of the Holy Spirit (Ac 2). The dove and tongues of fire, New Testament symbols of the third person of the Godhead, are represented.

THE HOLY SPIRIT—A PANORAMIC VIEW

Traits	Names	Ministries
Omnipresent (Ps 139:7)	Spirit of God (1Co 3:16)	Active in creation (Gen 1:2)
Omniscient (1Co 2:10–11)	Spirit of Christ (Ro 8:9)	Inspired the writing of the Scriptures (2Ti 3:16)
Omnipotent (Gen 1:2)	Eternal Spirit (Heb 9:14)	Helped Israel in the wilderness (Neh 9:20)
Eternal (Heb 9:14)	Spirit of truth (Jn 16:13)	Restrains Satan's power (Eph 6:10–18)
Equal with the father and with the Son (Mt 28:19–20)	Spirit of life (Ro 8:2)	Anointed Jesus (Mt 3:16)
He has a will (1Co 12:11)	Advocate (Jn 14:26)	Empowered Jesus (Mt 12:28)
He speaks (Ac 8:29)	Spirit of the Lord (Jdg 3:10)	Empowered the church (Ac 2)
He loves (Ro 15:30)	Spirit of the living God (2Co 3:3)	Indwells the believer (Ro 8:9)
He grieves (Eph 4:30)	Holy Spirit of promise (Eph 1:13)	Assures and guides the believer (Ro 8:14–15)
He prays (Ro 8:26)		Raises Christians from the dead (Ro 8:11)

Little is known of the personal life of the great Old Testament prophet Isaiah, represented in this 16th-century Russian icon. He was married to a woman who was also a prophet. She bore him two sons, each of whom was given a symbolic name as a sign of what God was going to do among his chosen people.

The Old Testament records a number of intermittent interactions between the Holy Spirit and a variety of people—from childless women to babes in the womb, from soldiers in battle to fugitives in hiding, from kings to peasants, and from priests to beggars.

In the New Testament, the image of the Spirit's work is specifically tied to the life of Jesus, to his coming at Pentecost, and to the life of the believer and the work of the church. God's Spirit not only lives in the believer and helps in the daily living of spiritual life (Ro 8), but he also gives spiritual gifts for the good of the church (1Co 12:7), and equips the church for ministry to others (Eph 4:12).

Isaiah (8th century B.C.)—An outstanding poet, writer, and statesman who lived in Jerusalem, Isaiah is considered the greatest Old Testament prophet. He lived during the reigns of Uzziah, Jotham, Ahaz, and Hezekiah. When he was about 25, he had a profound vision of God, and from that day on devoted himself to the vocation of prophecy.

Isaiah had a wife and two sons, both of whom were given symbolic names as a sign of what God was going to do among his people: the oldest was Shear-jashub ("the remnant will return") and the youngest was Maher-shalal-hash-baz ("the spoil speeds and the prey hastens")—a reference to the impending downfall of Samaria.

The two small kingdoms of Israel and Judah, often at odds with each other, were under the threat of advancing Assyria (the dominant power in Mesopotamia) and Egyptian military assaults from the south. Throughout this time of political and military threat, Isaiah's basic message warned against looking for safety in armies and ever-shifting alliances with various nations. His faith and vision led him to proclaim that God, and only God, had established and would protect the Hebrew nation.

More than a prophetic advisor to Judah's kings, Isaiah spoke out against idolatry, religious hypocrisy, and the rich and famous who ignored the plight of the poor. The prophet cared passionately about righteous living, and he did not hesitate to drive home the truth about social justice (Isa 58–59).

Even though Judah could not escape the consequences of their disobedience, Isaiah's message of warning included an element of hope. In time, God would destroy the enemies of the Jews and bring them back from exile. Isaiah also looked forward to the day when God's suffering servant—the Messiah—would come. (2Ki 19:2)

Jacob (20th century B.C.)—When he was born, Jacob was clutching his first-born twin brother's heel. From that moment on, there was rivalry and conflict between Jacob and Esau that would last for years to come. Matters were exacerbated years later when Jacob persuaded Esau to give up his rights as the first-born son in exchange for a bowl of stew. Thus Jacob—pretending to be Esau—gained Isaac's special blessing. When the plot was uncovered, Esau was enraged and planned to kill his cunning twin brother.

This dramatic depiction of Jacob and an angel illustrates the account in the Book of Genesis of Jacob's nocturnal wrestling match with a "man," also described as God. It was at this place, Peniel, that Jacob was given the name "Israel."

Jacob escaped to relatives in Haran. On the way there, God vowed to keep his promise to Abraham through Jacob and his descendants. Jacob worked for Laban, his uncle, for 20 years. He first married Laban's daughter Leah through the trickery of his uncle, then her younger sister Rachel, whom he loved.

While in Haran, Jacob became the father of many sons and a daughter by Leah and two maids in his household. He waited years for the birth of Joseph, then later Benjamin, by his beloved Rachel (who died giving birth to their second son). Jacob favored these two boys over his other children, and long-established family patterns of favoritism and jealousy continued.

Although Laban continued his practice of cheating and deceiving his nephew, Jacob built up his own flocks of sheep and goats, and left with his household for home. He never returned to Haran again. On his way home, Jacob had an unusual and significant encounter with an angel in human form. At this point his name was changed from Jacob to "Israel" which means "one who strives with God."

After this, Jacob and Esau were warmly reunited, but afterward they went their separate ways. Jacob lived in the land of Canaan until his son Joseph invited him to settle in Egypt. Before he died, Jacob blessed his twelve sons, who became the twelve tribes of Israel—the fulfillment of God's promise to Abraham. (Gen 25:26)

Jesus (1st century A.D.)—The name Jesus (meaning "salvation") was common among Jews during the Greco-Roman occupation. However, Jesus of Nazareth was not simply a common man. He is the historical figure whom Christians believe to be the Son of God incarnate—that is, God-in-the-flesh.

Close to the end of the short three-year ministry of Jesus, it became clear that the Jewish leaders were afraid of his claims and power, and they wanted to kill him. Judas betrayed his leader for 30 pieces of silver, helping the enemies of Jesus find and capture him at night. Jesus was arrested in the Garden of Gethsemane, close to Jerusalem, and he was tried and condemned by a Jewish court before dawn. Pilate, the Roman governor, ratified his death sentence for the sake of the crowd, even though he knew that Jesus was innocent of any charges.

JESUS CHRIST—BOTH MAN AND GOD

The Humanity of Jesus	The Deity of Jesus
He had a human mother (Lk 1:31)	He healed disease (Mt 8:1–4)
He had a human body (Mt 26:12)	He cast out demons (Mt 8:16–17)
He grew (Lk 2:40)	He had authority over all people (Jn 17:2)
He increased in wisdom (Lk 2:52)	He had power over nature (Mt 8:26)
He prayed (Mk 1:35)	He had power over sin (Mt 9:1–8)
He was tempted (Mt 4:1)	He had power over death (Lk 7:14–15)
He learned obedience (Heb 5:8)	He knew all about Nathanael (Jn 1)
He was hungry (Mt 4:2)	He knew all about Judas (Jn 6:70)
He was thirsty (Jn 4:7)	He knew all about the Samaritan woman (Jn 4:24)
He was tired (Jn 4:6)	He is omnipresent today (Mt 18:20)
He slept (Mt 8:24)	He was worshiped as God by a leper (Mt 8:2)
He loved others (Mk 10:21)	He was worshiped as God by Thomas (Jn 20:28)
He was angry (Mk 3:5)	He was worshiped as God by his disciples (Mt 14:33)
He wept (Jn 11:35)	He judges (Jn 5:22)
He was troubled (Mk 14:33–34)	He forgave wrongdoing (Mk 2:5)
He sweat profusely (Lk 22:44)	He gives eternal life (Jn 10:28)
He suffered (1Pe 4:1)	Paul called him God (Gal 2:20)
He bled (Jn 19:34)	Peter identified him with God (1Pe 3:22)
He died (Mt 27:50)	Jude called him God (Jude 25)
He was buried (Mt 27:59–60)	He rose from the dead (Mt 28:5–6)

Jesus was crucified and buried in the tomb of Joseph of Arimathaea. Three days later, a group of women found the tomb empty and an angel told them that Jesus was alive. During the next 40 days, his followers and many others saw him, and were convinced by his resurrection that he was truly the Son of God. Then Jesus ascended to the glory of heaven, and his followers were left with the assurance that he would return one day. (Mt, Mk, Lk, Jn, Ac 1:1–11)

Mary (1st century B.C.)—The young Jewish virgin was engaged to Joseph the carpenter, a descendant of Abraham and David, when the angel Gabriel visited her with some startling news. Mary was amazed to learn that she would soon become the mother of Jesus. When the angel told her that she would become pregnant by the power of the Holy Spirit, Mary accepted this assignment in spite of the shame associated with a pregnancy before marriage.

Before Jesus was born, Mary visited her cousin Elizabeth, who was also expecting a baby. When the women greeted each other, the baby in Elizabeth's womb (John the Baptist) moved in delight at hearing the voice of the mother of Jesus. Overcome with joy, Mary broke out in a song of praise (historically known as the Magnificat). She praised God for his mercy to the humble and poor and for his justice upon the rich and the proud.

Mary and Joseph left Nazareth to register in Bethlehem for a Roman census, and it was there that Jesus was born. His humble birth in an animal holding was acknowledged by angels and shepherds. When Jesus was presented at the temple eight days after his birth, Simeon and Anna honored him as the long-awaited Messiah. Some time later, after a visit from wise men from the East, the family had to escape to Egypt because King Herod, perceiving the baby Jesus as a rival, wanted to kill him.

The Annunciation by El Greco (1541–1614) depicts Mary receiving the words of the angel Gabriel: "Greetings favored one! The Lord is with you . . . And now, you will conceive in your womb and bear a son, and you will name him Jesus. He will be great, and will be called the Son of the Most High, and the Lord God will give to him the throne of his ancestor David. . . . " (Lk 1:28, 31–32)

A caring and loving parent, Mary was present at all the major milestones in her son's life. She was searching for her missing 12-year-old when he was at the temple confounding the teachers. Mary was there at Cana when Jesus—prompted by her—performed his first miracle. She stood at the foot of the cross and watched her son suffer an excruciating death. And Mary was with the disciples when they met together to pray after Jesus' ascension. Mary led a life of quiet dignity and strength, strong faith, and enormous purpose. (Mt 1:18)

Moses' sister, Miriam, led the Israelite women in a dance and a song of praise to God for their deliverance from the Egyptians and the waters of the Red Sea (Ex 15:20).

Miriam (15th century B.C.)—The sister of Moses and Aaron, Miriam played an instrumental role in saving the nation of Israel. When she was just a girl of 12, the King of Egypt ordered all Jewish baby boys slaughtered as a means of population control—including her newborn brother Moses. Her mother put the young boy in a makeshift lifeboat and floated him down the Nile. He was discovered by Pharaoh's daughter, who decided to keep the Jewish child. Miriam, who had watched from a distance, struck up a conversation and offered to fetch a Hebrew woman to nurse the baby. She then brought her own mother. Miriam had saved Moses' life and returned him to his mother's arms!

During the Exodus of the Israelites from Egypt and their subsequent 40 years in the desert, Miriam shared leadership with her two brothers, Moses and Aaron. Her strength and guidance was evident. After the parting of the Red Sea, she led thousands of the women in joyful singing and dancing in triumphant worship. But Miriam did not always support her brother and sing praises. She spoke out against Moses when he married a Cushite (Ethiopian) woman, and later joined Aaron in public rebellion against Moses' leadership. For this, she was struck with leprosy by God. Moses cried out to the Lord to forgive her sins and Miriam was healed, but only after she was quarantined outside the camp for seven days. (Ex 15:20–21)

Moses (15th century B.C.)—Born and brought up in Egypt, Moses became a great leader who freed the Israelites from slavery, led them through the wilderness, and brought them to the borders of Canaan. Although a Hebrew, he was brought up by the daughter of the Pharaoh and educated at the palace as an Egyptian.

Angered one day by the cruel treatment of the Israelites, Moses killed an Egyptian overseer. For his own safety, Moses fled into the desert and lived there for years as a shepherd. He married the daughter of Jethro, the man who took him in when he escaped.

Forty years after leaving Egypt, God spoke to Moses from a burning desert bush. He told Moses to go back to Egypt to rescue the Israelites from the Pharaoh's grasp. Along with his brother Aaron, Moses spoke to the Pharaoh, who refused to let the people go. God plagued the Egyptians with trouble, until finally the Pharaoh released the Israelites. The Egyptian army pursued their former slaves as far as the Red Sea, but the Israelites escaped into the desert and the Egyptian army was drowned.

The daughter of Pharoah discovers a baby in a basket among the reeds by the river in this painting by Raphael. She named the baby Moses (which means "drawn out") because he was rescued from the water.

At Mt. Sinai, God gave Moses the Law and instructions for building the tent of worship (tabernacle). During their time in the wilderness, the people often turned against Moses, complaining about food, water, and other desert conditions. They even forgot about God's power and turned to idol worship. Because of their faithlessness, the people were condemned to wander in the desert until all those who rebelled had died.

Before Moses handed the leadership of the people to Joshua, he gave God's Law to the new generation of Israelites. When he gave the people his final blessing, Moses climbed Mt. Nebo so he could glimpse Canaan, the Promised Land that he could not enter because of his own earlier sin. Moses—a great man of God—then died in the desert of Moab. (Ex 2:2)

Paul (1st century A.D.)—A dominant personality in the early church movement, Paul was an outstanding champion of Jesus Christ—an apostle and missionary whose letters make up a large part of the New Testament. Born a Jew, Paul was a Roman citizen educated in Jerusalem by Rabbi Gamaliel. At first, a Pharisee who strongly opposed the Christian movement, Paul supported the persecuting of Christians and was present at the stoning of Stephen.

The wonders that Paul performed at Ephesus are recorded in the Book of Acts: "God did extraordinary miracles through Paul, so that when the handkerchiefs or aprons that had touched his skin were brought to the sick, their diseases left them, and the evil spirits came out of them." (Ac 19:11–12)

In a dramatic incident on the Damascus road, Paul became converted to Christianity. After his baptism in Damascus, Paul immediately started preaching. When the Jews plotted to kill him, Paul moved on to Jerusalem. The Christians there were skeptical of Paul but Barnabas, a kind, encouraging Christian leader, introduced him to the apostles, and the Christian community embraced the new convert. Again, Paul's life was threatened, so he returned to Tarsus. Paul and Barnabas helped establish the church at Antioch in Syria.

Later, the two men embarked on a missions trip to take the Christian message to many people in Cyprus and Asia Minor. The missionaries then reported back to the church in Antioch. Paul went on to help the Jewish Christians in Jerusalem understand and accept that Jesus Christ came to be the Savior of all ethnic groups, not just the Jews.

Silas was Paul's helper on his second missionary journey. They visited the church in Galatia, then Timothy joined them in Lystra. From Troas they sailed to Greece, where they were joined by Luke, the author of the Gospel and Acts. At

Philippi, Paul and Silas were beaten and imprisoned. After their release, they traveled through Greece and Paul ended up in Corinth, where he stayed for more than a year.

On his third missionary trek, Paul did intensive ministry in Ephesus. Days were long as he worked to support himself and did preaching and teaching. After three winters there, working among Jews and Greeks, Paul moved on to Corinth to prepare for his visit to Rome. Then once more he traveled on to Jerusalem to tell the believers there of the spread of the Christian faith. He was arrested in Jerusalem, then sent to Caesarea to be tried. Imprisoned for two years, Paul was eventually sent to Rome for trial.

In this 19th-century painting, Peter denies knowing Jesus the Galilean. Later, filled with remorse because of his words and actions, Peter wept bitterly (Mt 26:69–75).

The sea journey to Rome included a shipwreck, lack of food, and an encounter with a venomous snake bite on the island of Malta. Yet God preserved Paul and his company through it all. When Paul got to Rome, he was kept under house arrest for more than two years. During this time he boldly preached the good news.

The Bible does not record Paul's death, but in his last message to Timothy, Paul indicates that his end is near. The fourth-century church historian Eusebius states that Paul was executed in Rome by Nero in 67 A.D. (Ac 7:58)

Peter (1st century A.D.)—A fisherman by trade, Peter was called by Jesus to be a disciple. Along with the call came a change of name: Known by everyone as Simon, Jesus changed his name to Peter (which means "rock"). It was this disciple who would later identify Jesus as the Christ, the Son of the living God. And in response to Peter's confession, Jesus would promise to establish the church on him, and give him the keys to the kingdom of heaven.

Peter was one of Jesus' closest followers. He was with Jesus at the transfiguration and in the Garden of Gethsemane just before his arrest. Although fiercely loyal to his leader, he was quick to deny ever knowing Jesus, and he deeply regretted this betrayal. However, Jesus loved and understood this impetuous disciple of his, and at Lake Galilee told him to be a shepherd to the Christian "flock." Jesus was certain of Peter's strength of character, his ability to lead, and his commitment to the kingdom of God.

At Pentecost, Peter preached about Jesus to the pilgrims in Jerusalem, and about 3,000 became believers. At first Peter only shared the gospel with the Jews, but God convicted him in a special vision to show him that he must take the message of the kingdom of God to non-Jews also.

Later, King Herod saw to it that Peter was arrested and imprisoned, but the apostle escaped because of the fervent prayer of believers at the house of Mary, and an angel of the Lord who was sent to release him. Herod was furious at the news, and Peter went elsewhere to avoid further harm. Not much is known of Peter's activities after this point, but he is credited with the authorship of two New Testament letters. Church tradition holds that he suffered martyrdom at the hands of the Roman Emperor Nero in the middle of the 1st century A.D. (Mt 4:18)

And Jesus answered him, "Blessed are you, Simon son of Jonah!... you are Peter, and on this rock I will build my church, and the gates of Hades will not prevail against it." Mt 16:17,18

Ruth (12th century B.C.)—The story of Ruth is an inspiring tale of a non-Jewish woman whose romance with an Israelite resulted in her becoming an ancestor of the Messiah. During a great famine, Naomi, along with her husband and two sons, were forced to leave Bethlehem in search of food. While in Moab, her husband died and her sons, Mahlon and Chilion, married the Moabite women Ruth and Orpah. The sons also died, leaving the women widowed. Naomi planned to return to Bethlehem and told the two women to go back to their mothers, but Ruth refused to leave Naomi. (Ancient customs held that a widow was a servant of the dead husband's family.) Once in Bethlehem, the hand of God guided Ruth to work in a wheat field, where the owner, Boaz, was drawn to her. Under Jewish law, a dead man's nearest relative had the right to marry or "redeem" the widow. If he refused, that right would pass on to the nearest kin. Boaz was a distant relative of Mahlon, so he waited at the city gate for a closer relative to claim redemption rights to Ruth. One was willing to buy the dead husband's land, but not marry Ruth; thus giving the rights to Boaz. Ruth and Boaz were married and had a son named Obed, who became the grandfather of David. (Ru 1–4.)

This painting by James Tissot depicts Ruth gleaning wheat in the field of Boaz. The Book of Ruth shows that the ancestry of Jesus came about through the marriage of a Jew and a Gentile.

Samuel (11th century* B.C.*)—The long-awaited son of Elkanah and Hannah, Samuel grew up to be the last great judge in Israel and one of its fine prophets. When Samuel was a toddler, Hannah kept her promise to God and brought the child to the shrine at Shiloh to be raised by Eli the priest.

One night while he was under Eli's care, God spoke to Samuel about the downfall of the house of Eli because of the corruption of Eli's two sons. When Israel was defeated by the Philistines at the battle of Aphek, Eli's two sons were killed and the sacred ark of the covenant was captured. When Eli heard the news, he was devastated and fell over backward, breaking his neck.

Samuel was now faced with a difficult situation. The Israelites felt that God no longer cared about them. At Mizpah, Samuel told the people to turn away from pagan gods, to repent, and to serve the God of Israel only. Once again the Philistine army began to attack God's people, and Samuel cried to the Lord for help. God answered Samuel's prayers. The Philistines were thrown into confusion and retreated. Samuel marked this victory by setting up a stone to the Lord and naming the place, Ebenezer, meaning "stone of help." After this, Samuel settled in Ramah, close to Jerusalem, and ruled Israel all his life.

A rich and royal representation of Samuel and David by Dutch artist Jan Vitors (1598–1684). Samuel took the horn of oil and anointed David, the handsome young son of Jesse, as king of the people of Israel (1 Sa 16:13).

When Samuel was old, he appointed his sons Joel and Abijah as judges and handed his work over to them. But the Israelites were displeased with their lack of justice and asked for a monarch instead. Samuel was against this idea at first, but God guided him to anoint Saul as Israel's first king. After Saul proved to be a disobedient and willful king, Samuel secretly anointed David as the next in line for the monarchy.

All of Israel mourned when the distinguished prophet and judge died. Samuel was an uncompromising man of God, diligent in a variety of roles in the religious and political life of Israel. The New Testament upholds Samuel as one of the great heroes of faith. (1Sa 1:20)

Satan—Appropriately, his name means "adversary," and Satan is portrayed in the Bible as the foremost enemy of God and humanity. Known by a host of names that serve to iden-

Satan, who was cast out of heaven, is portrayed in hell. The Bible says his final defeat will be the "lake of fire and sulfur," a place of torment that has been prepared for the devil and his angels at the end of time (Rev 20:7–10).

tify him as the source of all aspects of evil, Satan began his earthly career with the temptation of Adam and the woman. The prophet Ezekiel portrays Satan as a created being who once resided in heaven in a perfect, blameless state. However, he grew proud and desired to be like God and rule over him. Because of his flawed ambition and self-deification, Satan was thrown out of heaven and given the limited position of "ruler of the power of the air" (Eph 2:2). Thus began the adversarial relationship between God and Satan, good and evil, holiness and sin, life and death.

Even though Satan is without the powers of God, he still has the ability to seduce the human race. Thus the struggle between Satan and people is a constant theme throughout the Bible. Even though subject to God's ultimate authority, Satan afflicted Job with tragedy, tempted Jesus when he was hungry and weak, and ensnared the heart of Judas. Job ultimately prevailed as good won over evil, Jesus rebuked the enemy with the word of God, but Judas fell victim to the devil's temptation.

However, the New Testament teaches that Satan's ultimate power was broken through the work of Jesus on the cross (Heb 2:14). The victory over sin and death was won by God then, but the final defeat of Satan, his angels, and his followers will not be realized until after the final judgment (Rev 20). Until then, Satan continues his attempts to destroy God's plan and usurp his position.

SATAN'S NAMES

Most commonly known by the name Satan (adversary), this designation appears some 52 times in the Bible. Another frequent name—devil (slanderer)—appears 35 times. He is also called by many other descriptive names that help to identify the nature and work of Satan.

The ruler of the power of the air *(Eph 2:2)*
The god of this world *(2Co 4:4)*
The ruler of this world *(Jn 12:31)*
Day Star, son of Dawn *(Isa 14:12)*
The dragon *(Rev 12:7)*
The angel of the bottomless pit *(Rev 9:11)*
Abaddon or Apollyon (destruction, ruin) *(Rev 9:11)*
Beelzebul *(Mt 12:24)*
Beliar *(2Co 6:15)*
The evil one *(Mt 13:38)*
The tempter *(1Th 3:5)*
The accuser of our comrades *(Rev 12:10)*
An angel of light *(2Co 11:14–15)*
A murderer *(Jn 8:44)*
The father of lies *(Jn 8:44)*
The enemy *(Mt 13:39)*

Absalom, gifted and handsome, was the rebellious and ambitious son of David. He was a constant source of division and suffering to both his family and the nation. Absalom's death came when he got caught in an oak tree. He became an easy target for his enemies, who pierced his heart as he dangled from the tree (2 Sa 18).

WHO'S WHO FROM ABEL TO ZERUBBABEL

The Bible identifies at least 4,000 individuals, as well as nations and groups of people. This abbreviated list highlights a cross-section of Bible personalities. Almost every entry includes a definition of the person's name. (However, readers should know that the meanings given are merely educated guesses by scholars.) A brief description of each character is also provided, as well as the first Biblical reference for that person.

Abel (breath or vapor or son; possibly 'meadow'): The second son of Adam and Eve, he was murdered by his brother Cain (Gen 4:1–10).

Abishag (possibly 'my father was a wanderer'): A capable and attractive woman chosen to nurse the elderly David. She may also be the central female figure of the Song of Solomon (1Ki 1:3).

Absalom (father of peace): David's son; he tried to usurp the throne from his father (2Sa 3:3).

Adam (human being or humanity): The first man, and husband of Eve. Their sin caused a curse on all humanity (Gen 1:26–27).

Adonijah (the Lord is my Lord): One of David's sons; he was executed by Solomon for attempting to usurp the throne (2Sa 3:4).

Amalek (warlike): A son of Eliphaz and the forefather of the Amalekites (Gen 36:12, 16).

Amram (the kinsman is exalted): A descendant of Levi and an ancestor of Aaron, Moses, and Miriam (Ex 6:18, 20).

Ananias (the Lord is gracious): A follower of Christ who was struck dead for trying to deceive the apostles (Ac 5:1, 3, 5).

Anna (grace): A prophet and woman of prayer in Christ's time; she was of the tribe of Asher (Lk 2:36).

Apollos (possibly 'a destroyer'): A Jewish Christian and enthusiastic student of the Scriptures (Ac 18:24).

Aquila (eagle): Husband of Priscilla and friend of Paul (Ac 18:2, 18, 26).

Augustus (consecrated or holy) Caesar: The imperial name of Octavian, Julius Caesar's nephew who became emperor of Rome. Jesus was born during his reign (Lk 2:1).

Balaam (possibly 'devourer'): A prophet that the king of Moab persuaded to curse Israel. However, God put words of blessing in Balaam's mouth instead (Nu 22–24).

Barabbas (father's son or son of Abba): A murderer who was released to the people instead of Jesus (Mt 27:17).

Barnabas (son of consolation): A Jewish Christian who traveled with Paul; he was known for his ability to encourage others (Ac 4:36).

Bernice (victorious): She and her brother Agrippa (with whom she had an incestuous relationship) sat in judgment on Paul (Ac 25:13).

Caesar: The name of a branch of the family of the Julii that eventually gained control of the Roman government. Later it came to be known as the formal title of the Roman emperors.

Caiaphas (meaning unknown): The high priest who played a major role in the trial of Jesus (Mt 26:3).

Cain (to acquire): The eldest son of Adam and Eve; he murdered his brother Abel (Gen 4:1–25).

Caleb (dog or rabid): One of the spies sent out by Moses to evaluate the Promised Land (Nu 13:6)

Candace (pure): A dynastic title of the queens of Ethiopia (Ac 8:27).

Claudius Caesar (meaning unknown): The Roman emperor who banished the Jews from Rome (Ac 18:2).

Cyrus the Great (son): Founder of the Persian Empire; he returned the Jews to their land (Ezr 1:1–4).

Delilah (small or dainty): The Philistines paid Delilah to find out the secret of Samson's strength—and then betray him (Jdg 16).

The Israelite Samson courted and married the Philistine Delilah. He allowed his dominating passion for her to lead him to violate his Nazirite vow: He revealed to her the source of his amazing strength. In turn, she gladly betrayed him for a large sum of money (Jdg 16:4–21).

Dinah (justice): The daughter of Jacob and Leah who was violated by Hamor. This act resulted in tribal war (Gen 34).

Elizabeth (God is my oath): Married to Zechariah the priest, and mother of John the Baptist (Lk 1:5–57).

Elymas (meaning unknown): This false prophet opposed Saul and Barnabas at Paphos (Ac 13:8).

Epaphroditus (handsome or charming): A Philippian Christian who worked so strenuously that he lost his health (Php 2:25).

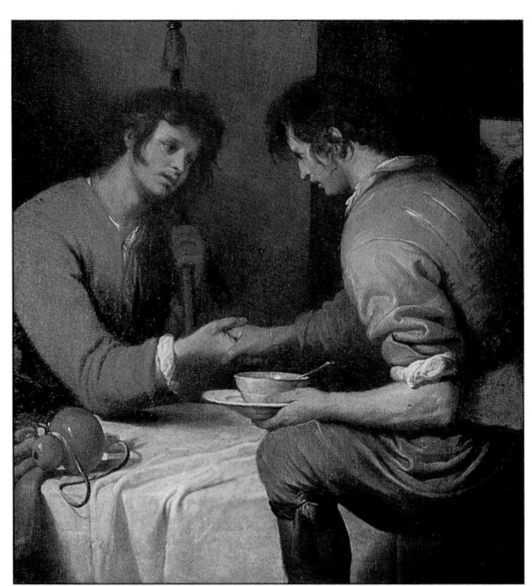

In a moment of hunger, Esau gave away his father's covenant to his brother Jacob for a bowl of stew and some bread. The moment when Esau "despised his birthright" (Gen 25:34) is captured by Italian artist Giovanni Andrea Ferrari (1598–1669).

Esau (hairy or shaggy): Jacob's twin brother and ancestor of the tribe of Edom. He sold his birthright to Jacob (Gen 25:25).

Ezekiel (God strengthens): A prophet who was taken captive to Babylon. He prophesied to the exiles in Mesopotamia (Eze 1:3).

Felix (happy): The Roman governor of Judea who presided over Paul's trial at Caesarea (Ac 23:23–27).

Festus (joyful): The successor of Felix; he continued the trial of Paul (Ac 25).

Gideon (cutter or hewer): The outstanding judge of Israel who delivered his people from Midian (Jdg 6–8).

Habakkuk (embracer or wrestler): A prophet during the reigns of Jehoiakim and Josiah who predicted the Exile (Hab 1:1).

Hosea (the Lord has saved): A prophet of Israel; he spoke out against the idolatries of Israel and Samaria (Hos 1:1–2).

Hur (meaning unknown): One of the men who held up the arms of Moses during the battle with Amalek (Ex 17:10).

Isaac (laughing or he laughed): The son born to Abraham and Sarah in their old age. The father of Esau and Jacob and an ancestor of Jesus (Gen 21–25).

Ishmael (God heard): The son of Abraham and Hagar; he established a clan of desert dwellers considered to be the ancestors of today's Arab nations (Gen 16:11–16).

Jairus (the Lord Enlightens): A ruler of the synagogue near Capernaum; Jesus raised his daughter from the dead (Lk 8:41).

James (supplanter): One of Jesus' 12 disciples; he was the son of Zebedee and brother of John. James was put to death by Herod Agrippa I (Mt 4:21).

James: The brother of Jesus who became a believer after Christ's resurrection. He became a leader of the church at Jerusalem, and he wrote the Letter of James (Ac 12:17).

Jemimah (little dove): The first daughter of Job to be born after he was restored from his troubles (Job 42:14).

Jeremiah (the Lord establishes or the Lord is exalted): A prophet whose work covered the reigns of the last five kings of Judah (Jer 1).

Jesse (meaning unknown): David's father and an ancestor of Jesus (1Sa 17:17).

Job (meaning unknown): A godly man; he endured fierce trial that resulted in tremendous blessing (Job 1–3).

Jochebed (the Lord is glory): A descendant of Levi and the mother of Moses (Ex 6:20).

John (the Lord has been gracious) the Baptist: He came to prepare the way for the Messiah (Mt 3).

John the Apostle: One of the 12 apostles. The fourth Gospel, three epistles, and the Book of Revelation are all ascribed to his authorship (Mt 4:21).

Jonah (dove): A Hebrew prophet sent to preach to the people of Nineveh (2Ki 14:25).

Jonathan (the Lord has given): Saul's son and David's close friend (1Sa 14).

Joseph (may God add): The son of Jacob and Rachel; he was sold into slavery in Egypt but then rose to the position of prime minister there (Gen 37).

Joshua (the Lord is salvation): Moses' successor; he led the conquest of the Promised Land (Ex 17:9–14).

Lazarus (God has helped): The brother of Mary and Martha. Jesus raised him from the dead (Jn 11:1).

Lot (concealed or covering): Abraham's nephew; he escaped from corrupt Sodom (Gen 13:1–14).

Mark (large hammer): A Christian convert and Paul's helper; he wrote the second Gospel (Ac 12:12).

Martha (lady): The sister of Mary and Lazarus who lived in Bethany (Lk 10:38).

Mordecai (consecrated to Marduk [a pagan god]): A Jewish exile who helped Esther save the Jews from destruction (Est 2–10).

Naaman (pleasantness): A Syrian general healed of leprosy by bathing in the Jordan (2Ki 5).

In the style of the High Renaissance, Raphael (1483–1520) shows Lot and his family fleeing Sodom. Lot's wife disobeyed the angels' warning: She looked back at the city and was turned into a pillar of salt (Gen 19).

Nehemiah (the Lord comforts): The governor of Jerusalem who helped rebuild that city (Ne 1:1).

Nicodemus (victor over the people): A pharisee who visited Jesus at night, and assisted in Christ's burial (Jn 3:1–15).

Noah (rest or comfort): The patriarch chosen to build the ark. He and his family survived the Flood (Gen 5:28–32).

Onesimus (profitable or useful): A Christian slave whom Paul defends as a brother in Christ in a letter to Philemon (Phm 10, 15).

Orpah (possibly 'neck'): Naomi's daughter-in-law (Ru 1:4–14).

Philip (lover of horses): One of the 12 apostles of Christ (Mt 10:3).

Pontius Pilate, the procurator of Judea, washes his hands before declaring himself innocent of the death of Jesus in this 17-century painting by Mathias Stomer. After this gesture, Pilate turned Jesus over to the crowd, who crucified the Messiah.

Pontius Pilate (javelin carrier): Fifth govenor of Judea. After trying several times to exonerate Jesus, Pilate was swayed by the angry crowd into crucifying him (Mt 27:24–26).

Potiphar (who Re [the sun god] has given): The Egyptian captain of the guard who became Joseph's master (Gen 37:36).

Publius (common or popular): The governor of Malta who graciously received Paul and his group when they were shipwrecked (Ac 28:1–10).

Rachel (ewe): The daughter of Laban, beloved wife of Jacob, and mother of Joseph and Benjamin (Gen 29–35).

Rahab (broad): The prostitute of Jericho who helped the Hebrew spies; she became an ancestor of Jesus (Jos 2:1–21).

Rebekah (meaning unknown): Isaac's wife and the mother of Jacob and Esau (Gen 24–28).

Samson (sun's man or distinguished): A judge of Israel for 20 years; his great physical strength and moral weakness made him notorious (Jdg 14–16).

Sapphira (beautiful or sapphire): The wife of Ananias; she was struck dead by God for her deception (Ac 5:1–10).

Sargon (he [the god] has established the kingship): An important Assyrian king who completed the siege of Samaria and carried the Israelites into exile (Isa 20:1).

Silas (of the woods): Companion of Paul on his second missionary journey; he was imprisoned with Paul at Philippi (Ac 15:22).

The apostle Thomas is most well-known for the doubt he expressed concerning the resurrection of his beloved Master. Thomas is seen here touching Jesus' side in this 17th -century painting by Giovanni Guercino.

Simon (he hears): One of Jesus' 12 apostles; he was called "the Zealot" (Mt 10:4).

Stephen (crown or crown-bearer): One of the seven deacons in the early church; he became the first martyr of the church (Ac 6:5–9).

Syntyche (fortunate): A woman of the church at Philippi (Php 4:2).

Tabitha (gazelle): The Christian woman of Joppa whom the apostle Peter raised from the dead (Ac 9:36–42).

Thomas (the twin): One of the 12 apostles; at first he doubted Christ's resurrection (Jn 20:24–29).

Tiglath-pileser (my trust is in the heir of [the temple] E-sharra): A king of Assyria who conquered northern Palestine and deported many from Naphtali (2Ki 15:29).

Timothy (man who honors God): The son of a Jewish mother and Greek father; the young convert traveled extensively with Paul (Ac 16:1).

Vashti (beautiful woman): The queen of Persia who was divorced by her husband because she refused to attend his great feast (Est 1:10–22).

Zacchaeus (pure): A tax collector whom Jesus visited when he was in Jericho (Lk 19:1–10).

Zerubbabel (seed of Babylon): The leader of the remnant who returned from the Exile; he began the rebuilding of the temple (Ezr 3–5).

CLANS, PEOPLE GROUPS, AND NATIONS

The 12 Tribes of Israel: Each Hebrew tribe was made up of all the descendants from one of the sons of the patriarch Jacob. The leader of each clan was known as a ruler, head, or a chief. The 12 tribes of Israel were grouped according to their fathers' houses while they were in Egypt. After they left the Pharaoh's land, the whole group began to operate as the 12 clans of Israel (Ex 24:4). And while they traveled through the wilderness, each group was assigned its place in which to march and to camp. When the Israelites were numbered, the tribe of Levi was not counted because God had set them apart

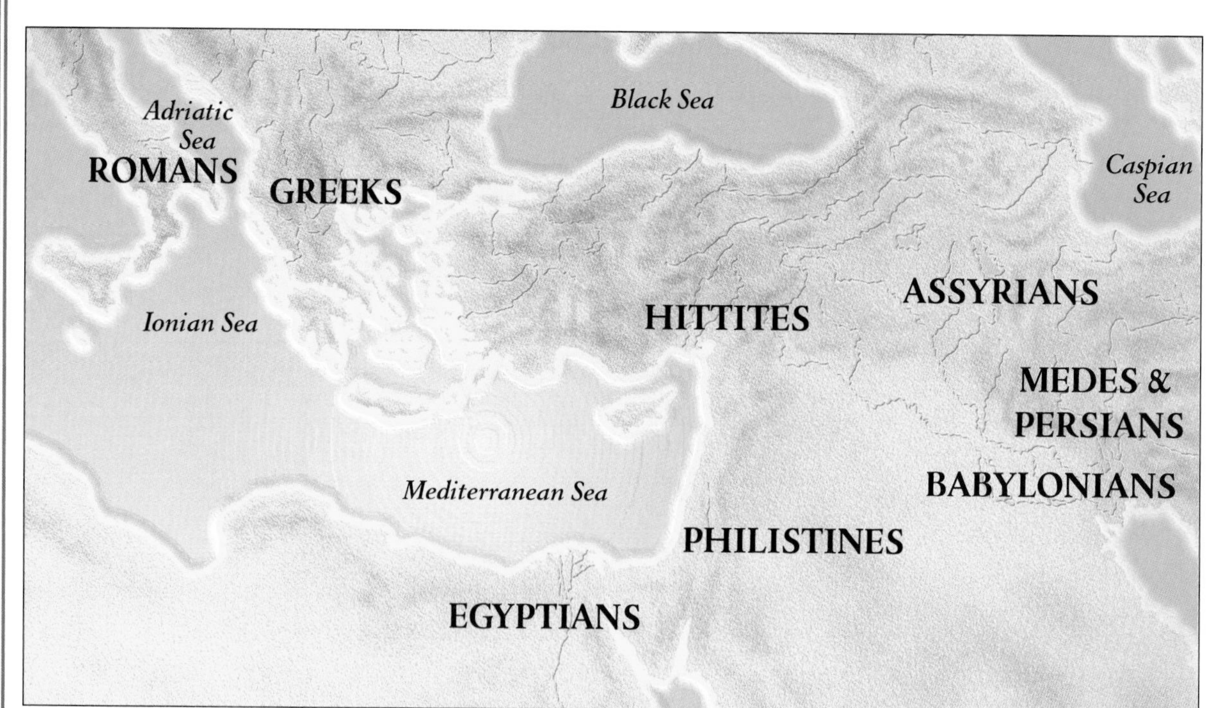

The Bible mentions many nations and groups of people. This map shows where some of the major groups of people were located during biblical times.

to take care of Israel's religious life. They had to keep and transport the tabernacle and its furniture, and they were responsible for worship and sacrifices.

The 12 sons of Jacob were Reuben, Simeon, Levi, Judah, Zebulun, Issachar, Dan, Gad, Asher, Naphtali, Joseph, and Benjamin. Although they were all fathered by Jacob, they had four mothers: Leah and Rachel (Jacob's wives), and Bilhah and Zilpah (household maids and concubines).

Before the Hebrew people entered the Promised Land, two tribes, Reuben and Gad (and part of Manasseh) decided to settle on the east side of the Jordan. When Canaan was conquered, its territory was divided among the remaining nine-and-a-half tribes.

During the time of the Judges, each clan determined its own laws and lifestyle. When David became king, he ruled over the whole land and Israel was unified. Jerusalem became the capital of the country—the political as well as the religious hub of the nation (2Ch 12:13).

After the death of Solomon, the tribes divided into two groups. Judah and Benjamin became one nation, the kingdom of Judah. And to the north of them, the remaining tribes formed the kingdom of Israel. This division continued until both kingdoms went into captivity, Israel in 721 B.C. to Assyria, and Judah in 586 B.C. to Babylon. These captivities marked the end of the tribal distinctions among the Hebrews.

The Egyptians: The might of ancient Egyptian culture and religion is well attested to by its many buildings, structures, and artifacts that still exist today. Besides the famous pyramids, the image of Pharaohs dominate many large building works, and huge pillars of the great hall in the Temple of Amun at Karnak still stand.

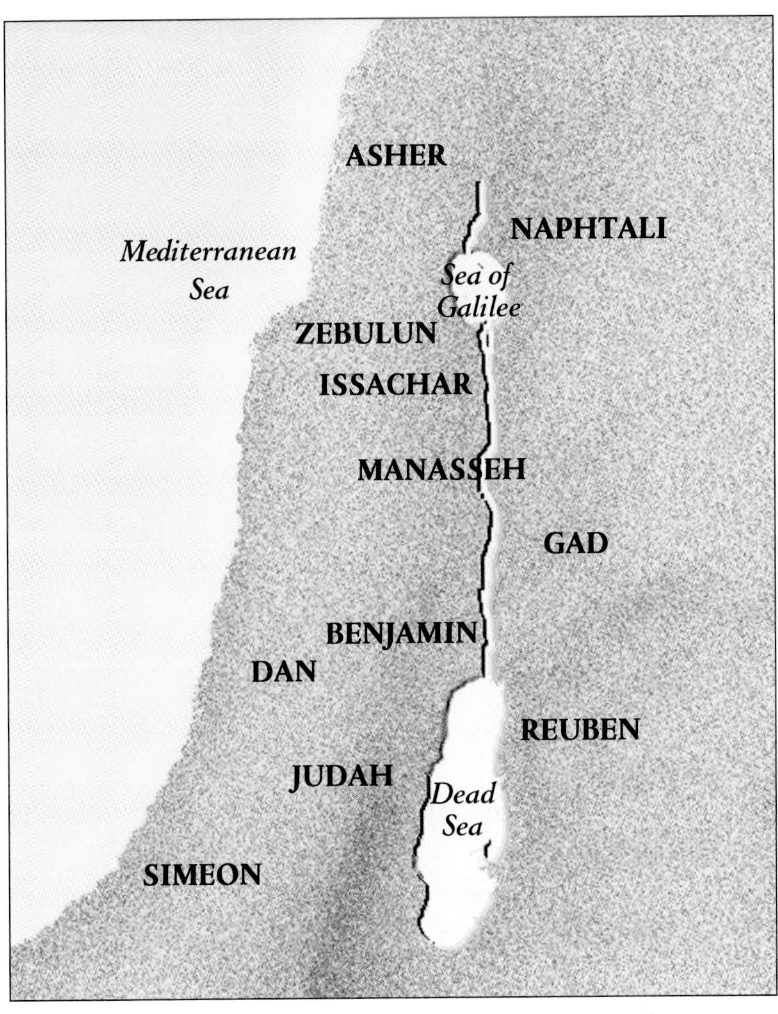

After the land of Canaan was conquered by the Israelites, its territory was divided among the descendents of the sons of Jacob. The capture of the kingdoms marked the end of these tribal divisions.

The life and culture of ancient Egypt centered around the great Nile river. Peasant farmers (most of Egypt's population during the time of Moses) depended on its annual flooding to irrigate crops and provide rich mud. At the end of the harvest, grain was always carefully recorded and stored. The Nile was also an important "highway" for travel. Egyptians quickly learned to make boats and use the waterway to their advantage. Besides the Nile, other parts of the region were also important. The deserts contained valuable metals, including copper and gold, and there was stone available for making the pyramids and temples of the Nile valley.

At the top of Egypt's social order was the Pharaoh, the king and chief negotiator between Egypt's pagan gods and the people. Second in command were two viziers who managed the vast political and social order of the culture. The people of this highly organized culture enjoyed many periods of greatness, but eventually became part of the Persian Empire, then later the Greek Ptolemies ruled Egypt until the coming of the Roman Empire.

The Canaanites: Renowned for their trading and crafts—and the first nation to develop an alphabet—the Canaanites were a people who settled at the eastern end of the Mediterranean Sea by about 2000 B.C. By Joshua's day, the land had been divided up into small, strongly fortified cities, each with its own king. The Canaanites traded up and down the Mediterranean Sea in their merchant ships. Their main ports were Tyre, Sidon, Berytus (Beirut), and Byblos.

The Philistines: The land of the Philistines consisted of five coastal cities: Ekron, Ashdod, Ashkelon, Gath, and Gaza. The settlers were originally warlike sea people who came from Crete in the 13th and 12th centuries B.C. They gave their name—Palestine—to the entire country. They brought iron to the area, using it to make tools and weapons, which gave them a great advantage in war.

The Assyrians: For much of the Old Testament period the Assyrians occupied the area that is now Iraq. From about 900 B.C. the Assyrian Empire was established. The Assyrians were known to be shamelessly cruel in war. They paraded their captors about before they blinded them and burnt them to death. The ruler, Ashurbanipal, made Nineveh the center for literature and the arts. There were thousands of clay tablets with the history and traditions of Mesopotamia written down on them. Assyrian carvings have survived that depict Ashurbanipal at his favorite sport of hunting. On one expedition he bragged about killing 30 elephants, 370 lions, and many other wild animals.

Hammurabi was the powerful king of Babylon from 1792–1750 B.C. Even though his name is not mentioned in the Scriptures, we know about him and his famous legal code from discoveries made by archaeologists. In this representation by artist Robert Thom, a Babylonian who has grieved King Hammurabi falls before him.

The Babylonians: One of the oldest cultures in the Middle East, Babylonia first rose to prominence about 1850 B.C. Their first prominent king was Hammurabi, who was known for his diplomacy and his work in revising the laws of Babylon and having them engraved on stone. Another well-known king (who came along 1200 years later) was Nebuchadnezzar. He was responsible for Babylon's hanging gardens (one of the ancient wonders of the world) and the construction of superb buildings that made Babylon famous. During Nebuchadnezzar's reign, Jerusalem was struck down and many Jews were taken captive to Babylon.

The great Babylonian empire was known for its system of writing (which spread throughout the Near East) and its developments in astronomy and mathematics. The divisions of the circle, the hour, and the day were all Babylonian in origin, and were later borrowed and developed by the Greeks.

The Persians: The setting of the Bible books of Ezra, Nehemiah, Esther, and part of Daniel belonged to the time of the Persian Empire under Cyrus the Great and the kings after him. Their borders stretched east to India, northwest to Macedonia, and south to Egypt. Cyrus divided the far-reaching empire into provinces that were controlled by rulers or *satraps* (who were Persian or Median nobles).

Aramaic became the diplomatic language of the empire. The different cultures of the empire, however, were encouraged to keep their own customs and religion. When Babylon was captured, the exiled Jews were given assistance to go back home to Judah. It was during the reign of Darius I that Haggai and Zechariah began to prophesy and the work on rebuilding the temple resumed (Ezr 5–6).

The Greeks: In the 5th century B.C., the most famous city in Greece was Athens. It was rich, powerful, had beautiful buildings—including the acclaimed Parthenon still standing today—and was known to be a model of democracy. This remarkable city became the home of many creative thinkers—Socrates, Plato, and Euripedes among them.

The brilliant soldier Alexander the Great defeated the Persians in 334 B.C., conquered Syria and Egypt (founding Alexandria), and went east to India. Wherever his armies went they spread the language, culture, and ideas of Greece (Hellenism). Greek became the international language of the Mediterranean lands, and even the Jews were influenced by it. In the second century B.C., the Old Testament was translated into Greek for the Jews who lived in Alexandria. This translation—known as the Septuagint—was most familiar to the first Christians.

The magnificent Parthenon, built on the Acropolis in Athens, is one of the world's best-known sites. Designed by architects Iktinos and Kallikrates, it was constructed in 448–432 B.C. First a Greek temple, then a Christian church, it later became a Turkish mosque—even an ammunition dump. Today, this ancient epitome of classical Greek architecture is partially restored.

The Romans: Following the Greeks with their philosophies, ideals, and culture came the practical Romans with their excellent roads, sturdy aqueducts, public baths, and spectator sports. From the time that Carthage (modern Tunisia) was destroyed in 146 B.C., the Romans became a world power, extending their control all around the Mediterranean Sea.

In New Testament times, Palestine was under Roman authority, and Roman army personnel are part of the everyday scenery in the Gospels, Book of Acts, and Letters. The apostle Paul, although a Jew by birth, was himself a Roman citizen.

However, there were many years of war as various generals and dictators vied for power throughout the sprawling empire. Eventually, in 27 B.C. Octavian (Augustus) brought peace to the region. It was during his reign that Jesus was born. Palestine, under Roman jurisdiction, was ruled by a king of the Herod dynasty at the time. When this family failed to rule, Rome sent a procurator to govern Judea.

At first, Rome protected and took care of the Jews, but they eventually grew tired of Jewish nationalism and religion. In turn, Jews were angered by Roman misrule, foreign oppression, and heavy taxation; and Jewish Zealot guerrillas constantly badgered the Roman troops.

By the time of the spread of Christianity, believers paid dearly for their faith. Rome's paganism led to the cult of emperor worship. Christianity was not tolerated and many believers were thrown into public arenas, made to fight wild animals, and then burnt to death.

BIBLE PEOPLE—UNUSUAL AND FASCINATING FACTS

- Methuselah, the oldest person in the Bible, lived to the ripe old age of 969 years. He fathered his first son, Lamech, when he was 187 years old!
- Jacob buried his beloved wife Rachel near Bethlehem, and built a pillar on her grave. Today nomadic Arabs bury their children near her tomb.
- Naomi lost her husband and two sons. Her name means "pleasant" but she told people to call her Mara, which means "bitter," because of her misfortune.
- Ahilud, who lived during the time of the judges, must have been rather short. Supporting pillars for roof beams in his house were only five feet three inches tall!
- The Phrygians were a warlike people who traded in copper and slaves. Several of their rulers were named Midas and were buried in richly furnished tombs.
- Several good Bible characters had troubled sons: Aaron's two sons offered unsanctioned sacrifices (Lev 10); Eli's two sons were scoundrels (1Sa 2); and Samuel's two sons took bribes and perverted justice (1Sa 8).
- Riding along on his mule, the rebellious Absalom caught his head in an oak tree and was left there hanging while his

mule rode on. Joab, knowing that Absalom had revolted against his father King David, came along and took three spears and thrust them into Absalom's heart (2 Sa 18).

- The Edomites, descended from Esau, often clashed with the Israelites. They were delighted when Israel fell, and the prophet Obadiah condemned them for this (Ps 137:7).
- The Moabites can be traced to Lot, Abraham's nephew. The Moabite king Mesha had dealings with the Israelite kings Omri and Ahab that are recorded in the Bible. These dealings were also inscribed on the famous Moabite Stone.
- Onesiphorus was a real friend to Paul. When Paul was imprisoned in Rome, Onesiphorus went to Rome and eagerly searched until he found the apostle. There Onesiphorus encouraged him greatly. Paul could not help but contrast his friend's example with that of Phylegus and Hermogenes, who abandoned him and the Gospel he preached (2Ti 1:15–18; 2:17–18).
- There are five different Mary's recorded in Scripture:

  1) Mary, Jesus' mother.

  2) Mary, Martha's sister, who anointed Jesus with precious oil and wiped his feet with her hair.

  3) Mary Magdalene, who was the first person to see Jesus after his resurrection.

  4) Mary, the mother of James and Joseph, who was present at the crucifixion.

  5) Mary, the mother of John Mark. The first Christians met at her home in Jerusalem.

16th-century Italian artist Caravaggio captures Mary Magdalene in soul repose. This Galilean woman, whom Jesus had healed during his time of ministry, wept when she discovered that the body of her teacher was missing from the tomb.

- Even in Jesus' day, name-calling was a problem. Jesus enjoyed a good meal like anyone else, and his enemies unfairly called him a glutton. Jesus was never drunk, but his enemies labeled him a "winebibber." And even though Jesus was a Galilean, those who hated him—historically prejudiced against the Samaritans—called him a Samaritan, hoping to insult him. Some even said that Jesus was demon-possessed. Yet in spite of all the ugly barbs, Jesus never retaliated (Lk 7:34; Jn 8:48).
- The first Christians jailed for their faith were Peter and John.
- Salome, the mother of James and John, is best remembered for her zealous attempts to gain high positions for her sons in heaven. She asked Jesus if one of her sons could sit at his right hand and the other at his left in the kingdom. Jesus explained that those positions would be granted by his Father. Needless to say, the other disciples were quite indignant about such a request!

IDEAS AND BELIEFS OF THE BIBLE

THE BIBLE is much more than a colorful history of people, places, and events. Beyond a collection of fascinating facts, interesting stories, and compelling literature, the Bible is God's word to us. It is his written instruction book for those he calls to follow him. So, what can we learn from the Bible? God shows us the difference between heaven and hell. He gives us a path to follow toward redemption or salvation. He teaches us about his gifts of grace and peace. In this section, we will look at many of the key teachings and themes in the Bible.

ANGELS

These important messengers of God are supernatural beings who surround God's throne in heaven. Their work in heaven is to worship God. On earth they are God's couriers, bringing his word to people. Gabriel and Michael are the only two angels named in the Bible; it was Gabriel who announced the birth of Jesus. The Old Testament term "the angel of the Lord" was used as a way of describing how God sometimes came to people in human form (Ps 103:20–21; Mt 1:20; Lk 1:26–38).

Angels are messengers from God, holy beings created to serve him. Among their tasks, these ministering spirits protect and help God's people, give witness to God's creative and redemptive acts, and constantly give praise to the Lord.

ANGELS—20 QUICK FACTS

1. They are created by God (Eph 3:9).

2. They report directly to the Lord (Job 1:6).

3. They are mentioned 273 times in 34 books of the Bible.

4. They proclaim the word of the Lord (Rev 14:6).

5. They announced the birth of Jesus to the shepherds (Lk 2:9–14).

6. They were created to live forever (Rev 4:8).

7. Their heavenly work is to worship and glorify God (Rev 4:8).

8. Their earthly work is to help believers (Heb 1:14).

9. They are spirit beings, not human beings (Heb 1:14).

10. They are numberless (Dt 33:2).

11. They possess free will (Jude 6).

12. They express joy (Job 38:7).

13. They express longing (1Pe 1:12).

14. They are mighty (Ps 103:20).

15. They provide wisdom (Da 9:21–22).

16. They do not die or marry (Mk 12:25; Lk 20:36).

17. Some are cherubim—four-winged angels (Eze 10:20).

18. Some are seraphim—six-winged angels (Isa 6:1–8).

19. They do not know everything (Mt 24:36).

20. They will join all believers in the heavenly Jerusalem (Heb 12:22–23).

APOSTLES

Jesus chose 12 apostles to be his special followers—to preach, to heal, and to carry on his work after he left earth. They were a select group who were with Jesus from the beginning.

These are the names of the twelve apostles: first, Simon, also known as Peter, and his brother Andrew; James son of Zebedee, and his brother John; Philip and Bartholomew; Thomas and Matthew the tax collector; James son of Alphaeus, and Thaddaeus; Simon the Cananaean, and Judas Iscariot, the one who betrayed him.

Mt 10:2–4

They also saw Jesus after he rose from the dead, and they watched him ascend into heaven. Before he left, Jesus told the apostles to take his message to all nations, and he promised to be with them always.

Before the death of Jesus, Judas Iscariot fell away from this group. He was replaced by Matthias. After Pentecost and the death of Stephen, the evangelist Paul became an apostle. Paul's dramatic conversion on the Damascus road transformed him into a great missionary witness for Jesus Christ (Lk:12–16; Ac 9).

The Mount of Olives was a prominent spot in the life of Jesus: Not only was it the place of Gethsemane, where Jesus prayed in anguish before he was crucified; it was also the site of Christ's ascent into heaven following his resurrection.

ASCENSION

After Jesus rose from the dead, he spent many days with his disciples. Gathering at Mt. Olivet with his faithful followers, Jesus gave them his final message, and then was carried up into heaven. After Jesus left, heavenly messengers assured the disciples that Jesus would come back one day in the same way that he had left.

Although the ascension marked the end of Jesus' ministry on earth, it was certainly not the end of his work. He left to be with God his father, and to share the glory of heaven. From there, he now reigns over the entire universe, represents his followers before God, and sends the Holy Spirit to be their helper (Ac 1:6–11; Heb 1:1–4; 4:14–16).

BAPTISM

In New Testament times, baptism meant more than ceremonial cleansing. It marked a real change of heart, it was a public declaration of faith, and it was a symbolic picture of a complete break with sin and the start of a new life in Jesus Christ (Ro 6:3–11).

BODY

The apostle Paul uses the idea of the human body as a rather unique picture of the church. He depicts Christians as different parts of the body with specific functions and roles, all working together and relying on one another in order to operate well as the church.

In the New Testament, the Christian is told to take care of his or her physical body. Scripture teaches that the body is the dwelling of the Holy Spirit, and it is to be used for God's glory (Ro 12:1–2; 1Co 12:12–30).

CHURCH

In the New Testament, the word church always refers to a community of true believers—not to a building. In fact, for several generations the first Christians did not have specific buildings for worship. They met in homes and other places. Paul taught that Christ was the head of the church, and that the gatherings of Christians everywhere were part of his body. In these early church communities, there were few official leaders. Some gatherings were guided by elders or bishops, but it was normal for everyone to share his or her gift and to take part in service and worship (Mt 16:18; Eph 4:11–16; 1Co 12:12–28).

SIGNIFICANT SIGNS

Just as baptism is a sign of repentance, the Bible mentions other important events or symbols that have special significance.

Sign	Meaning
Rainbow	God will never send another flood to destroy everyone (Gen 9:13–17)
Ten plagues in Egypt	a demonstration of the power of God for both the Egyptians and the Israelites to see (Ex 10:2)
Unleavened bread	a sign of the deliverance of Israel from the bondage of Egypt (Ex 13:7–9)
Sabbath	a holy day set apart to honor the Lord and to rest (Ex 31:13)
Twelve stones	a reminder of God's power in parting the Jordan so that Israel and the ark of the covenant could cross over (Jos 4:1–7)
Manna in the ark of the covenant	a reminder of God's provision of food in the desert (Ex 16:32)
Purim	a feast to remember the salvation of the Jews from the wicked Haman (Est 9:28)
Virgin birth	a sign of the incarnation (Isa 7:14)
Lord's Supper	a remembrance of the broken body and shed blood of Christ (Lk 22:19)
Speaking in tongues	a sign of God's power to unbelievers (1Co 14:22)

COVENANT

Although there are several covenants, treaties, and agreements mentioned in the Bible, there are two major biblical covenants that the Bible itself is arranged around: the Old and the New. In the Old Testament, God made the "old" covenant with Moses when the Ten Commandments were given to God's people to live by. In the New Testament, the "new" covenant is based on the death of Jesus—the final sacrifice for sin. The letter to the Hebrews compares both these covenants and points out that the new covenant offers freedom from sin, something the old covenant could never do (Ex 19:3–6; 20:1–17; Heb 10).

In 107 A.D., Ignatius of Antioch defined the triple division of the ordained ministry as bishop, priest, and deacon. Less than 100 years later, ministers were commonly known as priests.

CREATION

The Bible says that God created everything. He made a perfect, good world that included plants, animals, sunshine, water, and people. In this delightful environment the first humans enjoyed a close relationship with each other and with God. However, this perfection was spoiled by sin when the woman and Adam chose to disobey God. From that point on, the perfection of creation vanished. The Bible teaches, however, that one day in the future all things will be made new, and the believer (who is called a "new creation") will share in the fullness of that new order (Gen 1–3; Ro 8:18–23; Rev 21–22).

A Secret Password

The drawing of a fish was an important sign to the first Christians. It was written as graffiti and used as a secret password when Christians were being persecuted by the Romans. The fish symbol stood for five words of special importance to the early believers:

I	X	Θ	Υ	Σ
Jesus	Christ	God's	Son	Savior

The first letter in each of these words formed an acrostic of the Greek word for fish, ichthus. Thus, whenever a Christian saw the sign of a fish, it was an instant reminder of Jesus, and of the need to tell others about him.

Besides a quickly etched mark, drawings and paintings by the early Christians might include beautiful renderings of the fish symbol. Often the markings on a grave included a fish to suggest that the person was a Christian. Today, some Christians wear a fish pin on their clothing, or some place a plaque in a church or home with a fish on it. There are even bumper stickers that sport the fish symbol.

***For in him [Jesus Christ] all the fullness of God was pleased to dwell, and through him God was pleased to reconcile to himself all things, whether on earth or in heaven, by making peace through the blood of his cross.* Col 1:19–20**

Cross

Jesus was executed on a criminal's cross because of false charges brought against him by Jewish leaders. However, he was called to this sinless death by God himself to pay for the sins of the world. In Jesus' death on the cross, we see the profound nature of God's love for humanity. Because of Jesus' perfect and complete sacrifice, people can be reconciled both to the Lord and to each other. In the cross, we see all the powers of evil defeated by God. Thus the cross has become the universal symbol of the Christian faith (Mt 27; Ro 5:6–11).

Faith

The key to walking with God is to have faith in him. This means to put thoughtful trust and confidence in a God who can be counted on. The Christian faith is not a religion of self-effort, good deeds, and keeping the Law. Rather, it is a life of reliance on Jesus Christ and the Holy Spirit to give the help needed to live in a way that pleases God. The Scriptures provide basic teaching about Jesus, the Holy Spirit, and living the life of faith (1Jn 5:1–5; Gal 3).

The Fall

The Bible traces sin back to the dawn of history. When Adam and Eve disobeyed God, the "Fall" began. Instead of open fellowship with God, they were banished from the beauty and ease of the garden to a life of back-breaking hardship. Since the fall of Adam and Eve, all of creation has joined in their rebellion against God. Sin and death has spread throughout humanity like a hereditary disease, so that every part of the universe is tainted by the Fall (Gen 1–3; Ro 1:18–32).

Adam and Eve's disobedience—described in the Book of Genesis—led to their sin, guilt, and shame; and a deep sense of alienation from God. In this sorrowful scene, the pair face their expulsion from the Garden of Eden.

Forgiveness

God loves us and delights in forgiving us. The Bible clearly teaches that when people repent and turn away from wrongdoing, God quickly blots away their sin. In turn, Christians should excuse others because they themselves have been pardoned by God. And although there may be times when believers fall into sin, they can turn to God for forgiveness and restoration (Eph 4:32; 1Jn 1:9).

Gospel

The word "gospel" means "good news." The Bible teaches that people do not need to be cut off from God because of their sin. Jesus Christ can bring forgiveness and new life—that is the Bible's good news (Mk 1:1; Jn 3:16).

Grace

God is good to us because he loves us, and for no other reason. This, in essence, is the "grace" of God. In the Old Testament, God demonstrated his goodness to Israel countless times. In the New Testament, the grace of God is evident in the coming of Jesus.

Through the work of Jesus, God freely gives salvation to undeserving humans, and extends his grace into the believer's life from beginning to end. The apostle Paul often started or finished his letters to Christians with a prayer for God's grace (Dt 7:6–9; Eph 2:8–9).

Healing

Many miraculous healings are recorded throughout the Scriptures, but they take on particular theological significance in the New Testament. When Jesus came, he announced a whole new creation in which sin, sickness, and death would be overpowered. Although not completed yet, the new creation began with Jesus' resurrection and looks forward to being completed in the future.

Many of the wonders Christ performed involved giving sight to the blind. From the Gospels we learn that in separate incidents Jesus restored sight to two men. He also healed another man who could not speak or see, and he gave sight to a man who had been blind from birth.

While on earth, Jesus not only demonstrated the power to forgive sins but to heal sickness, disease, and disability. Since then, the healing work of Jesus has been carried on by some of his disciples. However, the final removal of all illness will not happen until the kingdom of God is fully established—only then will all tears, pain, and death cease (Nu 21:4–9; Mt 8:5–13; Jas 5:14–16; Rev 21:1–5).

HEAVEN

Where is heaven? Although the Hebrews used this word to refer to the sky, and the biblical phrase "heaven and earth" implies the whole universe, we do not really know where heaven is located. The Bible, however, clearly teaches that heaven is the home of God, Jesus Christ, and the

THE HEALING MIRACLES OF JESUS

	Matthew	Mark	Luke	John
Leper	8:2–3	1:40–42	5:12–13	
Centurion's servant	8:5–13		7:1–10	
Peter's mother-in-law	8:14–15	1:30–31	4:38–39	
Two demoniacs	8:28–34	5:1–15	8:27–35	
Woman with hemorrhages	9:20–22	5:25–29	8:43–48	
Two blind men	9:27–31			
Demoniac who was mute	9:32–33			
Man with a withered hand	12:10–13	3:1–5	6:6–10	
Demoniac who was blind and mute	12:22			
Canaanite woman's daughter	15:21–28	7:24–30		
Boy with epilepsy	17:14–18	9:17–29	9:38–43	
Two blind men	20:29–34	10:46–52	18:35–43	
Deaf man with a speech impediment		7:31–37		
Man with an unclean spirit		1:23–26	4:33–35	
Blind man at Bethsaida		8:22–26		
Woman bent double			13:11–13	
Man with dropsy			14:1–4	
Ten lepers			17:11–19	
Slave's ear			22:50–51	
Official's son				4:46–54
Sick man at Beth-zatha				5:1–9
Man born blind				9:1–7

angels. It is also the future home of all believers—the place where they will worship God forever:

> *"Do not let your hearts be troubled. Believe in God,*
> *believe also in me. In my Father's house there are*
> *many dwelling places. If it were not so, would I have*
> *told you that I go to prepare a place for you?*
> *And if I go and prepare a place for you,*
> *I will come again and will take you to myself,*
> *so that where I am, there you may be also. . . . "*
>
> Jn 14:1–3

What is heaven like? Not only will it be "home" for all God's people, but it will be a place to rest and share in God's work. The Bible gives us some broad clues about what to expect when we get to heaven. Here are ten facts that help fill the picture of the celestial home:

In the rich imagery of biblical language, heaven is described in a variety of ways. It is the celestial dwelling of God, the true home of the believer, and the experience of eternal life in the presence of the Lord.

Heaven is joyful. The Bible tells us to expect joy and pleasure in God's presence (Ps 16:11).

Heaven is healthy. Clearly, this aspect of heaven will be very unlike our earth. In the new order, there will be no place for pain, sorrow, or death (Rev 21:4).

Heaven is full of music. What type of music will be in heaven? The Bible at least mentions harps and choirs of angels (Rev 5:8–9).

Heaven is busy. The Bible does not say that we will recline on clouds and play heavenly harps all eternal day long. Our work in heaven will be to serve Jesus Christ (Rev 22:3).

Heaven is multicultural. The worldwide community of believers, from all periods of history and all cultures will join together in heaven to worship God in perfect unity (Php 2:10–11; 1Th 4:17).

Heaven has other names. It is called the holy city and the new Jerusalem (Rev 21:2).

Heaven is beautiful. It is described as having the glory of God, the radiance of a rare jewel, and appearing clear as glass (Rev 21:12, 18).

Heaven is being made ready. Jesus told his followers that he was going away to prepare a place for them, but that he would return for them one day and take them to be with him (Jn 14:3).

Heaven is for believers. Jesus told Nicodemus that no one can be part of the kingdom of God without being born again by the Spirit of God (Jn 3).

Heaven is a city. In several instances the Bible calls heaven a glorious city being prepared for the "bride" of Christ, which is the church (Rev 21).

In heaven, all Christians across the centuries will be safe, happy, and perfect in God's presence. There will be unending joy and life in this new land of perpetual day (Ne 9:6; 1Pe 1:3–5; Rev 4:21–22).

HELL

The Bible teaches that hell is the place of eternal punishment for those who live in disobedience to God. It is described in the Scriptures in horrifying terms: the hell of fire (Mt. 18:8–9); unquenchable fire (Mt 3:12); the lake of fire and sulfur—and a place of perpetual torment (Rev 20:10–15). Clearly, this vivid imagery implies that hell is a place of constant misery. It is reserved for Satan, his angels, and all those who reject God.

In some instances, the word "hell" has been used with another meaning to describe the Hebrew word "Sheol" ("Hades" in Greek). In this instance, "hell" means the place of the dead, not the place of eternal punishment. There is some mention of Hades in the Bible, and several more references in the apocryphal books (Ac 2:27; Tob 4:19; Sir 51:6).

This detail from Hans Memling's painting of the last judgment shows a horrifying picture of the damned being cast into hell, the place of punishment.Hell is also known as Gehenna or Hades.

JUDGMENT

God is the supreme ruler and judge of the universe. At the last judgment, everyone will be judged according to the knowledge they have about God. Those who do not know the Law, or the good news about Jesus, will be judged by what they know of God from creation, and how they have followed their own conscience. Believers will be judged according to the quality of their Christian lives. At this final sorting out of good from evil, the Judge of all the earth will act fairly and mercifully. The actual task of judging will be given to Jesus Christ himself (Ps 96:10; Ac 10:42; Heb 12:22–27; Rev 20:12–15).

The last judgment, presented in visionary and imaginative language in biblical apocalyptic literature, has been the subject of many visual artists. In this representation, the Dominican painter-monk Fra Angelico (c. 1400–1450) gives his interpretation of the end of time.

JUSTIFICATION

Because sin cuts us off from a holy God, there is nothing we can do to measure up to his standards. Only God's action on our behalf can "justify" us in his eyes. God accepts us into his family because of the work of Christ on the cross. Christ took our punishment for sin on himself so that we could be acquitted and made righteous before God. The believer is therefore justified by God's grace, and accepts this position in Jesus Christ through faith (2Co 5:21; Ro 3).

KINGDOM OF GOD

In his preaching and teaching, Jesus declared that the kingdom of God had arrived. He used parable stories to explain the meaning of this concept. The Jews thought that deliverance from the Romans would usher in the kingdom. However, Jesus taught that the life of the kingdom started from small beginnings that would then grow and spread throughout the world.

The kingdom of God is in action where God rules: it was demonstrated in the life and work of Jesus; it is alive in the hearts of repentant sinners; it shows up in the life and actions of the obedient believer. The kingdom will be completed in the future, at the time of the new heaven and the new earth (Mt 5:1–20).

RULES AND COMMANDMENTS— TEN QUICK FACTS

- The Ten Commandments are listed twice—first in Exodus 20, and then in Deuteronomy 5. They are also called "the ten words" (Exodus 34:28; Deuteronomy 4:13; 10:4).
- The Jewish rabbis counted 613 separate commandments in the Law of Moses.
- Jesus summarized the entire Law of Moses by saying that "You shall love the Lord your God with all your heart, and with all your soul, and with all your mind . . . And . . . You shall love your neighbor as yourself." (Mt 22:37–40)
- The Book of Leviticus contains instructions for the Levites—the order of priests for whom the book is named.
- In the Law of Moses, 365 commandments are stated negatively.
- In the Law of Moses, 248 commands are stated positively.
- In the Book of Numbers, the Israelites are counted and given instructions before entering the land of Canaan.
- Deuteronomy means "second law"; this book repeats and adds to many of the laws found in Exodus, Leviticus, and Numbers.
- It was said that 611 of the 613 commandments were given through Moses. Interestingly enough, the number 611 is the numerical value of the word Torah, which means "law," "commandment," or "instruction."
- The great Jewish rabbi Hillel was asked by a skeptic to teach him the entire Torah while standing on one leg. Hillel's response was, "What is hateful to yourself do not do to another. This is the whole Torah; go and study it; the rest is commentary."

THE LAW

The Law (Torah) was given by God to help his people know how to live. This body of law presented in the first five books of the Bible includes the Ten Commandments, religious, social, and dietary rules. These guidelines were basic to right living back then, and they are still a type of moral imperative for all humanity.

However, the coming of Jesus marked a change. Since it was impossible to keep the Law perfectly and atone for sin, a perfect one-time sacrifice was necessary to bring freedom from bondage to the old system. Jesus became that sacrifice. He fulfilled the deepest meaning of the Law, and introduced the age of "grace." The New Testament teaches that salvation does not come by obedience to the Law; it comes through Christ and the pardon he offers for sin (Ex 20–34; Ro 8:3–4; Heb 7:18–19).

LIFE

From the time that God created the world and infused the first person with the breath of life, the whole of creation has been dependent on God for life itself. Not only life, but death for every living thing is in the hands of the creator and sustainer of the universe. The Bible also speaks about "eternal life" as a free and lasting gift to anyone who becomes a Christian (Gen 2:7; Jn 10:10, 28).

LOVE

The character of God is love. Several Old Testament writers emphasize God's tender love and care for the people of Israel. The New Testament stresses the self-giving love of Jesus (agape) as the kind of love that joins God the Father with his son, Jesus Christ:

" 'You shall love the Lord your God with all your heart, and with all your soul and with all your mind.' This is the greatest and first commandment. And a second is like it: 'You shall love your neighbor as yourself.' On these two commandments hang all the law and the prophets."

Mt 22:34

It is this same love that God has for humanity, and it can only become part of the believer's life through the gift of God. This God-given love is the mark of God's presence in the life of every Christian. Believers who unselfishly love each other show the world that they are true disciples of Christ (Hos 11:1–4; Jn 3:16; 1Co 13).

Once you were not a people, but now you are God's people; once you had not received mercy, but now you have received mercy.
1Pe 2:10

MERCY

Although the Israelites often broke their side of the covenant-agreement with God, he showed great mercy to his people. Instead of abandoning them, he offered them his patient love and ready forgiveness—his mercy in action. It is because of God's mercy that he offers salvation through Jesus Christ to those who are lost and without hope (Ps 23:6; Ro 9:15; Eph 2:4).

MIRACLES

Many people witnessed the extraordinary miracles that Jesus performed. He healed the sick, turned water into wine, calmed a storm, and brought the dead back to life. These mighty works were done by the power of God. Jesus did miracles to show his compassion, and to demonstrate that the age of the kingdom of God had dawned. These "wonders" were signs that Jesus was the Messiah.

The disciples were also empowered by Jesus to do

OLD TESTAMENT "WONDERS"

There are many unusual wonders and dramatic signs recorded in the Old Testament that make the New Testament miracles seem almost tame by comparison. We read of Lot's wife turning into a pillar of salt (Gen 19:24–28), Balaam's speaking donkey (Nu 22:20–35), and Elijah dashing off to heaven in a fiery chariot (2Ki 2:9–11). Here is a list of some of the startling Old Testament marvels:

1. Moses at the blazing bush that did not burn (Ex 3:1–14)
2. Moses' leprous hand (Ex 4:6–12)
3. The ten plagues (Ex 4:8–12)
4. The Red Sea parting (Ex 14:21–31)
5. Aaron's budding rod (Nu 17)
6. The collapse of Jericho's walls (Jos 6)
7. Samson's destruction of Dagon's temple (Jdg 16:23–31)
8. The unfailing jar of meal and jug of oil (1Ki 17:13–16)
9. Elijah's triumph over the priests of Baal (1Ki 18)
10. Healing of the poisonous stew (2Ki 4:38–41)
11. The floating ax head (2Ki 6:1–7)
12. A dead man revived through Elisha's bones (2Ki 13:21)
13. Shadrach, Meshach, Abednego, and the fiery furnace (Da 3)
14. The mysterious handwriting on the wall (Da 5:5, 25)
15. Daniel in the lion's den (Da 6)

THE WAY OF PRAYER

In the Lord's pattern for prayer, he includes a number of important elements that should be part of our own prayers. Among these components are petition, confession, and praise and thanksgiving (Mt 6:9–13). Prayer was very much a part of the lives of many Bible personalities. Here is a partial list of significant Bible prayers which include some of the elements of the Lord's Prayer.

Petition

1. Abraham asked the Lord for an heir (Gen 15:2–3).
2. Moses prayed for a glimpse of God's glory (Ex 33:18).
3. David prayed for deliverance from his enemies (Ps 31).
4. Stephen prayed for his murderers (Ac 7:59–60).
5. Paul prayed three times for the removal of a personal difficulty (2Co 12:7–10).

Confession and forgiveness

1. David asked for forgiveness for numbering the people (2Sa 24:10).
2. David implored God to forgive him for his many sins, including his affair with Bathsheba (Ps 51).
3. Manasseh prayed for forgiveness and asked the Lord to restore to him his kingdom (2Ch 33:11–13).
4. Job confessed his pride and repented in dust and ashes (Job 42:1–6).
5. The prodigal son confessed his sin against God and his father (Lk 15:11–24).

Praise and Thanksgiving

1. Moses and Israel praised God for deliverance at the Red Sea (Ex 15).
2. Hannah praised God for the birth of her son Samuel (1Sa 2:1–10).
3. Mary praised God for being chosen to be the mother of the Lord (Lk 1:46–55).
4. The angels praised God for the birth of Jesus (Lk 2:13–14).
5. Paul and Silas praised God while they were in prison (Ac 16:25).

miraculous works, and these remained part of the experience of the early church. These signs and wonders were always done in the name and authority of God (Mt 8:2–3; 8:23–27; 9:18–19; Ac 3:6–10).

PARABLES

Jesus often taught in parables: these were stories about everyday life that were tied to spiritual truths (Mt 5:14–15; Mk 2:22; Lk 13:18–19).

PEACE

The Hebrew word for "peace" has several shades of meaning. It can imply safety, harmony, personal good health and long life, and unity in the community. The Bible is clear that God is the author of the precious gift of peace. And perfect peace will characterize the new age when God will finally establish the fullness of his holy kingdom.

Jesus is described as the "Prince of Peace" who came and preached the good news to everyone. His gift to every believer is peace with God and unity in the community of Christians. On the eve of his departure from earth, Jesus left the gift of his peace with the disciples—a deep inner assurance unaffected by circumstances (Isa 9:6; Jn 14:27; Ro 5:1; Eph 2:14–18).

PRAYER

People communicate with God through prayer. The Israelites in the Old Testament prayed three times every day.

In the New Testament (at the request of the disciples), Jesus taught his followers how to pray. The apostle Paul believed that prayer should have a central place in the life of the believer and the church as a whole. The Scriptures teach that it is the work of the Holy Spirit to assist Christians in prayer, turning their minds toward God, and bringing their requests to the heavenly father. Prayer involves confession of sin, petition, thanksgiving, and worship. God desires our fellowship with him through prayer, and is moved to act through the prayers of his people (1Sa 12:23; Ps 62:8; Mt 6:9–13; Php 4:6; Col 4:2; Ro 8:26).

PROPHECY

Prophets were an important part of the Bible panorama. Called to their line of work by God, they spoke with his authority, delivering messages of judgment, repentance, hope, and forgiveness. Prophecies were clear messages to the people about what God would do now and in the future to correct a particular problem or situation. Most prophetic messages referred directly to a specific situation in the prophet's own day:

In days to come
the mountain of the Lord's house
shall be established as the highest of the mountains,
and shall be raised above the hills;
all the nations shall stream to it . . .
He shall judge between the nations,
and shall arbitrate for many peoples;
they shall beat their swords into plowshares,
and their spears into pruning hooks;
nation shall not lift up sword against nation,
neither shall they learn war any more.

Isa 2:2, 4

Working right alongside the true prophets, there were times in biblical history when false prophets emerged. When their predictions did not come true, however, they were put to death because they tried to lead the people away from God, and they were a threat to Israel's faith and security.

In the Bible, there are certain prophecies that are different from the traditional God-inspired prophetic voice. These prophecies belong to a particular type of literature known as "apocalyptic." The prophecies of the Book of Revelation and the Book of Daniel fall into this category. This kind of writing contains imagery and symbolism best understood in the context of the time when these books were written.

In a series of detailed prophecies, God revealed the future to the prophet Daniel. These later chapters of the Book of Daniel include messianic prophecies and predictions about the end of time.

From that time Jesus began to proclaim, "Repent, for the kingdom of heaven has come near." Mt 4:17

A major topic in apocalyptic literature is the end of time. In the Bible, the significant apocalyptic portions are Ezekiel 40–48, Daniel 7–12, Zechariah 9–14, and the Book of Revelation. The Book of Revelation is the longest example of apocalyptic literature in the Bible. It presents the apostle John's visions and prophecies of the last days and the new spiritual order. The book is rich with symbols. It speaks of strange creatures—a great red dragon with seven heads and ten horns and seven crowns on its head, a beast that looked like a leopard with feet like a bear's and a mouth like a lion's! It also mentions hosts of angels, and it describes armies and battles, a lake of fire, and a bottomless pit. Throughout the book, however, the consistent message woven into the prophetic imagery is the ultimate and final triumph of Christ over the devil and all forces of evil.

With the coming of the Holy Spirit in the early church, all Christians were given the right to proclaim God's message of salvation. And the New Testament declares that the gift of prophecy is given to some believers to strengthen the church (Am 7:14–15; Dt 13:1–5; 1Co 12:10, 29).

REDEMPTION

By his life, death, and resurrection, Jesus paid the price that would set people free from sin. This work of his is known as redemption. By his blood sacrifice, he recovered those enslaved to wrongdoing. Christians are therefore redeemed, and the apostle Paul encourages them to live in freedom and to not fall back into old patterns of sin and entrapment. The apostle also points out that full freedom will have to wait until the end of the age when Christ returns, and all things will be made new (Mk 10:45; 1Co 6:20; Ro 6:12–14; 8:19–23).

REPENTANCE

Repentance involves turning away from sin and leaving it behind. In the Old Testament, people showed sorrow for sin by wearing sackcloth and ashes, offering sacrifices, and fasting. In the New Testament, Jesus called for a radical approach to repentance—an inward change of heart, not outward rituals. He commanded people everywhere to turn from their evil ways and repent in order to become a part of the kingdom of God (Joel 2:12–13; Lk 18:9–14; Lk 19:1–10; Ac 17:30).

RESURRECTION

One key fact of the Christian faith is that Jesus rose from the dead. The apostles saw him on a number of occasions

Opposite page: *Hans Memlin was considered one of the best painters in Christendom in the 15th century. His depiction of the Resurrection portrays the risen Christ in a perfectly balanced and serene composition. Christ's crucifixion wounds, the tomb guards, the women, and the angel all form an integral part of this luminous scene.*

after his resurrection, and in his first letter to the Corinthian church, Paul lists many people who encountered Jesus alive. Because of the empty grave, and the absence of the body, the authorities could not disprove the claim that Jesus had risen from the dead.

> *They found the stone rolled away from the tomb, but when they went in, they did not find the body. While they were perplexed about this, suddenly two men in dazzling clothes stood beside them. The women were terrified and bowed their faces to the ground, but the men said to them, "Why do you look for the living among the dead? He [Jesus] is not here, but has risen."*
>
> Lk 24:2–5

"Jesus said to her, 'I am the resurrection and the life. Those who believe in me, even though they die, will live, and everyone who lives and believes in me will never die. Do you believe this?" Jn 11:25–26

The power of the resurrection is vital to believers. The New Testament teaches that they will share in the resurrection at the end of the age. Naturally, Christians face physical death (part of the Fall) like everyone else, but they can count on a future with Christ. In this new spiritual existence, there will be the resurrection of the complete person in a new and perfect body (Mt 28; Mk 16; Lk 24; Jn 20; 1Co 15).

REVELATION

People know about God because he chooses to reveal himself. Since he is unapproachable in his purity, majesty, and holiness, we must rely on his revelation if we are to know anything about him. God has revealed something about himself through the world he has created. All during the history of Israel, God showed glimpses of himself through his actions and through the words spoken by his prophets and leaders.

In the New Testament, he fully revealed himself in his son, Jesus Christ. He became a person, and lived in community with others. Yet, many people did not recognize who he really was.

Another important revelation is the Bible itself—it is the revealed word of God. Divinely inspired, it is the record of God's actions from the dawn of creation, to the time of the New Testament apostles, including the growth of the early church (Ex 3; Am 3:7; Jn 1:14; Heb 1:1–2).

SALVATION

The Bible tells us that God sent his son into the world to save people from their sins. Jesus dealt with the sin problem in his death and resurrection. Those who put their faith in Christ and accept his work on their behalf are now "saved." This gift of salvation is offered to anyone who calls on the

Lord in repentance. However, the full significance of salvation will not be experienced until the end of the age and the return of Christ, the Savior.

Besides spiritual deliverance, the Old and New Testaments speak of salvation in broader terms. When God rescued the Israelites from Egyptian bondage, it was a major act of salvation. References to salvation in the New Testament include freedom from imprisonment, disease, and demon possession (Isa 60:16; Mt 1:21; Eph 2:8–9; Ro 10:13).

Second Coming of Christ

When Jesus came to earth as a baby, his arrival was hardly noticed. His impact on the world was definite, but small and quiet at first. During his time of ministry here, Jesus promised that he would return at the end of the world. His second coming would be unlike his first, because this time he would come with power and glory for everyone to see, and his second coming would mark the time of judgment.

The world still awaits the second coming of Christ. The Bible teaches that when he returns, it will be the moment of final salvation for all believers, both living and dead. At his

With great power and depth, 16th-century Italian artist Jacopo Tintoretto depicts the crucifixion of Christ. In his forceful, dramatic style, the artist presents Jesus as the central figure and the focal point of light in this masterpiece. In contrast, the two bandits who were crucified with Jesus are presented in somber, dark tones, away from the Lord himself (Mt 27:38).

second coming, Jesus will take all believers with him to live forever in the place that he has prepared for them. The Bible does not tell us when that day will be, but encourages us to live in readiness for Christ's unexpected return (Mt 26:64; Php 3:20; 1Th 4:13–5:11; Rev 19–22).

SIN

Although the Bible does not deal with the issue of where sin came from, it describes this condition and its effects clearly. Sin is basically rebellion against God, and it permeates all of society. People are instinctively at enmity with God. The Bible is full of stories that show this natural human bent in action.

From the biblical record we learn that although sin started with Satan, people are responsible (and guilty) for their own wrongdoing. Because sin is an offense to God, he defeated its power in the work of Jesus Christ on the cross:

. . . Christ also suffered for you, leaving you an example, so that you should follow in his steps.
"He committed no sin,
and no deceit was found in his mouth." . . .
He himself bore our sins in his body on the cross, so that, free from sins, we might live for righteousness; by his wounds you have been healed.

1Pe 2:21–22, 24

The ankle bone of a young man, crucified in the first century A.D.*, showing the metal spike used to nail his foot to a cross. Crucifixion was an atrocious method of execution first developed in the East. It was borrowed—and perfected—by the Romans to punish crimes such as sedition and murder. Tied or nailed to a cross, the victim died slowly and painfully.*

In this "fallen" world of ours, however, wrongdoing still abounds, and the full significance of Christ's work on the cross will not be experienced until Jesus returns to redeem his church. In that day, sin and evil will no longer exist (Gen 3; Ps 51; Isa 1:18–20; Ro 1:18–2:11).

SOUL

In the Bible the word "soul" means a person's entire being. Greeks had the idea that the immortal soul was caged in a decaying body, but this was not the Christian view. In biblical thought, the soul included mind, will, and personality—besides flesh and bone (Ps 103:1; Mt 10:28).

SUFFERING

Part of the consequence of sin is the misfortune of suffering. Pain and hardship strike at believer and unbeliever alike. Sometimes it seems that the innocent suffer while the guilty enjoy relatively pain-free lives. The Book of Job deals with the problem of suffering, innocent people, and the hand of God in it all.

In the life of Jesus, we see suffering as a way of life (Isa 53). Totally innocent, Jesus took on the rejection, hatred, and sin of others to bring salvation to the lost. God took responsibility for the problem of suffering in the death of his son. However, suffering will not finally go away until all things are made new in the future (Gen 3:15–19; 2Co 12:6–9; Heb 12:3–11).

For I know that my Redeemer lives, and that at the last he will stand upon the earth; and after my skin has been thus destroyed, then in my flesh I shall see God. . . .
Job 19:25–26

TEMPTATION

There are two classic accounts of temptation in the Bible. In the story of Adam and Eve, the serpent leads the woman into doubt and confusion about God's will, and she gives in to temptation by eating the fruit from the forbidden tree. In the second case, Satan tempts Jesus in the wilderness, but he rebukes the evil one by quoting the word of God to him.

Clearly, the Scripture shows that God allows his people to be tested, but it also points out that they should be on guard against temptation, assured that God will not allow his people to be tempted beyond what they can bear (Gen 3; Mt 4; Eph 6:10–18).

WORSHIP

God commands his people to worship him, and to give him the honor due him—not just because he is God, but for the world he has created, for his work of redemption through Jesus Christ, and for his blessings and gifts. God is not interested in outward forms of worship; he is only interested in praise that comes from the heart. True God-centered worship is reflected in a life lived to honor him. The Psalms are filled with eloquent words of worship and praise to the Lord.

In the New Testament, Christians joined to worship God. Empowered by the Holy Spirit, they sang hymns and psalms of praise to the Lord. Paul and Silas even praised him when they were imprisoned.

However, the Bible also teaches that worship is not simply restricted to life on earth. In heaven, the great hosts of angels worship the Lord, and when the entire church is finally redeemed, God's whole creation will praise and worship him forever (Ps 29; 136; Ac 2:43–47; Col 3:16; Rev 15).

A DOZEN WAYS TO WORSHIP GOD

1. Read the Scriptures (1Ti 4:13)
2. Study God's word (Ac 6:2)
3. Teach God's word (1Ti 4:6)
4. Proclaim God's word (2Ti 4:2)
5. Maintain Christian traditions (1Co 11:2)
6. Sing psalms, hymns, and spiritual songs (Eph 5:19)
7. Pray in the Spirit (Eph 6:18)
8. Present your whole person to God (Ro 12:1)
9. Offer a sacrifice of praise (Heb 13:15)
10. Confess his name (Heb 13:15)
11. Do good (Heb 13:16)
12. Share what you have with others (Php 4:18)

Bible Questions and Answers

HE BIBLE is a lively collection of information. There are stories, anecdotes, trivia, well-known and lesser-known facts, oddities, humor, and much more between its pages. Readers everywhere are fascinated by the Bible and have questions about the world's most treasured book. Some people wonder: Is the Bible true or just a collection of fables? Others ask: Did the miracles and wonders in the Bible really happen? Some people are curious about Bible characters: Was Goliath really a giant? Who were the wise men? The questions are as many and as varied as the readers themselves, and include concerns about every aspect of the Bible. This chapter explores many of these questions, from the importance of the Bible and how it came to be, to its stories, people, places, events, and customs.

ABOUT THE BIBLE

Q. What makes the Bible important?

A. The Bible is much more than an ancient religious book, a record of the people of Israel, or the rise of the early church. The Bible is a message from God. More than 2,600 times, the authors of the Bible profess to speak or write God's words—not their own! People read the Bible to be enlightened and encouraged, and to find a word to them from God himself. The Bible is important to people because of its spiritual value.

Q. How did God give his words to the Bible's authors?

A. God gave his message to the authors of the Bible by inspiring them to write down what he wanted them to say. Sometimes the writers had dreams and visions in which God told them what to write. At other times God spoke orally to them, or he put an idea in their minds and they wrote it in their own words. God was able to communicate with the writers so they wrote down exactly what God wanted to convey. The Bible says:

> *"All scripture is inspired by God and is useful for teaching, for reproof, for correction, and for training in righteousness, so that everyone who belongs to God may be proficient, equipped for every good work."*
>
> 2Ti 3:16–17

Q. How did the Bible's authors write?

A. Many authors probably did their own writing, but others told their words to a scribe or secretary who wrote them down. Some of the authors' words may have been collected and written down by their followers.

Micah the prophet not only spoke of sin, repentance, and renewal, he also prophesied about the future return of Hebrew exiles to their homeland. His recurring theme was: God would judge but he would also save his people. This dramatic depiction of the Old Testament prophet is found in St. Mary's Basilica, Minneapolis, Minnesota.

Q. How do we know that the Bible is true?

A. As a historical text, the authenticity of the Bible is proven by old records on monuments, by tablets recently deciphered, and by numerous on-going archaeological discoveries in biblical lands. The Bible—really an ancient collection of books—was copied accurately, kept safe, and passed on from century to century with very little change.

The Scriptures themselves display a wonderful unity, even though the writings reflect the work of 40 different people who lived hundreds of years apart. The prophet Micah foretold the town where Jesus would be born (Mic 5:2), and 700 years later Jesus was born in exactly that place. The prophet Isaiah described the death of Jesus hundreds of years before Jesus was put to death on a criminal's cross (Isa 53).

Apart from its historical accuracy and internal unity, the Bible itself claims to be true, and to be the authentic and authoritative word from God to humanity. Jesus himself trusted the Bible as God's word. He often quoted the Law and the Prophets, and he reproached his audience with these words:

> *"Oh, how foolish you are, and how slow of heart to believe all that the prophets have declared!"*
> Lk 24:25

Q. Has Bible history been validated?

A. Yes, by investigations in biblical lands. Old Babylonian tablets have been uncovered that attest to ancient stories of the flood. The discovery of Assyrian inscriptions has proven the identity of Sargon, one of the greatest kings of that nation. Most recently a *stela* (a carved or inscribed stone slab or pillar) was found—dated around the time of King David—that refers to the Israelites of David. Many ancient records of brick, stone, and papyrus confirm the history of the Bible.

What is the biblical view of creation? It is that God called into being all that exists. The view that a personal God created the heavens and the earth and all living things stands in sharp contrast to the creation myths of the ancient world. Renaissance artist Raphael (1483–1520) depicts his view of the Creator at work.

FROM GENESIS TO MALACHI

Q. The story of creation tells us that God made everything in a matter of a few days. How could this be?

A. Christians agree that the account of creation is not a myth or story without historical truth. They are, however, divided in the way they look at the seven days of creation. Several theories abound. However, many scholars of the Scriptures believe that the issue is not

TEN UNUSUAL BIBLE FIRSTS

Question	Answer
1. What was the first commandment given?	"Be fruitful and multiply" (Gen 1:28).
2. Who was the first to become drunk on wine?	Noah. After planting the first vineyard and making wine, Noah drank some of the fermented juice and became drunk (Gen 9:20–21).
3. Which was the first war mentioned?	The war of the four kings of the north led by Chedorlaomer (Gen 14:1–24).
4. Who celebrated the first birthday party?	Egypt's pharaoh, during Joseph's time in prison, celebrated his birthday with a feast, the restoration of one of his servants, and the hanging of another (Gen 40:20–22).
5. What was the first miracle performed by Jesus?	Jesus' first miracle involved turning water into wine. At a wedding in the town of Cana, the host ran out of wine. Mary asked Jesus to do something. He instructed the servants to fill stone jars with water, and serve it to the wine steward. He told the groom that he had saved the best wine for last (Jn 2: 1–11).
6. Who was the first Hebrew king?	Abimelech. He was the son of Jerubbaal (Gideon), and he killed his brothers—70 of them (the youngest, Jotham, survived)—to establish himself as king of Shechem, his mother's people (Jdg 9:1–6).
7. Who were the first female construction workers?	The daughters of Shallum who helped rebuild part of Jerusalem after the Exile (Neh 3:12).
8. Who held the first beauty contest?	King Ahasuerus of Susa. When the king divorced his first wife, Vashti, beautiful young girls were paraded before the king to compete for the position of queen. The year-long contest ended when the crown was placed on Esther's head (Est 2).
9. Who was the first to use a pseudonym?	Queen Esther. Her given name was Hadassah (meaning "myrtle"), but she used the Persian name Esther in the court of King Ahasuerus (Est 2:7).
10. When were Jesus' followers first called Christians?	In Antioch, many responded to the message about Jesus. When those in the church at Jerusalem heard this, they sent Barnabas, later joined by Paul, to meet with them. It was here that Jesus' followers were first called Christians (Ac 13).

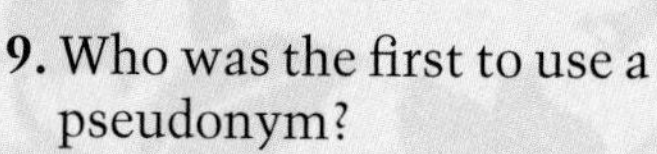

how long God took to bring everything into being, but that God did create it, and everything in the material and spiritual world exists because he brought it into existence. This, Christians affirm, is the unmistakable message of Genesis 1.

Q. When God made the world, did he create dinosaurs?
A. Yes. On the fifth day of creation, God made all kinds of beasts including sea monsters and winged birds of every kind. Such a variety of creeping and flying creatures and wild animals would certainly have included dinosaurs.

Q. What were the first human beings like?
A. In many ways, the Bible is silent about this. We do not know if they were tall or short, black, white, or brown. The Bible, however, gives three basic facts concerning the nature of the first human beings. First, they were made from the "dust of the ground" (Gen 2:7). Second, they were given the "breath of life" by God himself. Third—and most significant—they were made "in the image of God" (Gen 1:26–27), a fact that separates humanity from the rest of the animal world.

Q. Where was the Garden of Eden?
A. Although the exact location is uncertain, many scholars think that it was located in Mesopotamia.

Q. What was the Red Sea that divided to let the Israelites pass through and then joined together again to overwhelm the Egyptian army?
A. The Israelites did not, in fact, cross the Red Sea. It is believed that they passed through the "sea of reeds," one of the large, shallow bodies of water that lie between Goshen and the Sinai peninsula. The exact location of the crossing is not known.

Q. Why did Solomon have so many wives? Didn't this violate Old Testament law?
A. Solomon not only violated the Mosaic Law with regard to the number of wives he had, but also by building a large army and accumulating such great wealth (Dt 17:16–17). Solomon's passion for international relationships led him to amass many wives. In biblical times, treaties between nations were commonly cemented by marriage. Unfortunately, Solomon's marriage alliances were his eventual undoing.

***"So out of the ground the Lord God formed every animal of the field and every bird of the air, and brought them to the man to see what he would call them; and whatever the man called every living creature that was its name."
Gen 2:19***

Q. Why did God allow Job's awful suffering?

A. After all he went through, Job obtained a glimpse of God and realized that his only response was to worship and trust God. He learned that life must be lived by faith in response to who God is. He learned not to question the wisdom and goodness of God. Perhaps, then, Job's suffering was permitted in order to glorify God.

Q. How many Old Testament prophecies concerning Jesus Christ were fulfilled?

A. There were many predictions made concerning Jesus Christ hundreds of years before he was born, yet each was literally fulfilled in specific detail. These are a few examples of possibly 300 prophecies about Jesus that are found in the Old Testament:

Prophecy	Prediction	Fulfillment
Jer 23:5	would be a descendent of David	Lk 3:23, 31
Mic 5:2	would be born in Bethlehem	Mt 2:1
Isa 7:14	would be called Immanuel	Mt 1:23
Isa 35:5–6	would perform healing miracles	Mt 9:35
Isa 53	would be crucified	Mt 27
Zec 12:10	would be pierced	Jn 19:34
Isa 53:9	would be buried in a rich man's tomb	Mt 27:57–60

One of the prophet Joel's most important contributions is the concept of "the day of the Lord." This depiction of Joel is part of Michelangelo's great Sistine Chapel painting.

Q. What is the "day of the Lord" mentioned five times in the short Book of Joel?

A. This is a theological term that refers to any period of time in which God acts to bring about a specific purpose in his dealings with the Israelites, his Old Testament people. The "day of the Lord" is also a phrase frequently used by the prophets to speak of events that will take place at the end of time.

Q. Was Jonah swallowed by a whale?

A. The Hebrew text does not say that Jonah was swallowed by a whale. From the account in Scripture, it is clear that God prepared a great fish to swallow the drowning prophet and preserve his life. Jonah clearly describes a miracle that was orchestrated by God himself to fulfill his purposes for Jonah and the people of Nineveh.

OLD TESTAMENT NAMES AND TERMS

Q. What was "manna"?

A. This question has puzzled people for ages. It was a spe-

cial food provided for the Hebrews during the Exodus. It came at night, falling with the dew, and it resembled coriander seed. After it was gathered, it was ground in mills then boiled, and made into delicious and nutritious cakes. As soon as Israel entered the Promised Land, the manna ceased to fall (Jos 5:12).

In grand classical style, 16th-century French artist Nicolas Poussin represents the Israelites gathering manna. The special food was provided for them by God during their Exodus from Egypt to the Promised Land.

Q. What does "selah" mean?
A. The word selah occurs 71 times in the Book of Psalms, and it is also found in the Book of Habakkuk. The meaning of the term is unknown. It is generally believed to be a musical or liturgical sign, a note to the singers of the psalm or to the musicians who were accompanying the singers.

Q. Who were the Nephilim?
A. The Nephilim (a Hebrew word of uncertain meaning) of Genesis 6:4 is the first mention of giants in the Bible, and refers to a group of tall, large-framed, powerful warriors. Nephilim were found in Canaan when the Hebrew spies explored the land (Nu 13:33). The spies felt like grasshoppers beside their immense height. Giants

But Moses said to God, "If I come to the Israelites and say to them, 'The God of your ancestors has sent me to you,' and they ask me, 'What is his name?' what shall I say to them?" God said to Moses, "I am who I am."...
Ex 3:13–14

(called by a variety of names in the Scriptures) intimidated the Israelites from their entry into Canaan until the time of David. He killed the most famous colossus of all, Goliath of Gath, whose height was "six cubits and a span" (over eight feet) (1Sa 17).

Q. How did the Jews get the name "Hebrews"?
A. The name is thought to be derived from Heber or Eber, which means a sojourner or immigrant. Abram was the first to be called a Hebrew (Gen 14:13), and in his case, it was probably used in the immigrant context. The name is sometimes used to identify the Israelites in the Old Testament.

Q. What is the distinction between Sunday and the Sabbath?
A. The word Sabbath comes from the Hebrew "Shabua" meaning "seven." It was used to mark the seventh day of the Jewish week—from sunset on Friday to sunset on

OLD TESTAMENT DEFINITIONS

There are a number of words used throughout the Old Testament that have more than one meaning. The following list of words indicate the various ways in which each word is used.

Word: Israel

1. The name given to Jacob by an angel.
2. The name given to the children of Israel. The collective term for the 12 Hebrew tribes.
3. When the united kingdom split into a southern and a northern kingdom after the reign of Solomon, the name given to the northern kingdom.

Word: Judah

1. The name of the patriarch who was the fourth son of Jacob.
2. The name of the tribe or clan descended from Judah.
3. The name given to the southern kingdom after the united kingdom split in two, following the death of Solomon.
4. After the northern kingdom fell apart, this name was used to identify all Hebrews left in the Promised Land.

Word: Jews

1. A word that refers to God's holy people. It is of Latin and Greek derivation.
2. A word that does not occur before the period of Jeremiah in Old Testament literature.
3. The word that was first used to identify the tribe of Judah, the country of Judah, or the southern kingdom and its inhabitants.
4. The name given to Hebrews who returned after the Captivity.

Saturday. Under the Mosaic law, it was a day of absolute rest, with clear rules as to how it should be observed. To honor the Sabbath, a person could not light a fire, carry a handkerchief, or walk more than a short distance on the Sabbath.

The New Testament indicates that Jewish Christians held the Sabbath and a second day, the Lord's Day—the first day of the week—sacred (Ac 20:7). The apostle Paul preached in the synagogue on the Sabbath, but it was on Sunday that the Gentile believers met to celebrate communion, and this was likely the only holy day observed by the Gentile converts. In an edict issued by the Emperor Constantine in A.D. 321, the Lord's Day was officially honored as the Christian holy day, and in subsequent Council rulings, direction was given concerning the forms of Christian worship on that day, and how rest and work should be observed on it.

Today, in memory of Jesus Christ's resurrection, Christians throughout the world continue to celebrate their faith on each Sunday of the year. However, the Sabbath is still observed by some Christians as their sacred day, and it is the weekly day of rest and worship of the Jews.

God empowered Samson, one of Israel's Judges, with superhuman strength. Among his many feats, Samson removed the heavy doors from the gates of the Philistine stonghold of Gaza and carried them a quarter of a mile to the top of a hill (Jdg 16:1–3).

ANCIENT BIBLE TRIVIA—50 QUICK QUESTIONS

1. What was the name of the man who worked 14 years to get the wife he truly wanted?
A. Jacob (Gen 29:18–30)

2. How old was Joseph when he was given his beautiful robe?
A. 17 years old (Gen 37:2–3)

3. After David stoned Goliath to the ground, whose sword did he use to cut off Goliath's head?
A. Goliath's (1Sa 17:50, 51)

4. What was the name of the person who was blind, yet killed about 3,000 people at a pagan religious feast?
A. Samson (Jdg 16:23, 27–30)

5. What group of people complained about their food?
A. The Israelites (Nu 11)

6. What was the name of the Old Testament prophet who was fed by ravens?
A. Elijah (1Ki 17:1–6)

7. What is the name of the man whom King David arranged to have killed because he wanted the man's wife?
A. Uriah the Hittite (2Sa 11:2–17)

8. Which came first in Egypt—the plague of frogs or the plague of gnats?
   A. The plague of frogs (Ex 8:1–18)
9. On what mountains did the ark of Noah come to rest?
   A. Mt. Ararat (Gen 8:4)
10. Who traveled a great distance to see for herself the wisdom of Solomon?
    A. The queen of Sheba (1Ki 10:1–10)
11. What kind of wood did Noah probably use to make the ark?
    A. Cypress (Gen 6:14)
12. What was the name of the person who was both cupbearer to King Artaxerxes and a builder?
    A. Nehemiah (Ne 1:11; 2:5)
13. How many men did King Nebuchadnezzar see walking in the fiery furnace?
    A. Four (Da 3:25)
14. After the flood subsided, what did Noah see in the sky?
    A. A rainbow in the clouds (Gen 9:11–17)
15. What was the source of Samson's strength?
    A. His uncut hair (Jdg 16)

The ten plagues of Egypt were the means God used to convince Pharaoh to let the Israelites leave the land of Egypt. This 15th-century stained-glass depiction of the plagues is found in St. Lorenz Church, Nuremburg, Germany.

16. Who prayed three times every day in front of a window?
    A. Daniel (Da 6:10)
17. Which Old Testament king is known for his fame, riches, and wisdom?
    A. Solomon (1Ki 10)
18. Who was turned into a pillar of salt because of disobedience?
    A. Lot's wife (Gen 19:24–26)
19. What type of false god did Aaron the high priest create out of gold?
    A. A calf (Ex 32:1–6)

20. How old was Joseph when he died?
A. 110 years old (Gen 50:26)

21. What was David's occupation before he became king?
A. Shepherd (1Sa 16:11–13)

22. Who was Baal?
A. The chief god of the Canaanites (1Ki 18)

23. Who was the priest that struck his donkey in anger three times, and then was reproached out loud by the hurt animal?
A. Balaam (Nu 22:22–30)

24. Who wore clothes out of fig leaves that were sewn together?
A. Adam and Eve (Gen 3:7)

25. Who was the wife of Boaz, the prominent rich man of the family of Elimelech?
A. Ruth (Ru 4:13)

26. Who was the older son of Adam and Eve—Cain or Abel?
A. Cain (Gen 4:1–2)

27. What was the name of the commander who gave each man in his army of 300 a trumpet and an empty jar?
A. Gideon (Jdg 7:15–16)

28. What was Gideon's other name?
A. Jerubbaal (Jdg 7:1)

29. Which Old Testament prophet brought back to life the widow of Zarephath's son?
A. Elijah (1Ki 17:17–24)

Twelve spies went into Canaan from the Israelite camp in the wilderness. When they returned, ten doubted that the Israelites were capable of defeating the inhabitants of the Promised Land. Only Joshua and Caleb, seen here, believed that God would enable the people of Israel to conquer their enemies.

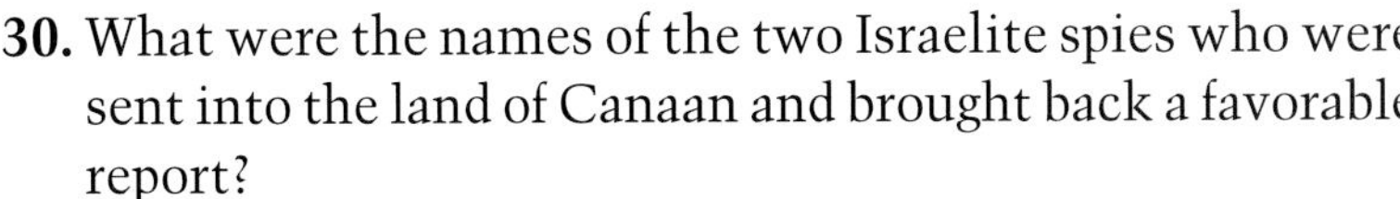

30. What were the names of the two Israelite spies who were sent into the land of Canaan and brought back a favorable report?
A. Joshua and Caleb (Nu 14:6–9)

31. Which twin was born first—Jacob or Esau?
A. Esau (Gen 25:24–26)

32. What did the spies say that the fruitful land of Canaan flowed with?
A. Milk and honey (Nu 13:27)

33. On what day of creation were Day and Night created?
A. The first day (Gen 1:1–5)

34. Who had 700 princesses and 300 concubines numbered among his wives?
A. Solomon (1Ki 11:3)

35. Who sold their younger brother into slavery for 20 pieces of silver?
A. The brothers of Joseph (Gen 37:26–28)

36. What was the name of the prophet who ordered the execution of 450 pagan priests?
A. Elijah (1Ki 18:22, 40)

37. What was the name of the mother of Abraham's first son?
A. Hagar (Gen 16:15)

38. When Sarah bore Abraham his second son, Isaac, how old was the patriarch?
A. 100 years old (Gen 21:5)

39. What city walls fell down when the soldiers marched around the city, blew trumpets, and shouted?
A. Jericho (Jos 6:2–5)

40. What was the name of the prostitute who was Hosea's wife?
A. Gomer (Ho 1:3)

41. What was the name of the leper who was also the commander of the army of the King of Aram?
A. Naaman (2Ki 5:1)

42. What group of men could not wear garments that would cause them to sweat while they were in the holy sanctuary?
A. The priests of Israel (Eze 44:15–18)

43. What was the name of the mother who hid her son in the reeds on the bank of the river?
A. Jochebed, the mother of Moses (Ex 2:3; 6:20)

44. What was the name of the prophet who foretold that Jesus would be born in Bethlehem?
A. Micah (Mic 5:2)

45. Who was hung on a gallows 50 cubits (approximately 75 feet) high?
A. Haman, the enemy of the Jews (Esther 7:9–10)

46. In order to win the battle against Amalek, how did Aaron and Hur help Moses?
A. They held his hands aloft (Ex 17:11–13)

47. What was the name of the wife of Lappidoth, and what was she famous for?
A. Deborah, a judge and prophet, who led a successful Israelite revolt against Canaanite domination (Jdg 4–5)

So Joshua son of Nun summoned the priests and said to them, "Take up the ark of the covenant, and have seven priests carry seven trumpets of rams' horns in front of the ark of the Lord."
Jos 6:6

48. When David pretended to be mad, scratching marks on the doors of the gate, and letting his spittle run down his beard, from whom was he attempting to escape?
A. Achish, king of Gath (1Sa 21:12–22:1)

49. How many stones were placed in the Jordan River after the children of Israel had crossed over onto dry land?
A. 12 (Jos 4:3)

50. When the ark of the covenant was being transported on a cart back to Jerusalem, the oxen shook the ark, and a man reached out his hand to steady the ark and keep it from falling. He was struck dead because he had touched the sacred chest. Who was this man?
A. Uzzah (2Sa 6:6–7)

This stained-glass image is a reminder of the Bible story that wise men from the East followed the star of the king of the Jews to Bethlehem. However, it is not clear how the wise men identified the Messiah's star, and we do not know the exact number of wise men who visited the child Jesus.

FROM MATTHEW TO REVELATION

Q. What was the star of Bethlehem?

A. Many theories have been set forth to explain the star that was the ever-present guide of the wise men, and then came to a standstill over the spot where the child was (Mt 2:9). One explanation for the star is that it was an unusual coming together of bright planets. Another theory is that it was a nova (a star that suddenly brightens considerably). Others think that it was the planet Venus at its most brilliant. The biblical description of the moving star, however, leave many dissatisfied with inadequate scientific theories. Many choose to believe that the star of Bethlehem was a miracle.

THE TRUTH ABOUT CHRISTMAS

1. Was Jesus born on December 25?
Most scholars believe that the birth of Jesus was never known and that the December date is merely a tradition.

2. What year was Jesus born?
Although Bible scholars are not certain about the actual year of Jesus' birth, there is astronomical evidence that puts the date around December of 7 B.C. During that time, there was a highly unusual occurrence in the heavens thought to be the star of Bethlehem. Chronologists date the birth of Jesus around 5 B.C. based on the census decree of the time and the death of Herod.

Under the direction of Marcus Aurelius, Christians were systematically persecuted. The Roman emperor and Stoic philosopher considered religion a threat to the peace of the empire. Ironically, he also established the date that Christians would later celebrate as Christmas.

3. How was December 25 chosen as the day to celebrate the birth of Jesus?
In 274 A.D., the Roman emperor Aurelian fixed December 25 as the date for the winter solstice. It is believed that the early Christians adopted this day for their "Christmass," their celebration of the coming of Jesus as the light of the world.

Saint Boniface, the Benedictine missionary known as the "apostle of Germany," was a man of profound religious commitment. Born and educated in England, Boniface devoted his life to making Christian converts of the people of Germany and the Netherlands. He was killed in 754 or 755 in Friesland, and today his life and death are remembered on June 5, the feast day of St. Boniface.

4. When and where was the earliest known observance of Christmas on December 25?
In the year 336 in Rome, as recorded in a Christian calendar of the period.

5. What is the Epiphany?
It is the commemoration of the appearance of the wise men and it is celebrated on January 6.

6. Was Epiphany always celebrated on January 6?
No. The earliest Christians celebrated their Christmass on this date, commemorating the baptism of Jesus—not his birth or the Epiphany. It was not until centuries later that the appearance of the wise men was celebrated on January 6.

7. How did the Christmas tree originate?
The origin of the Christmas tree is generally traced to Saint Boniface of the eighth century. He chose the fir as a symbol of everlasting life in Jesus.

8. When were Christmas trees first decorated?
It is believed that Martin Luther may have been the first to adorn a Christmas tree when he fixed candles to a fir.

Q. Who were the wise men from the east who visited the child Jesus?

A. The Bible text does not tell us that the wise men were kings or that there were three of them as popular tradition holds. The wise men of the nativity story are often referred to as magi, and it is believed that they came from southern Arabia. Originally a religious group among the Persians, they were a scholarly circle devoted to astrology. At the time of Jesus, it is conceivable that the wise men may have had knowledge of the expected coming of the Messiah (Nu 24:17). We do know that a vibrant Jewish community thrived in the east from the time of the Babylonian conquest.

Q. Why did Herod the king order the death of male children in Bethlehem?

A. Herod, an extremely ambitious and ruthless leader, stopped at nothing to advance himself and protect his interests. Proclaimed king of the Jews by the Romans, he was troubled when he learned that the wise men were seeking a newborn Jewish king. Sensing that his position might be in jeopardy, he resolved then to destroy all the male children who were in the area, thereby killing the unknown usurper (Mt 2).

Q. What were the locusts that John the Baptist ate in the wilderness?

A. In Bible times, the common locust or grasshopper when prepared and dried, tasted somewhat like shrimp and was a popular food. Ethiopians were known to be locust eaters, locusts were relished by the Greeks and preserved by the Assyrians. It was reported that entire armies had been saved from starvation by eating locusts. However, later Bible scholars surmised that the "locust" mentioned in the Book of Mark (1:6) as the food of John the Baptist, was actually the carob, a sweet

When Jesus was born, King Herod the Great feared that his throne might be in jeopardy. The cruel ruler ordered all boy babies and toddlers in the Bethlehem area murdered in an effort to get rid of Jesus. The execution of this horrifying edict is graphically displayed in this stained-glass scene from St. Luke's Church, St. Paul, Minnesota.

bean, and the fruit of an evergreen tree found in the region.

Q. How were the men able to let the paralytic down through the roof of the house?

A. The flat roof of any ordinary home in Palestine in New Testament times was constructed of layers of dried branches and mud laid on top of poles. The friends of the paralyzed man literally dug their way through the layers to let the man down through the hole they made (Mk 2:1–5).

Q. Who were the Pharisees and teachers of the law who so quickly sided with one another against Jesus?

A. The Gospels take note of many groups who opposed Jesus. The ones most often mentioned are the Pharisees, the Sadducees, the chief priests, and the teachers of the law. The Pharisees and the Sadducees were religious parties that held differing theological views within Judaism. The chief priests were generally Sadducees. They were the top religious figures in the temple hierarchy. The teachers of the law were the rabbis, who were the primary authorities on Old Testament teachings. They used their knowledge of the law to serve as judges in trying civil and criminal cases. Although a fairly small group, the Pharisees and Sadducees had immense power and social position. These two groups were generally at odds concerning religious and political issues, but they joined forces to malign and discredit Jesus—and finally in the plot to get rid of him for good.

"But woe to you, scribes and Pharisees, hypocrites! For you lock people out of the kingdom of heaven. For you do not go in yourselves, and when others are going in, you stop them."
Mt 23:13

Q. Why were the disciples surprised when Jesus said it is difficult for someone wealthy to enter the kingdom of God?

A. First-century Judaism held that riches were an evidence of God's favor. Besides, wealth allowed a person to do generous deeds that were thought to earn even more of God's approval. This perspective was rooted in a misapplication of the Law: In the Book of Deuteronomy, the nation of Israel was promised prosperity if they gave God their devotion and obedience (Dt 30:1–10). During the time of Jesus, this perspective was inappropriately applied to individuals. In his teaching, Jesus made the point that a person with great material possessions would be unlikely to give priority to spiritual issues—that is, to matters of the kingdom of God.

Three of the four Gospels recount the story of Jesus raising the daughter of Jairus, a leader of the synagogue. In this, one of Jesus' many "mighty works," the Messiah showed his godly power by bringing the dead girl back to life. Here the miracle is portrayed by German artist Johann Friedrich Overbeck (1789–1869).

Q. Included among the many miracles of Jesus are the accounts of bringing people back to life after they had died. How many people did Jesus bring back to life and why did he do it?

A. There are three such incidents recorded in the New Testament. In the Book of Matthew, Jesus was asked by a leader of the synagogue to lay his hand on his daughter who had just died. When Jesus arrived at the house, he told the hired mourners to leave, and he went in and helped the girl to her feet, bringing her back to life. After this incident, the reputation of Jesus spread throughout the region (Mt 9:18–26). Perhaps Jesus performed this miracle in order to establish who he was in the minds of the people early on in his ministry.

Luke's Gospel records another resuscitation, the raising of the widow's son (Lk 7:11–17). The story states that Jesus was filled with compassion for the widow whose only son had just died. Jesus brought the young man back to life, and returned him to his mother. In biblical times, a widow was in a vulnerable position both socially and economically. Without a husband to support her, one of the widow's options was to count on any son she had for financial support. Because of his concern for her well-being, Jesus likely returned the son to his mother.

In the Book of John, we read the account of Jesus raising Lazarus of Bethany from the dead. In this story, it is clear that Jesus loved Lazarus and his sisters, and was troubled by the death of his friend. He wept at the tomb and ordered Lazarus to come forth. When Lazarus emerged alive and well, many onlookers—amazed at the power of the carpenter of Nazareth—came to believe that Jesus was in fact the promised Messiah (Jn 11:1–45). In this instance, Jesus may have performed this miracle because of his love for his friends and to demonstrate his power and authority to those around.

Q. Why was Jesus flogged before he was crucified?
A. The soldiers used a leather whip intertwined with sharp-edged weights to whip the victim before crucifixion. This kind of flogging was customary, and it was intended to weaken the condemned so that they would take less time to die once they were crucified.

Q. Why was there a summary of charges against Jesus attached to the cross?
A. Roman custom held that a person about to be executed should wear, or have carried, a board on which the sum-

Before being crucified on a cross, a Roman official supervised the beating of the victim. A leather whip laced with pieces of metal or bone was used for the flogging. Because Christ was condemned to death by crucifixion, he had to endure all the barbaric practices that were part of this form of execution.

Very early on the Sabbath, the women in Jesus' close circle hurried to his grave in order to embalm his body with spices. They were startled to discover that their beloved Lord was no longer there. This painting by German artist Carl Julius Milde (1803–1875) shows the angel telling the women that Christ had risen from the dead.

mary of charges against him were written in ink or burned into the wood. At the execution, the board with the charges was attached to the cross, above the victim's head. In the case of Jesus, the Gospels report that the charges against him read: This is Jesus of Nazareth, the king of the Jews.

Q. What happened on the morning of Jesus' resurrection?
A. The sequence of events most likely occurred as follows:

1. Three women go to the tomb (Lk 23:55–24:1).
2. They discover the stone rolled away (Lk 24:2–9).
3. Mary Magdalene leaves to tell the disciples (Jn 20:1–2).
4. Mary, the mother of James, encounters the angel (Mt 28:1–2).
5. Peter and John inspect the tomb (Jn 20:3–10).
6. Mary returns to the tomb, sees angels, and then encounters the resurrected Lord (Jn 20:11–18).
7. Mary, the mother of James, goes to the tomb with other women (Lk 24:1–4).
8. These women see angels (Lk 24:5).
9. An angel assures them that Jesus is risen (Mt 28:6–8).
10. Jesus greets the women (Mt 28:9–10).

Q. What happened to the apostle Paul following his story in the Book of Acts?

A. The Book of Acts ends with Paul in prison awaiting trial. From his New Testament letters, however, further information is given about the rest of his life. Paul was released from prison, whereupon he traveled to Spain on a missions trip. Some time later, Paul was arrested once more and taken back to Rome. He was condemned and executed there before 70 A.D.

New Testament Names and Terms

Q. Who were the Gentiles?

A. Gentiles, which simply means "nations," was a term used by Jews to describe all peoples other than themselves. The term eventually took on a hostile meaning, as Jews gradually set themselves apart as a "holy nation."

Q. What is the meaning of the word "Abba"?

A. Found three times in the New Testament, the word Abba is the Aramaic word for "father," best translated "Dad" or "Poppa"—a child's term of endearment for his or her beloved father. Abba was a term given by Jesus to his followers, as an acceptable, even preferable way of addressing God, their heavenly father (Mk 14:36; Ro 8:15; Gal 4:6).

Q. What language did Jesus speak?

A. During his life and ministry, the common language of Palestine was Aramaic, a language related to Hebrew. After the Exile, it replaced the original Hebrew. It is reasonable to assume that Jesus spoke Aramaic, the everyday language of the people. He may have also spoken some Greek, which was the commercial and literary language of the day.

Q. Who were the Herods?

A. Backed by the Roman government, the family of the Herods brought iron-fisted control to the area of Palestine during the time of Jesus Christ and the founding of the early church. To their credit, the Herods strengthened the military power of Judea and built many fine structures.

However, they are best known for their dysfunctional family history and mean-spirited political dealings. Herod the Great was in power during the time of Christ's birth. Herod Antipas (the son of Herod the Great) had John the Baptist beheaded (Mt 14:1–12) at the request of Herodias (his second wife—and also his

"When you are praying, do not heap up empty phrases as the Gentiles do; for they think that they will be heard because of their many words. Do not be like them, for your Father knows what you need before you ask him." Mt 6:7–8

Opposite page: *This painting by 17th-century artist Eustache Le Sueur depicts Paul giving a great sermon in Ephesus. Moved by his words, the converted magicians brought their books of magic before Paul and burned them (Ac 19:19).*

This poignant portrayal of John the Baptist is found in St. John the Baptist Church, Wausau, Wisconsin. It shows the imprisoned forerunner of the promised Messiah just moments before his death. John the Baptist was beheaded by Herod Antipas at the urging of his wife Herodias, who asked for the head of John the Baptist on a platter (Mk 6:17–28).

sister-in-law). The early church was persecuted during the reign of Herod Agrippa I (the grandson of Herod the Great). It was under his orders that the apostle James was executed (Ac 12:1–2).

Q. What was the census recorded in Luke 2:1–3?

A. Governments in biblical times counted their citizens, just as the United States government keeps track of its population every ten years. There are four censuses mentioned in the Bible: one during the time of Moses (Nu 1:1–3); one during the time of David (1Ch 21:1–2); one after the captivity, during the time of Ezra and Nehemiah (7:4–72); and the one mentioned during the time of Jesus' birth, when Quirinius was imperial legate in the Roman province of Syria. The census was an important tool for taxation, administration, tithes and offerings, as well as military and labor planning.

Q. What is the significance of Jerusalem in the Bible?

A. Jerusalem (also called "Zion" and the "city of God" in the Bible) was the main city of Palestine during biblical times. It appears in the Bible as early as the time of Abraham (Gen 14:18). It was captured by David and made the capital of Israel. This ancient place became the site of Solomon's temple—and then in the first century, Herod's temple.

During the time of Jesus, the population of Jerusalem was somewhere between 70,000 to 100,000. Jesus' death, resurrection, and ascension to heaven all occured there. The city was besieged and destroyed by Rome in 70 A.D. Matthew the writer called Jerusalem "the holy city" (Mt 4:5). It was the sacred center of Judaism and Hebrew culture, and the place over which Jesus anguished because of its rejection of him (Mt 23:37–39).

Using the imagery of holy Jerusalem, the Book of Revelation speaks of a coming new Jerusalem. It will be a holy city, descending from heaven as a light to the nations, a place of peace and justice, and the primary city and dwelling place of God (Rev 21).

NEW TESTAMENT TRIVIA—25 QUICK QUESTIONS

Three of the Gospels record the event known as the Transfiguration, witnessed by three of the disciples. Jesus, bathed in miraculous light, appeared with Moses and Elijah. The voice of God was heard, and a bright cloud covered Jesus and the prophets. This depiction of the holy event was painted by Raphael.

1. What was the name of the angel who told Mary that she would be the mother of Jesus?
A. Gabriel (Lk 1:26–28)

2. What were the names of the three disciples who were with Jesus on the mountaintop when he was transfigured?
A. Peter, James, and John (Mt 17:1)

3. What were the names of the two disciples who were called Sons of Thunder?
A. James and John (Mk 3:17)

4. What name was also used for Bethlehem?
A. The city of David (Lk 2:4)

5. Who was the brother of Andrew?
A. Simon, also known as Peter (Mt 10:2)

6. An angel told Joseph to leave Bethlehem with his wife Mary and the baby Jesus. Where did the angel tell them to travel?
A. Egypt (Mt 2:13)

7. In what town did Joseph, Mary, and Jesus live?
A. Nazareth (Mt 2:23)

8. How much older was John the Baptist than Jesus?
A. About six months (Lk 1)

9. When Jesus was in the wilderness, how many temptations did the devil offer him?
A. Three (Mt 4:1–11)

10. How did Jesus refute the devil's temptations?
A. By quoting the Scriptures (Mt 4:1–11)

11. What was the name of the man who wore clothes made out of camel's hair?
A. John the Baptist (Mt 3:4)

12. Where did Jesus perform his first miracle?
A. Cana of Galilee (Jn 2:11)

13. Bartimaeus wanted Jesus to heal him in what way?
A. He asked to receive his sight (Mk 10:46–52)

14. Who wrote with his finger on the ground?
A. Jesus (Jn 8:6)

Christ and Nicodemus, the Pharisee whom Jesus called "a teacher of Israel," portrayed in stained glass. Nicodemus' surreptitious visit to Jesus at night, his hesitant defense of Jesus, and his quiet contribution of spices to embalm Jesus' body all reveal tentative steps along the road of faith.

15. Jesus mixed something with clay and anointed the eyes of the blind man with the mixture to make him see. What did Jesus mix with the clay?
A. Saliva (Jn 9:6)

16. What was the name of the religious leader who visited Jesus at night to discuss spiritual matters?
A. Nicodemus (Jn 3:1–2)

17. Who was Judas Iscariot?
A. The disciple who betrayed Jesus to his enemies (Mt 26:14–16)

18. What was the name of the high priest's servant who had his right ear cut off by the apostle Peter?
A. Malchus (Jn 18:10)

19. When the Roman soldiers pierced Jesus in the side with a spear, what flowed out?
A. Blood and water (Jn 19:34)

20. What happened at Pentecost?
A. At the great annual Jewish Feast of Weeks (also called Harvest or Pentecost), God's Holy Spirit chose to descend on 120 new converts to Christianity, gathered in the upper room. This turned into a spiritual harvest where 3,000 new converts were added to the church (Ac 2).

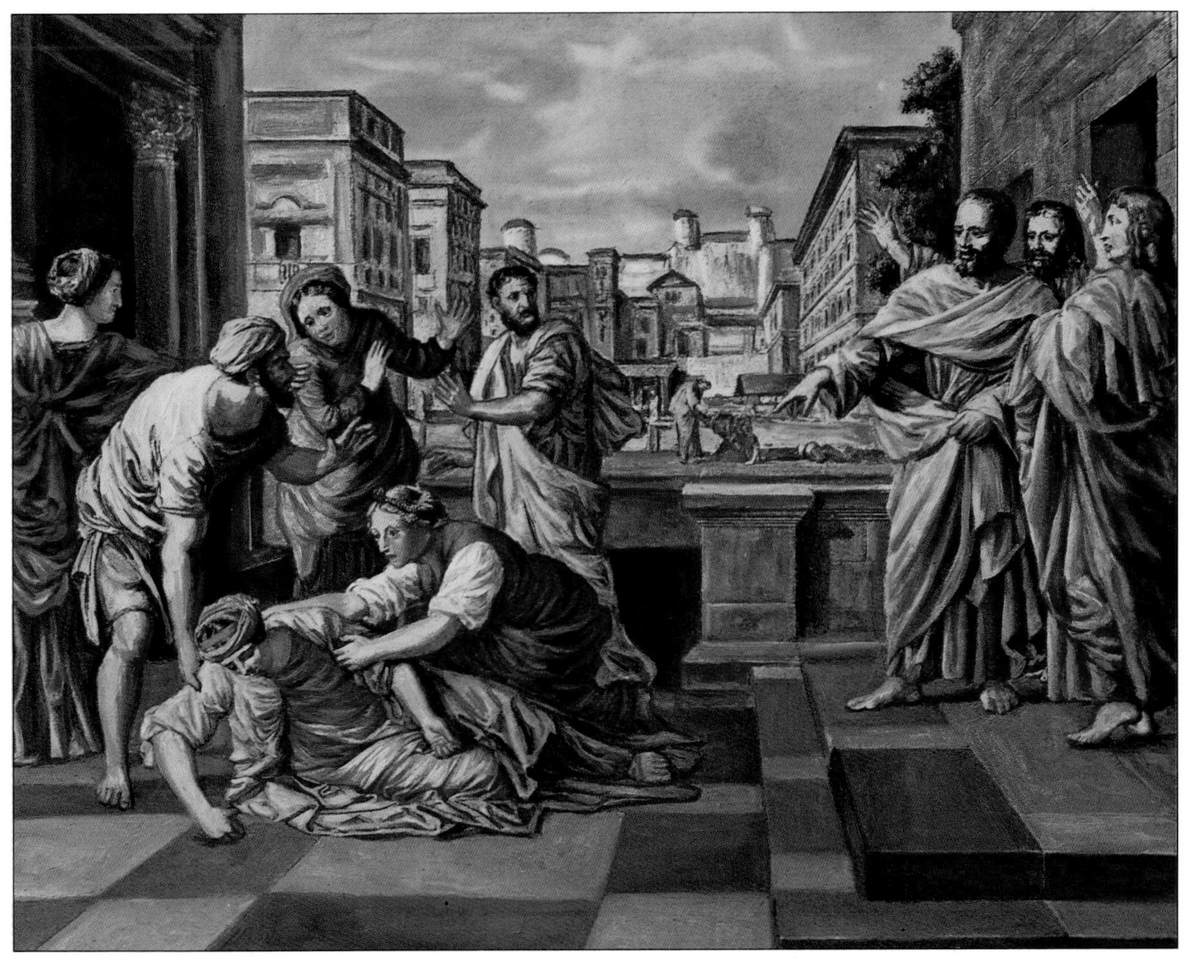

21. What was the name of the man who was released from prison by an angel?
    A. Peter (Ac 12:5–11)
22. What was the name of the couple who died because they lied to the Holy Spirit?
    A. Ananias and Sapphira (Ac 5:1–10)
23. What was the name of the woman in the early church who was known as a dealer in purple cloth?
    A. Lydia (Ac 16:14)
24. The apostle Paul preached on Mars' Hill. In what city is Mars' Hill located?
    A. Athens (Ac 17)
25. What is Armageddon?
    A. The word "Armageddon" is only found in the Book of Revelation. Armaggedon describes an immense army gathered to resist God at the end of history (Rev 16:16). Many think that this verse refers to a wide valley below Mount Carmel in Israel.

The tragic story of Ananias and his wife, Sapphira, is told in the Book of Acts. The couple sold land they owned and pretended to give all the proceeds to the early church to support the poor. In truth, they held back part of the profit for themselves. This plotting and deception led to their sudden death, which had a great impact on the early church (Ac 5:1–11).

Index